Deep Discipling

My Flesh Is Mine, But It Is *Not* Me

By John Byron Shank

Acknowledgments

I would like to thank the following for their help and encouragement in the editing, feedback, and support in writing this book: Bob Hazen, Joe Novak, Lanny Lundquist, Victoria Larkowski, Deanna Anderson, Greg Marsh, and Marie & Jonathan Shank.

Also, the Beta Book class: Shannon & Mary Mack, Elisha Fraley, Lynda Inglesia, and Jose Castillo.

I would also like to thank many friends and teachers who have personally encouraged and corrected me over the years, to grow in faith, especially: Donald and Mildred Shank, Ernest O'Neill, Fred Herzog, Norman Grubb, Bob Hazen, Brian & Tandy Coatney, Tom & Paige Prewitt, Fowler & Sanda Cooper, Scott Breckenridge, Ron & Pat Mace, Virginia Brown, Gail Bedell, and Mimi Anderson.

All opinions and conclusions of this book are mine. My mention of the names above, should not be taken as an insinuation to imply endorsements by them, since none but the editors have read this book. I am grateful to them for their help in my times of need and only wish to acknowledge my gratitude.

Deep Discipling

My Flesh Is Mine, But It Is *Not* Me

By John Byron Shank

Peniel Publishing

ISBN 9780692889411

To my wonderful wife Marie, who has made me so happy,
and my beloved son Jonathan, who has made me so proud,
I dedicate this book.

About the Author

At this writing, I serve as a part-time Chaplain at Ramsey Jail, in St Paul, MN, and as a teacher-counselor at Metro Hope in Minneapolis MN.

As for me, I am a branch snatched away from the fire. There was never any intrinsic good found in me. The good that I do now does not come from me, but from Him Who lives inside, living out as me.

He called me when I did not know Him and fed me from a Vine I did not plant; He set me to work in fields I did not plow, in cities I did not build. He gave me victories over enemies that did not come from my strength. He bent me away from destruction, even checked me hard up against the wall. He wounded me that I might not die and hindered me from deeper disasters. He has given me a wonderful wife I did not deserve, a house I did not choose. He paid my debt with money I did not earn and gave me honor among His people I did not deserve, for their sake, not mine. He has loved me in spite of my sin; He has been sweet to me. I am His; I am not my own. He loves me because He cannot deny His Own Nature. My security is in His loving-kindness and faithfulness, not in anything I could ever do. Therefore, I boast in my weakness.

He has opened up His Word to show me the wonders of His Law and the beauty of His Righteousness. He has given wisdom to a simpleton. He has exposed my treachery, ruthlessness, and weakness for the seduction of evil, and has called me to separate myself from my enemy who originated my sin, and He has shown me how to overcome by His power. He is teaching me to walk with Him; He has taken me by the hands, leading me with cords of kindness, with His loving bands. I am amazed and astonished that He has set me at His Right Hand in Christ. He has given me His Ear and answered many prayers. He has delivered many from bondage and brought freedom to many fellow captives.

When we sow, we do not sow the body that will be, we sow the seed. God gives it the body that we shall see, and I have been burning to sow this seed and to see what kind of body it will be. I have written these pages to share the truths which have helped me to really change.

I also have a strong desire to help and bless you as the Lord has blessed me. I may differ with you in my theology at times, but my desire is not to offend or be contentious. We all come from different backgrounds and traditions. I have tried to let the Spirit have His way in what

I proclaim. He has laid a new foundation in me with insights and perspectives that were once new to me but have always been part of the deeper revivals in church history. Sometimes the old wars that shaped our denominational brand loyalties have left us unable to see some vital truths the Lord still wants to restore to us in His Word.

I argued about some of these ideas at first hearing, in order to test the truth. But we must endeavor to see what is of God and what is not. Patient perseverance is always rewarded with revelation.

If you will be patient with what you are about to read, you will begin to understand more fully what is being said by about Chapter 5, because the foundational ideas must be understood before seeing the deeper meanings. It is my prayer that the Lord will also expose and deliver you from many hidden and destructive conceits, in order that He may do for you what He is so graciously doing for me. – Shank

CONTENTS

Forward   All Belongs to God   1

I: The Passionate Embrace of My Identity in Christ

Chapter 1   What is Man?   10
       A Vessel   12
       A Branch   12
       A Temple   14
       A Wife   15
       A Bond Slave   16
       A Body Part   17

Chapter 2   I Am Dependent   21
       Partakers of God's Nature   23
       The Unregenerate Friend   25
       The Unregenerate Enemy   26
       He Identifies with Me   29
       I Must Identify with Him   30
       United in Him   31

Chapter 3   My Nature Is in My Spirit   33
       Who Reigns   36
       Sold to Sin   37
       Perfect Symmetry   39
       My Flesh Is Mine but It Is Not Me   42
       Two Laws at War in Me   42
       God's Part and My Part   45
       The Bride Revisited   46
       Predestination & Free Will   49
       Sola Scriptura   57

Chapter 4	The Law & The Tree	59
	Sin & Sins	61
	Sanctification Poem	62
	True Self Versus False Self	63
	Misplaced Hope	65
	Image of God	66
	The Carnal Christian	68
Chapter 5	Soul & Spirit	71
	Body/Soul/Spirit Diagram	75
	A Definition of the Soul	77
	Personal Application	80
	Proper Consideration of the Soul	82
	Left Hand & Right Hand	89
Chapter 6	To Will and To Do	92
	Andrew Murray	94
	Absolute Surrender	98
	Rhema and Logos	100
	Disqualifying the Holy Spirit	102
	Spiritual Laws, Principles & Proverbs	107
Chapter 7	Faith and the Will	109
	Faith Diagram	110
	The Progress of Corruption	112
	A guide for forgiving	115
	A guide for making amends	116
	Who Am I?	
	Personal Meditations	118
	Lifted to the Right Hand	120

I Will Change Your Name
by JD Butler   127

II: The Passionate Breaking of My Fallow Ground

Chapter 8   The Role of Suffering
              & Rewards   129
              My Loaded History   133
              Ancestral Curses and the Demonic 137
              The Christian and Demonic
              Possession   140
              Accountability and Discipleship   147

Chapter 9   The Root of Bitterness   150
              Processing Resentment   153
              Processing What You Did &
              What I Did   156
              Bitterness Chart   158

Chapter 10   The Root of Fear   160
              Healthy & Toxic Fear   161
              Processing My Fears   164
              My Fear Inventory   165
              Fear Chart   166
              Processing Five Examples   167

Chapter 11   The Root of Shame   172
              Shame Versus Conviction   174
              Shame Sources   176
              Shame Chart
              My Shame Inventory   179
              Summary   182

Chapter 12   The Root of Lawlessness
              or Root of Shamelessness   183
              The Parable of the Sower   186
              Unconditional Eternal Security
              & the Perseverance of Faith   190
              The Greek Tenses   192
              Crisis   202
              My Lawless Inventory   203

Chapter 13   Male & Female Relationship
              Conceits   204
              Magical Thinking   207
              Victim Mentality   210
              The Chameleon   213
              The Knight and the Nurse   215
              The Predator   216

Chapter 14   Narcissism & Relationship
              Addictions   221
              Sexual Addiction   222
              Romance Addiction   224
              Relationship Addiction   225
              Addiction Cycle Diagram   227
              Healing and Brain Training   229
              Real Relationship Skills   230
              True Love   233
              Why Wait?   234

III: The Passionate Worship of True Spirituality

Chapter 15	Magic, Mysticism & Curses	239
	Laws of Contagion or Contact	241
	God Created Fixed Laws	243
	Ceremony and Ritual	247
	Mysticism	248
Chapter 16	True Worship & Prayer	251
	The Holy Approach	252
	Kinds of Prayer:	
	Praise & Adoration	254
	Thanksgiving	257
	Confession	259
	Petition	260
	Intercession	262
	Fasting	267
	Imprecation	269
	Excommunication	271
Chapter 17	Personal Gifts of the Spirit	273
	Gifts of Grace	276
	Gifts of Revelation	279
	Gifts of Power	279
	Gifts of Edification	280
	How Do I Know the Voice of God?	281
	The Gifts in More Detail	
	Word of Wisdom	282
	Word of Knowledge	284
	Faith	286

Chapter 18   The Only Autonomous Being
             Operations of Powers   290
             Gifts of Healing   294
             Ministry of Healing   299
             Discerning Spirits   301
             Prophecy   306
             Tongues   310
             Interpreting of Tongues   314

Chapter 19   Offices & Gifts of the Spirit   320
             The Apostolic Office   321
             The Prophetic Office   326
             Pastors and Teachers   327
             The Evangelist   329
             Workers of Miracles   329
             Healers   330
             Helpers and Ministry of Service   331
             Spiritual Motivation   333

Chapter 20   Judgment & the Household
             of Faith   336
             Persevering Faith   339
             Topheth   341
             Leaving Denomination X   343
             Persecution of the Church   347
             Unity, Duality & Contention   349
             Image of God & you are gods   351
             Reckoning   354
             The Word That Does Not Lie   355
             Yes I Am *Song*   358

       Bibliography   360

FOREWORD
Deep Discipling
My Flesh Is Mine *but* It Is Not Me
by John Byron Shank

For the most part, I am using the ESV translation, copyright 2001 by Crossway Bibles, a publishing ministry of Good News Publishers. However, wherever I have personalized the text, or made special emphasis, I have listed my name so as to distinguish each quotation from the ESV, KJV, RSV, et cetera, on which my personalizing emphasis is based. I have also capitalized all pronouns referring to Deity.

"You shall love the Lord your God with all your heart and with all your soul and with all your mind, and you shall love your neighbor as yourself." These are the words of Jesus to you and me from **Matthew 22:37-40**. This is the command of heaven to be heavenly—to join in the widening circle of love that flows out unceasingly from the Father to the Son, from the Spirit to the Son, from the Son to the Father, from the Spirit to the Father, from the Father to the Spirit, from the Son to the Spirit, from the Spirit to us, and from us to each other and back to the Father in Christ, by the Spirit! How else shall we keep His command except by the love that flows out and back through us all to Him and to each other? Why else are we made in His image? Have we any comprehension of the height and depth of the love of God for us?

Do you have any idea how profoundly you are loved by God? This is **agape love**, the love in New Testament Greek that is for the benefit of others. Agape is not the kind of love that desires what self-fulfillment inspires. It is primarily a *giving* love that nurtures, builds up, and extends grace to others. This is the love that God gives. It is also what we are meant to give the Lord in return, not because He needs anything from us, but because He wants us to be as He is, in His ways. We are made in His Image to be in sweet fellowship with Him and with one another, and to share That Love with the lost that they may be inspired to join us.

1 John 4:7-21 says:

> Beloved, let us love [agape] one another, for love is from God, and whoever loves has been born of God and knows God. Anyone who does not love, does not know God, because God is love. In this the love of God was made manifest among us, that God sent His Only Son into the world, so that we might live through Him. In this is love, not that we have loved God but that He loved us and sent His Son to be a propitiation [*atoning sacrifice*] for our sins. Beloved, if God so loved us, we also ought to love one another. No one has ever seen God; if we love one another, God abides in us and His love is perfected in us.
>
> By this we know that we abide in Him and He in us, because he has given us of His Spirit. And we have seen and testify that the Father has sent His Son to be the Savior of the world. Whoever confesses that Jesus is the Son of God, God abides in him, and he in God. So, we have come to know and to believe the love that God has for us. God is love, and whoever abides in love abides in God, and God abides in him. By this is love perfected with us, so that we may have confidence for the Day of Judgment, because as He is, so are we to be in this world.
>
> There is no fear in love, but perfect love casts out all fear. For fear has to do with punishment, and whoever fears has not been perfected in love. We love because He first loved us. If anyone says, "I love God," but hates his brother, he is a liar; for he who does not love his brother whom he has seen cannot love God Whom he has not seen. And this commandment we have from Him; whoever loves God must also love his brother."
> – ESV

By the abiding of Christ, by His living in me, the love-nature of God is also in me. I must believe it! The capacity to love as Christ loves is now mine—I must say it is now mine and believe by living *as if* this now is the truth about me, with an act of obedience. If I can say I am forgiven and saved by the love-nature of Christ in His sacrifice for me, why do I still doubt? Doubt comes from fear that God's love may not be really intended for me, that He still wants to punish me because of the bad things I have done, and because of those bad things, He lets bad things happen to me. Some of those bad things happened to me because of my own sin. But bad things also happened to Jesus when He came into this cruel and sinful world with God's love-nature for me. But He did not sin. He felt the fear of what was going to happen to Him on the cross, but His love-nature cast that fear away. His love for me overcame fear and the power of sin, for my sake. That same *love-nature* of Christ is now mine because He is in me. Perfect love casts out all fear because the Perfect Lover is now in me.

Psalm 19:7-14 says:

> The Law of the Lord is perfect, converting the soul:
>> the testimony of the Lord is sure, making wise the simple.
>
> The statutes of the Lord are right, rejoicing the heart:
>> the commandment of the Lord is pure, enlightening the eyes.
>
> The fear of the Lord is clean, enduring forever:
>> the judgments of the Lord are true, and righteous altogether.
>
> More to be desired are they than gold, yea, than much fine gold:
>> sweeter also than the honey and the honeycomb.
>
> Moreover, by them is Thy servant warned:
>> and in keeping of them there is great reward.
>
> Who can understand his *own* errors? Cleanse Thou me from secret *sins.*
>
> Keep back Thy servant also from presumptuous sins;
>> let them not have dominion over me:
>> then shall I be upright,
>> and I shall be innocent from great transgression.
>
> Let the words of my mouth and the meditations of my heart be acceptable in Thy sight,
>
> O Lord, my Strength and my Redeemer. – KJV (*Shank*)

"The Law of the Lord"—the Torah of the Lord—the Word of the Lord, "is perfect, reviving the soul," this means that the truth of God's love-nature now comforts the anguish of my soul in Christ.

"The Testimony of the Lord is sure, making wise the simple," means what the Lord says is true: The Word of the Lord does not lie. If I believe by obeying Him, I will become wise.

"The Statutes"—the ruling principles "of the Lord are right, rejoicing the heart," means I am blessed in following His ways and having joy in my heart as I bear His fruit.

"The Commandment of the Lord is pure, enlightening the eyes," means His Spirit will mercifully speak to me and show me the way to go. He sees what I cannot see, and I benefit from His perspective and foreknowledge; my eyes are opened.

"The Fear of the Lord is clean, enduring forever," means the awesome respectful fear that I should not offend the Holy God I love keeps me holy and keeps me from the foolishness of contempt.

"The Judgments of the Lord are true and righteous altogether," means His decisions are always correct, flawless, and coming from the highest goodness. These are all more desirable than gold and sweeter than honey. They warn and keep me in the loving benefits of God.

"Who can understand *his* errors?" The italics in the King James Version (KJV) indicate the absence of a Hebrew word for *his* or *his own*, but they help make the context clear—we are unable to objectively comprehend the subtlety or depth of our own moral errors, because sin is blinding.

"Cleanse Thou me from secret *faults*." If there is no Hebrew word here for faults, it could also be read as "cleanse me from secrets." In Part II of this book, we will deal with breaking up our fallow ground. This is where secrets hide as **conceits** that misdirect us with an unseen hand. Unconfessed sin keeps us from knowing ourselves and will deceive us.

"Keep back Thy servant also from presumptuous sins; let them not have dominion over me." This means sins with a high hand or willful disobedience. Let me not have an attitude of contempt in response to the beauty of God's love-nature and grace.

"Then shall I be upright and be innocent from great transgression. Let the words of my mouth and the meditations of my heart, be acceptable in Thy sight, O Lord, my Strength and my Redeemer." This points to my being in Christ and Him being in me; He is my Savior and my Keeper, the Rock Who upholds me.

All belongs to God.
Psalm 24:1 says:

> The earth is the Lord's and the fullness thereof. The world and those who dwell therein. – ESV

God's original intention for man came from His *loving nature*, which expressed itself in the *perfect* Garden of Eden. But Satan defiled it by infecting mankind with his *sin-nature*. God had to quarantine that contamination with death, or all of His creation would eventually be ruined, if fallen man lived forever. So, the Tree of Life was withheld from us and we must now eat from the Tree of the Knowledge of Good and Evil until we die. But God will eventually have His creation restored to the way He originally wanted it. It is all His. The day will eventually come when He will say something like this:

> "Everyone who loves Righteousness and wants to be with Me and My kingdom, by the Blood of My Son, has come. I will now shut the Book of Life because it is full. All who are Mine will go on to be with Me forever. All who reject Me will be without Me in the outer darkness, forever."

In other words, everything that is good will remain with God. Everything that is not good will be with Notgod, who is evil. Those saying they don't want God will have their request granted—but will find they have nothing good. They will be in the kingdom of Notgod, their Unmaker, forever! All creation is moving toward this ultimate resolution. Now is the choosing time.

At this point, many would say: How can a God with this love-nature you just described send anyone to eternal destruction? We hate this idea. It's terrifying. This doesn't seem fair; there must be a softer third option. We don't want to believe it. Why can't those who reject God just die? But this is God's Word, which does not lie. We will not escape by pretending we will not have to answer for our sins before the Living God. If the Judgment was not revealed, many would just say they will enjoy sin now while they live, then just die—not caring what their sin has done to others. The only way to truly be grounded in God's love-nature is to understand how both the kindness and severity of God are part of that love-nature, and this we shall pursue in what follows in the rest of this book.

For now, consider the well-reasoned argument I once heard from Vishal Mangalwadi, a well-known Christian teacher from India. I will adapt it to the question at hand. He asks something like this: What is the ultimate reality for eternity, life or death? If one says *death*, life is a temporary accident of chance; there is no living Creator God, no resurrection, no judgment; you have no fear of consequences; do as you please. The universe will eventually die a heat death, returning to the dead matter it originally was. But if this is to be believed, how did this accidental interval of life come from dead matter? And more so, how did some accidental flash of life find the ability to reproduce itself to keep life going? What did it eat? And how did it later become intelligent? Why should dead matter ever be more than dead matter, forever?

On the other hand, if *life* is the ultimate reality for eternity, the interval of death is temporary. Everything that has died will eventually revert back to its eternal living state because an Always-Living Creator God can restore everything that once lived back to life again. That Living God has warned us that we will be judged for our deeds, because all of us have sinned.

If our deeds don't matter, life has no meaning. But the Living God says life choices have great meaning. What right do I have to be offended by what you do to me if life is meaningless? If you have suffered loss because of me, why are you angry? Why do we both have a need for justice? Why do we have a drive to find meaning in life in spite of a world so full of appalling sin, making us all suffer?

With or without God, the eternity to come will not be like the world is now. The eternity with Notgod will be hell, no God, no good. For those who have embraced the mercy of God in the Blood sacrifice of His Son and have believed God—they will be in paradise. They will have admitted the guilt of their sin, repented, and received His Spirit. The just condemnation they deserve has been gratefully paid for by Jesus. They will now be in agreement with God and want to love and obey Him. They will live forever with Him. This is what God has commanded of us, to be saved.

Those who reject this simple solution reject the God Who offered it and insult the Christ Who suffered and died for them. This rejection has eternal meaning. God our Maker has warned us not to reject eternal life with Him. You will not like eternity with Notgod, the Unmaker.

Warning
Romans 1:18-31 says:

> For the wrath of God is revealed from heaven against all ungodliness and unrighteousness of men, who by their unrighteousness suppress the truth. For what can be known about God is plain to them, because God has shown them. For His invisible attributes, namely, His eternal power and divine nature, have been clearly perceived ever since the creation of the world in the things that are made. So, they are without excuse. For although they knew God, they did not honor Him as God or give thanks to Him, but became futile in their thinking, and their foolish hearts were darkened. Claiming to be wise, they became fools, and exchanged the glory of the immortal God for images resembling mortal man and birds and animals and creeping things.
> Therefore, God gave them up in the lusts of their hearts to impurity, to dishonoring their bodies among themselves, because they exchanged the truth about God for

a lie and worshipped and served the creature rather than the Creator Who is blessed forever! Amen.

For this reason, God gave them up to dishonorable passions. For their women exchanged natural relations for those contrary to nature; and the men likewise gave up natural relations with women and were consumed with passion for each other, men committing shameless acts with men and receiving in themselves the due penalty for their error.

And since they did not see fit to acknowledge God, God gave them up to a debased mind to do what ought not to be done. They were filled with all manner of unrighteousness, evil, covetousness, malice. They are full of envy, murder, strife, deceit, and maliciousness. They are gossips, slanderers, haters of God, insolent, haughty, boastful, inventors of evil, disobedient to parents, foolish, faithless, heartless, ruthless. Though they know God's decree that those who practice such things deserve to die, they not only do them but give approval to those who practice them. – ESV

God knows our hearts. He knows the besetting sins that each of us has from our youth, which will overwhelm us if we are not transformed by His life in us. Besetting sins are established sin patterns of behavior and believing that grow out of our inherited dispositional weaknesses from the Fall. The Fall affected our genetics as well as the culture of our families of origin. One may have a disposition towards addiction, to another depression, or violence, or sexual perversion. Some must deal with physical and mental handicaps. We are all scarred by abuse, abandonment, betrayal, and loss. These wounds and dispositional weaknesses will either drive us to Christ or destroy us in Satan. If we reject Christ, or just ignore Him, our sin will come to its full flower in the corruption of death.

Notice the sequence of progressive corruption of mind and body in the verses you just read. Sin causes a darkness of thinking that eventually swallows us whole if we don't repent. What does the Bible say can be done about it? How can we be transformed into the likeness of Christ? How can we overcome the weakness of the flesh in this life? The answer is found in first seeing what is Biblically true about what a human being *is* and what a human being *is not*, then rebuilding our faith on the faith of the One Who keeps us.

I: The Passionate Embrace of My Identity in Christ

1

What is Man?
A Biblical View of Humanity

My friend, there are many lies we have believed that were taught to us by our old master, Satan. He convinced us they were true when we who were born in sin, were still naive and defenseless. Once bent in the wrong direction, it was easy for him to entangle us in more sin and further blind us. He also hid from us the real truth about God. He laid down a false foundation of what normal life is.

We will now begin to dismantle some of these lie systems in ourselves, which still have influence over us, even if we are now born again. God has empowered us to change, but we have very little idea of how to do so. By grace, we are saved and made righteous in Christ. But what in the world does it mean to be in Christ and He in me? May the Lord give patience as you read on, and may the Lord bless you with revelation for your diligence, until that insight comes.

Foundation Concepts

The word often used for *man* in the New Testament is **an-thropos**, which refers to mankind in general, that is, human beings—man versus animal, not just the male sex. Greek words for male gender are **anaer** or **arsaen** (*my spelling*), a word never used to describe women. So, when **anthropos** is used in the New Testament, it means a person of either gender. The Bible refers to the old man (**anthropos**) as being the type of person we were before we were born again. The new man refers to the person one becomes after receiving the Spirit of Christ. The sense in which the Bible uses man for our purposes here is in reference to the moral character or nature of a person. Note also when the New Testament is using the word **phus-ikos** in its translation as **natural** person, it is not describing our talents, temperaments, or personalities. Our study here confines itself to the Biblical idea of old and new natures in the context of the old and new person. Another term for nature as we mean it would be moral identity, the way one is morally.

The following is an adaptation from *Romans 6 to 8, Paul's Key to the Liberated Life* by **Norman Grubb**. I have added some of my own comments.

Position A

The majority view in Evangelical Christianity is that we have two natures when redeemed. The old nature in **Romans 7** must be forever battled against by the new nature in **Romans 8**. This is said to be our daily struggle for the rest of our lives. While a very common view, it is technically inaccurate. The NIV translation even disregards the word flesh (**sarx**) and substitutes the phrase *sinful nature* in its place! This is a theological bias in interpretation and makes the right understanding of **Romans 6-8** almost incomprehensible, because the Bible says our old sinful nature was put to death in Christ. (*Further clarification will be provided in* **Chapter 4** *of this book where we will discuss the flesh and the spirit.*)

Position B

The minority view or Holiness Theology, following Wesley and Fletcher and finding modern expression among many Charismatic congregations today, holds that there is a two-stage *process*, the first being salvation or justification, the second being the baptism in the Spirit, or a purifying of the heart and an anointing with power. The reason for a second work of grace is said to be necessary because an incomplete foundation has been laid in many believers of what it actually means to be saved and in-dwelt with the Holy Spirit. (*See ignorance of the Holy Spirit in Apollos that was corrected in* **Acts 18:24-19:7**)

Both views hold that there is an old nature that we have as a result of The Fall. **Position A** says the new nature in Christ overrides the old, but the old nature remains. **Position B** says the new nature has completely replaced the old by a second work of grace, although there will be a continuance of fleshly weaknesses.

Position C

The Bible does not speak of human nature by itself as an identity but speaks of the human condition as containing a *deity nature* - as an operator, or energizer (**energeia**), as a *master*. In other words, we are the expression of the nature of Satan, the prince of the air and the god of this fallen world, or we are the expression of the nature of Christ, The King of kings and Lord of all, after salvation. We have no nature of our own to express! The origin of moral good and moral evil does not come from us. Our moral expression comes from the master we obey. The significance of this is profound, as we shall see as a more correct Biblical foundation is laid. Let me show you what I mean with the following examples in Scripture.

A Vessel

Romans 9:21-23 says:

> Has the potter no right over the clay, to make out of the same lump one vessel for honorable use and another for dishonorable use? What if God, desiring to show His wrath and to make known His power, has endured with much patience vessels of wrath prepared for destruction, in order to make known the riches of His glory for vessels of mercy, which He prepared beforehand for glory... – ESV

We are either vessels of wrath or mercy. If we are not saved and regenerated by the Holy Spirit, we contain and express the nature of Satan and will bear his sinful fruit. If we are saved, the Holy Spirit is in us and we contain and express the nature of Christ and can now bear His righteous fruit.

Inserting one's self into the text can make its power more real. I have substituted bold face type for **I** or **me** to emphasize your placement in the verse when you read it. I have also amplified the meaning with some paraphrasing where stronger emphasis is needed.

A Branch

John 15:1-6 says:

> Jesus is the True Vine, and His Father is the Vinedress-

er. Every branch in Him that does not bear fruit the Father takes away, and the one that does bear fruit He prunes, that it may bear more fruit. Already I am clean because of the word Jesus has spoken to me. I abide in Him and He abides in me. As a branch cannot bear fruit by itself, unless it abides in the vine, neither can I unless I abide in Christ. Christ Jesus is the Vine; I am a branch. Because I abide in Him, and He in me, I will be able to bear His fruit, for apart from Him I can do nothing. If I do not abide in Him I will be thrown away like a branch that withers; and those branches are gathered, thrown into the fire, and burned. -ESV (Shank)

See how your personal placement in the text opens it for you? I have not altered the meaning of the verses but made them more personally applicable.

The branch can bear nothing in and of itself. Any branch that is not joined to the Vine will wither and die. Dead dry branches are burned up in the fire. The branch that is joined to the Vine is part of the Vine and is nourished by the same sap. Nourished by the True Vine to which real Christians are joined, we're able to produce the fruit of the Vine in our lives. Christ is describing the relationship of the believer to Himself, or more precisely the relationship of you and me to Him. If I am joined to Him, I am able to express His character and fruit. In a similar way, it is not difficult to see how the old nature expresses the selfish character of Satan, the false vine, in an unredeemed person, by bearing the poison fruit of his sin nature. I either have the old nature (Satan) or the new nature (Christ). It is unbiblical to say I have both at the same time. How I can still sin when I have a new nature in Christ will be more fully discussed in **Chapters 4 and 5**.

Note: Again, I have no moral character or fruit to express by myself. If I am joined to Christ, I produce the life and righteousness that is in Him. If I am not grafted into Christ, I will be thrown away in the fire with the devil, because I will be unable to ever express this true righteousness. If I am joined to the Vine, but refuse to be fruitful, I will also be removed and burned.

When the Tree of Life is offered again in Paradise to those who are His, I will be permitted to eat from it. There will be no snakes allowed in that Garden. The testing will be over forever!

A Temple

I Corinthians 3:16-17 says:

> Do you not know that you are God's temple and that God's Spirit dwells in you? If anyone destroys God's temple, God will destroy him. For God's temple is holy, and you are that temple." – ESV

The word translated from the Greek as temple is **naos**. This word does not actually mean the temple as a whole but refers to the place in a temple where a god was located. The word for the temple precincts as a whole is **heiron**. For example, the Corinthians knew the **naos** of Athena was the place in her temple where the image of Athena *was* and where she was said to *be*. When Paul said, we are the **naos** of God, we are where the Spirit of Christ *is* because His Spirit indwells us, in our human spirits. The human spirit corresponds to the holy of holies—the **naos** of the temple Paul knew in Jerusalem. This does not make us God but makes us holy because His Spirit indwells our spirits.

There may be times when we feel as if God is far from us, but the Word says He is in us and we are in Him **(John 17)**. Feelings are not necessarily facts, but the Word does not lie. If we are real Christians, we are always with Him and He is always with us. He knows everything that is going on in our lives, whether He is manifesting His presence in some dramatic way or not. We must not put God to the test by demanding that He prove He is present with us by giving us visions, sensations or other wonderful experiences. He may encourage us sometimes with outward signs like these, but most of the time, He will withhold manifestations because He wants us to exercise faith in what is unseen but promised by the Word, which does not lie.

As a young man, I remember lying on the floor and praying to God Who was high atop a vast   spiral tunnel of clouds, way up high and far away, while I called out to Him as if from the bottom of a well, way down here. Now, it is true that God is high and lifted up and His train fills the temple, but Satan blocked me from seeing the Lord was joined to me by the Spirit—where I live on earth. Though I knew God's Spirit in me was real, the enemy convinced me the Lord was remote. I thought the Bible verses describing me at the Right Hand of God in Jesus were an unfathomable mystery that had only legal or symbolic meaning. The experience of being filled with the Spirit seemed to be something that would come and go; the Holy Spirit was my wonderful helper now and then. Otherwise, life was all up to me to figure out by myself. At that time, I still only saw God's transcendence, His distance from me—I did not yet understand His immanence—Christ in me! Now I know He is always in me and I am always in Him, regardless of how things look or feel at any given moment.

A Wife

Romans 7:2-4 says:

> For a married woman is bound to her husband as long as he lives, but if her husband dies, she is released from the law of marriage. Accordingly, she will be called an adulteress if she lives with another man while her husband is alive. But if her husband dies, she is free from the law, and if she marries another man she is not an adulteress.
>
> Likewise, my brothers, you also have died to the law through the body of Christ, so that you may belong to Another, to Him Who has been raised from the dead, in order that we may bear fruit for God. For while we were living in the flesh, our sinful passions, aroused by the law, were at work in our members to bear the fruit of death. But now we are released from the law, having died to that which held us captive, so that we serve in the new way of the Spirit and not in the old way of the written code. – ESV

I used to find this passage confusing. The first paragraph says the wife is bound to her husband until *he* dies. But the next paragraph says you (*the wife*)   also have died. Now I see it!

15

The first husband is Satan, controlling me through the Law, but his old nature is now dead in me. The second husband is Christ, Who freed me from the curse and snare of the Law; His new nature is now alive in me. A wife bears the fruit of her husband; she cannot bear children without his **seed**. The Church is the bride of Christ. The Law gets its power from the command of God when He said to Adam and Eve "...but of the tree of the knowledge of good and evil you shall not eat [*if you do*] you shall surely die" (**Genesis 2:17**). After disobeying God and obeying Satan, they were cursed to bear the sinful fruit of the serpent, the one they obeyed. So, death entered all of creation. Saying *yes* to Satan and *no* to God, they passed on to us the *nature* of the one they believed and obeyed. We who are born children of unbelief—who are children of the **seed** of Adam—cannot bear God's fruit without being born again. Since I have now been born of God, I can now bear His fruit!

A Bond Slave
Romans 6:16 -19 says:

> Do I not know that if I present **myself** to anyone as an obedient *slave*, I am a slave to the one I obey, either in sin, which leads to death, or of obedience of faith, which leads to righteousness? But, thanks be to God, that I who was once a slave to sin have become obedient from the heart to the standard of teaching to which I was committed, and having been set free from sin, have become a slave of righteousness. - ESV (Shank)

What if I say, "I will not obey either; I'll just do what I want?" These verses show *no third option* because there are only two ways to be. Two masters—two moral operators (**energeia**). "I'll just do what I want." is what Satan believes and he is separated from God.

Jesus Agrees
John 8:34.

> Jesus answered them, "Truly, truly, I say to you, every one who commits sin is a *slave* to sin." - ESV

I am a slave to sin or a slave to righteousness, but I have never lived as my own master. We may picture slaves as people in chains and laboring under the whip. That does happen to people under harsh punishment in captivity. Those of us who have fallen into full-blown addictions know bondage like that as well. But slavery, in this verse, refers to doing the *moral will* of our master, not our own. The master says do—and the slave does what the master says. The will of the master is reproduced in his servant/slave. When duplicating my music, I have a master disc on the hard drive. All the copies of what's on my master deck are faithfully reproduced in the rows of slave decks. The master is in the hard drive.

The word **doulos** can mean either slave or servant. Christians are to willingly present themselves as slaves or bond servants to our Righteous Lord. Satan tries to entice or force obedience to himself. The Lord commands, but He gives us grace to respond in faith by *choosing* to do what is right. How else will we become obedient from the heart? The Lord is Righteous in His heart, so are we to be. Righteousness is a *choice* to do good when there is an evil option. When tempted or provoked, we are to resist sin and take the same path Jesus would take because we believe we are now like Him in moral nature and have His power to overcome. Even if all my history up to this point contradicts what the Bible says is true about me, I must reject who my past says I am and start believing who God says I am now. Old patterns of behavior may take some time to break, but faith in who I am now, will break them because the Overcomer is in me and will overcome as me.

Faith = obedience. Faithlessness = disobedience. Jesus also counts obedience as love. **John 14:15** says:
> If you love Me, keep my commandments.

A Body Part
1 Corinthians 12:27 says:
> Now you [*plural*] are the body of Christ and individually members of it. – ESV

The body of Christ is the church and is led by the Head. A body without a head cannot   do anything. If a leg does not respond to the command from the brain to step, the whole man is unable to walk. The church cannot fulfill its purpose without Christ. Humans are dependent. The only One in the universe Who Is truly autonomous—completely self-sufficient, is God. Even Satan, the false god of this world for now, is dependent on God for how long he will live and move and have his being. (**Acts 17:28**) As a member of the body, I have a particular role to play that may not be the same as the role you are to play. One is a foot, one is an ear, et cetera. The Head will direct us both in what we are to do to make the body more effective as a whole.

Take a look at **Revelation 20:1-3, 7-10**:

> Then I saw an angel coming down from heaven, holding in his hand the key to the bottomless pit and a great chain. And he seized the dragon, that ancient serpent, who is the devil and Satan, and bound him for a thousand years, and threw him into the pit, and shut it and sealed it over him, so that he could not deceive the nations any longer, until the thousand years were ended. After that he must be released for a little while...
>
> And when the thousand years are ended, Satan will be released from his prison and will come out to deceive the nations that are at the four corners of the earth, Gog and Magog, to gather them for battle; their number is like the sand of the sea. And they marched over the broad plain of the earth and surrounded the camp of the saints and the beloved city, but fire came down from heaven and consumed them, and the devil who had deceived them was thrown into the lake of fire and sulfur where the beast and the false prophet were, and they will be tormented day and night forever and ever.
> – ESV

Notice that Christ reigns for a millennium on the earth, while Satan is bound and thrown into the bottomless pit. There is peace for 1000 years! Then Satan is allowed to come out for a short time. He deceives the nations again and the Gog-Magog war against Christ in Jerusalem begins. He and the deceived armies are destroyed by fire. Notice the obvious: When Satan is allowed to deceive, sin and destruction abound. When Satan is taken away, peace and righteousness prevail under Christ. When Satan comes back, he is able to deceive the world again, even after the whole world sees Christ and His Righteousness for 1000 years! Satan saw the Face of God in all His Glory and Righteousness in heaven above, but he rebelled and tried to overthrow God on His throne. On earth, Adam and *Eve saw and walked with* the Word of the Lord (*Jehovah-Elohim as He is called in the Hebrew*) in the garden, when all creation was still good. You may ask, if Adam and Eve were good, how could they sin? They were good, well made, but not yet righteous, which means they needed to be able to say **no** to Evil.

John 1 says:
> In the beginning, the Word was with God and the Word was God and the Word became flesh and dwelt among us. – ESV

Satan deceived Eve, and both Adam and Eve rebelled. In the future, all the people of the earth will see Christ on His throne in Jerusalem, ruling in Justice and Righteousness and prosperity. When Satan returns, many will again be deceived and rebel once more. We are all *vessels*. I believe this could be a reason the judgment is eternal, so that the eternal Paradise will never again be defiled by Satan and his children.

Remember: We have **never** been self-operating, or autonomous of either operator, in the moral sense. We have **never** been the originators of good or evil, but only *expressers* of the moral will of one or the other.

When Copernicus discovered the earth revolved around the sun instead of the sun revolving around the earth, the world had a significant change in perspective. This was called a paradigm shift, because it proved the earth was not the center of the universe, but a small part of something much greater than itself. The realization that we have no moral character or nature of our own to express but only that of Christ or Satan, is a paradigm shift in how we must now view ourselves.

Chapter 1 Study Questions.
Answer the following questions from what you have just read, *not from whatever your prior understanding of these things may be.*

1. Explain positions A ‑ C on pages 9 and 10, in your own words.

2. Does the Biblical definition of humanity—showing that we are not masters of ourselves but vessels who contain a greater being—make you feel devalued in some way, less than you thought you were? If so, how are you less?

3. In what way is this understanding of yourself liberating, making your life more valuable?

4. If the Bible is saying you do not originate either good or evil but only participate in the nature of the One Who is good or the one who is evil, why do you feel shame when you sin?

5. What is your role in the war between good and evil, and what is your sphere of responsibility?

2

I Am Dependent

In a powerful scene in the 1978 *Superman* movie, Lois Lane falls out of a helicopter at the top of a tall building. Superman flies up to catch her and says, "Don't worry, ma'am, I've got you." The startled Lois exclaims, "You've got me? Who's got you?" The only autonomous person in the Universe is Christ, the real Superman. He needs no one to sustain Him.

Fruit
Ephesians 2:2-5 says:

> Once I followed the ways of the world and the Prince of the power of the air. As a child of disobedience, I lived in the passions of my flesh ... carrying out the desires of the body and mind ... and I was by nature a child of wrath, like the rest of mankind. But God, being rich in mercy, because of the greater love with which He loved me, even while I was dead in my trespasses, made me alive together with Christ—by grace I have been saved.
> – ESV (Shank)

Before salvation, I followed the ways of the world and the Prince of the power the air. I carried out his desires because he was operating in me, a son of disobedience. He is the father of disobedience and I was his son. He was the spirit operating (**energeia** – *working*) in me, to corrupt my needs and desires. Satan was my operator.

My body has creational desires and needs designed by God. I'm hungry, so I know I need to resupply my body with food. I want to sleep when my body needs to be refreshed with rest. My soul has feelings of fear to keep me out of danger—a need to be safe. Satan, the Unmaker, wants to misuse those legitimate needs with his selfish agenda. My need for food is corrupted into gluttony. My need for rest becomes laziness.

My desires are also hijacked. My soul's desire to be safe can succumb to both real and imagined threats that paralyze decisive action with *anxiety*. My desire to mate becomes selfish fornication. My desire to succeed becomes domination and control. My desire for affirmation becomes vanity. Needs and desires are not wrong in themselves. But when we are attached to Satan, the Unmaker, they are corrupted.

But when we become believers attached to our Maker, Jesus the True Vine, our needs and desires can be met through grace and submission to God's context and purpose. We must practice the obedience of faith, for which God has given us the grace to learn to do. Faith is believing God's truth by choosing to take actions that are consistent with the Word. Unbelief is rebellion against God that is justified by a **conceit**. I'm defining **conceit** as a *lie of convenience* that sets up a false line of reasoning to disconnect us from following the truth. If we don't repent of our **conceits**, our conscience becomes dull and unresponsive to the Holy Spirit. Our foolish minds are then darkened, corrupting others as well as ourselves. A **conceit** is a *license to disobey*. A policy of disobedience is *licentiousness*, producing a complex of **conceits** in a whole system of sin. As believers, we must learn to break these motivational **conceits** which Satan previously planted in us when we were still his.

For example, I know that slander and gossip are wrong because they tear down people behind their backs. Instead of speaking to Bob directly about what he may doing wrong, I complain to others to build a false sense of privilege and confidence with them. Bob is diminished in what is revealed, as I elevate myself in the eyes of the one to whom I "confide," and they are flattered to share in my secret knowledge of what is really going on.

My motive might be revenge—blocking forgiveness. If Bob has hurt me, I can get even. I justify myself with a **conceit** that I'm entitled with a license to punish Bob, because I didn't deserve the way he treated me.

My motive may also be fear—blocking courageous faith. If I confront Bob about his sins, he may get angry. He may confront me about my sins. So, I say I deserve a safe hiding place to shoot my arrows from a distance. And Bob deserves to be the wide-open target.

My motive could be pride—blocking internal honesty about my sinful part. Nobody gets to do nasty things to ME.

There are legitimate reasons to confide in another: to make sure my motives, perceptions, and actions are right, or even to ask for prayer before I talk to Bob. However, I must be sure I follow through with the policy decided upon, and the person I confide in is trustworthy, and not one who could be corrupted by this shared confidence. The best intentions can have hidden agendas. I must not deceive myself with a **conceit**.

Partakers of God's Nature
2 Peter 1:3-4

> His Divine power has granted to **me** all things that pertain to life and godliness, through the knowledge of Him Who called **me** to His own glory and excellence, by which He has granted to **me** His precious and very great promises, so that through them **I** may become a partaker of *the Divine nature*, having escaped from the corruption that is in the world because of sinful desire.
> – ESV (Shank)

Who can resist the power of God? He has given me all I need for life and godliness. He has given me a new nature like His. It's a holy nature. I am made in God's image, but I am still mortal; my flesh will die. He created my life, but God's life is Uncreated Life. There was never a time when God did not be. When I receive His Holy Spirit, I receive a share in the eternal Life and Nature of God. I now want what God wants. He will teach me to walk in His ways by unpacking what He has promised, which has now been placed inside my spirit. Now I am a partaker or sharer in the Divine *nature*, called to His glory and excellence and promises, life and godliness!

The Right Hand
Ephesians 2:4-10 says:

> But God, rich in mercy because of the great love with which He loved **me**, even when **I** was dead in **my** trespasses, made **me** alive together with Christ—by grace **I** have been saved—and raised **me** up with Him and

seated me with Him in the heavenly places in Christ Jesus. In grace, I have been saved through faith. And this is not my own doing; it is a gift of God, not as a result of my works, so that I may not be able to boast. For I am His workmanship, created in Christ Jesus for good works, which God prepared beforehand, that I should walk in them. – ESV (Shank)

As a partaker in Satan's nature, he was my operator and I was Satan to others and to God. I was a child of wrath because I was like Satan in human form, expressing his selfish nature and justifying myself with the evil agenda of my **conceits**. Sins are the fruit of Sin, which is the nature of Satan, and he blinded me. Even what had the appearance of goodness in me came from his sin-nature because the best a person can do apart from Christ is enlightened self-interest (*soulishness*)—things like getting along to keep it smooth between people, or acts of kindness that prove to myself that I am good and don't need to change... to love people for what they mean to me or could do for me, not what I could be for them.

Before Christ, there had to be a payoff for me to stay in a relationship. Or I owed someone something by obligation or law. Or they owed me. Love without Christ is just another *deal*. There may be warm emotions and strong desires involved, even some sacrifice at times, but only as long as it had the promise of a reward for me. Because the flesh is weak, it gives up after a while when it gets tired of waiting for the *payoff.*

But as a partaker of Christ's nature, I can be Christ to others and to God, seated at His Right Hand in Christ in the heavenly places. In Him I surrender my self-justifying **conceits**. I plead no contest so far as my own merit is concerned. God loved me when I had no other way to live but in selfishness. He mercifully appealed to my self-interest by showing me the way I was living was headed for hell. Ironically, it was the self-interest of my **soul** that led me to repent, because—without Christ—I was still only capable of self-interest. But that was God's plan of grace to me; I could not do otherwise. Since I surrendered to Him, He has shown incredible patience with me as I go through the process of learning how to be more like Him. By

His Spirit being joined to my spirit, I have a new nature and grace to learn how to live by His love in the interest of others, that they may also be helped to salvation and enter the Kingdom to come. What God has lavished upon me, I now want to lavish upon others, even if it causes me some pain or loss along the way—and it has.

The people of the Old Testament were saved by faith in the Messiah to come, but their sins were only *set aside* by the sacrifices of innocent animals without blemish. In Christ, the sins of all are *atoned for* with His holy and perfect Sacrifice. At His death, He descended into Sheol and preached to those who were already dead in faith before His incarnation. Then He led a host of captives free to paradise. At Pentecost, all who received the Spirit of Christ were regenerated. Regeneration means being born again. One who is not born again is still unregenerated, even if that person is a part of a church congregation.

Before Christ, all men were still under Satan. It is possible to be part of the culture of Christianity but not be part of Christ. As Corrie ten Boom's father is reported to have said, "Just because a mouse is in the cookie jar, doesn't make him a cookie." If I try to live the Christian life without being born again, I live in futility because Christ is not joined to me and I am not joined to Him. I will not think as He thinks or see as He sees. I will not have the same heart or have His power to overcome my sins. My best intentions will be misdirected because Satan is still my operator.

The Unregenerate Friend
Mark 8:31-33 says:

> And He began to teach them that the Son of Man must suffer many things and be rejected by the elders and the chief priests and the scribes and be killed, and after three days rise again. And He said this plainly. And Peter took Him aside and began to rebuke Him. But turning and seeing His disciples, He rebuked Peter and said, "Get behind Me, Satan! For you are not setting your mind on the things of God, but on the things of man."
> – ESV

"Get thee behind me Satan!" Jesus called Peter "Satan" because he was the agent of Satan in tempting Him. Peter could not help himself or even see what he was doing because he was not yet a new creation (*regenerated*) in Christ. This would not happen until **Acts 2**. He was still like everyone else at that time, under the fallen mindset of the god of this world, even though he was a disciple of Christ. He wanted to do what he thought was right, but he could not because Satan had blinded him to what real goodness was, just like we were before the Spirit's indwelling. After the atonement of Christ, Peter became a new man in Christ when he was filled with the Holy Spirit, and he became capable of seeing and doing right because he was expressing his *new nature* in Christ.

The Unregenerate Enemy

John 8:38-47 says:

> I speak of what I have seen with My Father, and you do what you have heard from your father. They answered Him, "Abraham is our father." Jesus said to them, "If you were Abraham's children, you would be doing the works Abraham did, but now you seek to kill Me, a man who has told you the truth that I heard from God. This is not what Abraham did. You are doing the works your father did." They said to Him, "We were not born of sexual immorality. We have one Father—even God." Jesus said to them, "If God were your Father, you would love Me, for I came from God and I am here. I came not of My own accord, but He sent Me. Why do you not understand what I say? It is because you cannot bear to hear My word. You are of your father the devil, and your will is to do your father's desires. He was a murderer from the beginning, and has nothing to do with the truth, because the truth is not in him. When he lies, he speaks out of his own character [*nature*], for he is a liar and the father of lies. But because I tell you the truth, you do not believe Me. Which of you convicts Me of sin? If I tell the truth, why do you not believe Me? Whoever is of God hears the words of God. The reason why you do not hear them is that you are *not* of God." – ESV (Shank)

"You are of your father the Devil, and it is his works that you do!" Apart from God, the best we can achieve is enlightened self-interest—making a deal to get along. Self-centeredness is the *sin nature*. Satan is a self who lives for himself and his own selfish purposes. God is a Self Who lives to give to others. The Trinity pours out gifts and blessings to creation. When the creation gives back glory, the Spirit gives glory to the Son, the Son gives glory to the Father, the Father gives glory to the Son—in endless cycles of giving and blessing. In **Revelation 4:9**, we see all those around the Throne who have received crowns from God, bowing down and casting their crowns before the Lord in worship. God has given His love-for-others nature, to us. There was never any time in history when man had a nature apart from either Christ or Satan.

When God created man, He called him good (*well-made, no flaws*), but he was not yet righteous, because he had not yet learned to say no to evil. When Adam obeyed Satan, and ate from the forbidden tree, he was changed into an ashamed man and hid from the Father with Whom he once walked in confident fellowship.

Blinded by Sin and Unbelief

2 Corinthians 4:4 says:

> In their case the god of this world has blinded the minds of the unbelievers, to keep them from seeing the light of the gospel of the Glory of Christ, Who is the image of God." – ESV

It's interesting that when John was preparing the way of the Lord with the baptism of repentance, many of the common people responded to his call to repent. The rulers only came to test and speculate about what he was doing, from an academic distance. They did not repent, so their minds remained blinded to see Who Jesus really was, even when they saw His miracles! Those who obeyed John's call and were baptized were the ones whose eyes were opened, and they were able to see. Satan is the Unmaker, corrupting what God has made, with the cooperation of human spirits that will not obey the truth. Conversely, when one enters into repentance and agrees with God, one begins to see.

The Murderer

1 John 3:11,12 says:

> For this is the message you have heard from the beginning, that you should love one another. We should not be like Cain, who was *of* the evil one and murdered his brother. And why did he murder him? Because his own deeds were evil and his brother's deeds were righteous.
> – ESV (Shank)

"... not as Cain, who was *of* the wicked one..." The reason Jesus says anyone who hates his brother is guilty of murder in his heart is because the Murderer is expressing his nature through that hate. (**Matthew 5:21-23**)

Satan does not want you to be born again. If you are born again, he does not want you to know you are now one who contains the Holy Spirit and are joined to Christ by His Spirit. The enemy does not want you to discover you can boldly go before the Throne of God as His child. Your Father will answer your prayers, break bonds, and give you authority over the Evil One, if you really begin to believe you are seated at His Right Hand, in Christ.

If you have received the Spirit of Christ, Satan still wants you to see yourself falsely, as separated from God, keeping the conceit of thinking you can work out your problems, by your own fleshly will, with a little of God's help now and then. He wants you to see yourself as a beggar who must beg God to do what is good. He does not want you to know that God is only motivated by His Own Goodness, and because of the Blood, you now have the full benefit of that Goodness. Satan wants you to remain weak, wounded, outcast, filled with defeat, naked, and ashamed.

You may have seen that well intended but sentimental wall poster that has a poem called "Footprints." It describes how two pairs of footprints in the sand show Jesus walking with the author. Then only one set of footprints is showing through a rough patch. The author asks if he was abandoned during that time. Jesus is said to respond, "It was then that I carried you." I'm sure the author is a real Christian and means to encourage other believers, but this sentiment undermines the meaning of **Ephesians 2, John 17, Romans 6-8,** and others quoted here.

The leverage in overcoming is not just that God is *with* you. It's that you are *in* Christ and He is *in* you. Your old nature is dead. Believe it! You are now joined to Christ by the Holy Spirit, Who is indwelling your human spirit. Believe it! There is no time when He is not with you and you are not with Him. How long will we believe like children who need the constant reassurance of the perception of our senses? Blessed are those who believe without seeing, feeling, touching. And why are they blessed? Because they walk in the power of faith. God knows what encouragement we may need and when. He also knows when we need to just stand in faith, when our senses seem to testify against the promises of the Word.

He Identifies with Me
Hebrews 4: 14-16 says:

> Since **I** have a Great High Priest Who has passed through the heavens, Jesus the Son of God, **I** will hold fast to **my** confession. For **I** do not have a high priest who is unable to sympathize with **my** weakness [*in the flesh*], but One Who in every respect has been tempted as **I** am, yet without Him sinning. So, it is with confidence that **I** draw near to the Throne of Grace, that **I** may receive mercy and find grace to help in **my** times of need. – ESV (Shank)

The intercession of Christ for **me** was to be born in the flesh like **me**, to be tempted in every way as **I** am, but for Him to be completely victorious over sin. He knows what it's like to be **me**, feeling the pull of sin in His mortal flesh. Then Jesus offered Himself as the penalty for **my** sin, in **my** place, by His own death. God said death is the fruit of sin **I** deserve. As Co-Creator of the universe, Christ made the world and all that lives in it. He's worth more than all of us put together because He has the power to make another world and all the life in that world, and another and another. So, His Blood on the Scales of Justice weighs far more than all the worlds put together, and that surely covers all **my** sin. I will not let the **conceit**—of letting my vanity masquerade as humility—convince **me** that **I** am uniquely special at being capable of exhausting His sacrifice and grace!

Then He rose from the dead because death could not hold the Author of life. And He has raised you and me up to be with Him forever, now in spirit and later with a new incorruptible body at the resurrection.

I Must Identify with Him
Romans 6:1-4

> What will **I** say? Am **I** to continue in sin that grace may abound? By no means! How can **I who** died to sin still live in it? **I** know that **my** being baptized into Christ means **I** was baptized into His death. **I** was buried with Him by baptism into death, in order that, just as Christ was raised from the dead by the glory of the Father, **I** too might walk in newness of life.
> – ESV (Shank)

He identified with me, so now it's time for me to identify with Him. "Don't you know that all of us who are baptized into Christ Jesus are baptized into His death?" I used to *hate* that verse. What do you mean "Don't you know...?" How could I possibly know that? "I was buried with Him in His death?" I was not alive 2000 years ago to die with Him. But since I believe the Word of God does not lie, how can this be?

Now I see. It's not symbolic or by proxy alone. I am *actually joined* by the Spirit to The One Who died back then. His sin-overcoming nature is now mine because He is in me and I am in Him! My mind only begins to comprehend this now, but the Word does not lie, so I can stand on it by faith, and I now have some fruit from that faith. Every time I make a decision to obey Christ against my feelings, impressions or opinions to the contrary, I generate evidence that the Word is true, by the fruit that follows.

Union with Christ
Romans 6:5-11

> For if I have been united with Him in a death like His,
> I will surely be united with Him in a resurrection like
> His. I know that **my** old self was crucified with Him in
> order that this body of sin might be brought to nothing,
> so that I would no longer be enslaved by sin. For one
> who has died is set free from sin. Now, if I have died
> with Christ, I believe that I will also live with Him. I
> know that Christ being raised from the dead, will never
> die again; death no longer has dominion over Him. For
> the death He died He died to sin, once for all, but the
> life He lives He lives to God. So, I also consider **myself**
> dead to sin and alive to God in Christ Jesus. – ESV
> (Shank)

United in Him

Symphutos is the Greek for a similarity of experience and nature. I am united with Him in His death and in His resurrection. The temptation to sin remains, but the *nature* to want to sin has been crucified with Christ, who died to sin. When tempted, I must believe this by faith, which is to act *as if* the Word is true, not believe what my soul-feelings say is true. Feelings are not facts. The Word is fact. When I make choices *as if* the Word is true, I am walking by faith. If I make choices *as if* my feelings, opinions or even habits are true, I walk in unbelief and make myself a hypocrite, because I now have the mind of Christ. But when I make choices *as if* the Word is true, I begin to generate evidence that the Word is true, and then I begin to see I really am a *new creation* in Christ. As a vessel of Christ, I am now Christ in my form; learning to express His Christ life to the world around me.

Chapter 2 Study Questions

Answer the following questions from what you have just read, *not from whatever your prior understanding of these things may be.*

1. Where did my desire for sin come from and what part of me still wants it, if I am a real Christian?

2. Why do I have to suffer in my flesh as I learn to obey God?

3. How can I know I was crucified with Christ 2000 years ago before I was even born?

4. How do I know Jesus knows what I experience and suffer?

5. The Lord identified with me; how can I possibly identify with Him?

3

My Nature Is in My Spirit

1 John 4:4-6 My (*my reply*)

> Jesus, I am now from God and have overcome the anti-
> christ and the world. For He Who is in **me** is greater
> than he who is in the world. They are from the world;
> therefore, they speak from the world, and the world lis-
> tens to them. Christ is from God. Whoever knows God
> listens to Him (*and* I *do*); whoever is not from God
> does not listen to Him. By this I know the Spirit of
> truth and the spirit of error. – ESV (Shank)

He that is in me is Christ. The rest have the spirit of the world
in them. The nature of Christ and the nature of the world are
opposed to each other. There is no autonomous human nature
apart from either one.

Jesus said, "Out of the abundance of the heart, the mouth
speaks" (**Matthew 12:34**). He's referring to my attitude of believing. The human spirit is the intended receptacle for the
Spirit of God. It is what makes union with God possible and is
also why the Church is called the Bride of Christ, being one
spirit with Him. My spirit is joined to either the Spirit of
Christ, or the spirit of the antichrist: Satan. The result of the
Spirit's indwelling is a new nature that wants to do God's will.
That new nature begins to affect the attitude of my heart to
express the will and intentions of God with tenderness and
good deeds. Without a new spirit, there can be no new heart,
no matter how sincere a person may be.

This is why John calls me to test the spirits in people—
because the source of what they profess is either Christ or Satan, however appealing their arguments may seem. My confession is to be much more than what I say with my lips because
lips can lie. Those who are really in Christ have a consistency
in their words and deeds with the Word of God. John says that
if I am in Christ, the Word will resonate with me. If I am not in
Christ I will listen to false teaching prophets. If as a Christian I

disobey God, I will produce corrupt fruit and jeopardize my testimony, until I repent.

What does repentance really mean? Repentance is a change of mind. It's also a redirection of my ways. More importantly, it's a redirection of my heart's believing. My sinful-behavior choices can also be seen as coming from Satan's *Sin vine*. The fruit on those branches are sinful deeds. If I am a believer in Christ I am no longer joined to the *Sin vine*, but if I sin, I bare sin fruit *as if* I am not a believer, until I repent. Sins are nourished by branches of **conceits** or lies of convenience that give my flesh permission to act in accordance with Satan's selfish agenda, as well as habits of unbelief I have learned from years of obeying his evil will. The need for permission to sin comes from the conflict in my conscience between what God wants and the sinful entitlements I have believed I deserved. (*Because of what they did to me, I get to do that to them.*)

Satan wants me to believe I am still separated from God and have to resort to sinful ways to get what I want because God won't be enough for me. The deepest repentance is to change my core believing about myself: I am now *in* Christ and He is *in* me. I am now *like* Him; I *want* to do my Father's will. Because of Jesus, I am free from the power of sin. I have the grace to learn how to walk that truth out in this life because God is for me and not against me. If I stumble He will forgive me. I must confess and repent when I sin. Then I am to rule over the power of my flesh with the power of God in me. My flesh is mine, but it *is not* me. The Word of God *does not* lie.

Consider the Exodus

- The children of God and His Promise were slaves to Pharaoh, which is a picture of our being slaves to Satan.

- The blood of the Passover lamb is a picture of the Blood of Christ.

- Crossing the Red Sea is a picture of baptism.

- The pillar of fire by night and the cloud by day that led Israel presents a picture of the Holy Spirit, always in our midst and now, always in you and me who have believed.

- The generation to whom the Law was given, but who rebelled, is a picture of those who did not see themselves as free from their old ways—that slave-to-sin nature and mindset. So, they died in the wilderness. They could not overcome, and we cannot overcome unless we believe we are joined to Christ in His Nature and Power.

- The next generation represents those who learned to overcome and take possession of the promises of God. That generation is a picture of the new man, living in the grace of Christ with the Power of His Life.

It's interesting to see in **Hebrews 3:19**, concerning those who were overthrown in the wilderness: they were unable to enter in because of unbelief.

And in **Hebrews 4:1-2** it says:
> Therefore, while the promise of entering His rest remains, let us fear lest any of you be judged to have failed to reach it. For the good news came to us just as to them; but the message which they heard did not benefit them, because it did not meet with [*not having been mixed together with*] faith in the hearers.
> – RSV Interlinear Greek English New Testament

So how do I mix faith with the Word? How do I become more than just one who hears the Word? I must become a doer of the Word by believing I can do all things in Christ Jesus because I am a new creation in Him. My choices express my real faith. Faith is *acting as if* what the Word says about me is true with a righteous choice against evil. When I mix faith with the Word by an act of obedience, I generate a solid brick of evidence that the Overcomer is in me. The more bricks I make, the stronger I become. This is not by my strength. This is the fruit of faith—through my operator, Christ!

Who Reigns?
Romans 6:12-23

> I will not let sin reign in my mortal body to make **me** obey its passions. I will not present **my** members to sin as instruments of unrighteousness. Rather, I will present myself to God as one who has been brought from death to life. I present **my** members to God as instruments for righteousness. For sin has no more dominion over **me**, since I am not under the law but under grace.
>
> What then? Am I to sin because I am not under law but under grace? By no means! I know that if I present **myself** to anyone as an obedient slave, I am a slave to the one I obey, either of sin that leads to death, or of obedience, which leads to righteousness. But, thanks be to God, that I **who** was once a slave to sin have become obedient from the heart (*transformed by my new spirit nature in Christ*) to the standard of teaching to which I am committed, and having been set free from sin, I have become a slave of righteousness... For just as I once presented **my** members as a slave to impurity and to lawlessness leading to more lawlessness, so now I present **my** members as a slave to righteousness leading to sanctification.
>
> For when I was a slave to sin, I was a freeman in regard to righteousness. But I am now ashamed of the fruit I got from that way of living. For the end of those things is death to **me**. But now that I have been set free from sin and have become a slave to God, the fruit I get leads to sanctification and its end, eternal life. For the wages of sin is death, but the free gift of God is eternal life in Christ Jesus **my** Lord. – ESV (Shank)

When I was a slave (*or bond servant*) to sin, I was free from righteousness, that is, my conscience didn't bother me very much. I followed the self-for-me nature of Satan, doing what I thought was in my own interest. I was somewhat aware that what I was doing was wrong, but I didn't really want to stop myself, and largely ignored how my behavior was affecting others.

As a slave or bondservant to righteousness, I am now free from the power of sin. Now I am learning to walk after the self-for-others nature of God because He has freed me to do so and empowered me with His Spirit. My desire is to please my Lord, even though I am tempted through the weakness of my flesh. But I am *not* my flesh. My flesh is mine to manage, but it *is not* me.

Law Versus Grace

The Law gives sin its power because Satan appeals to God's justice against me to induce condemnation, saying, "See, he has broken Your law; do not bless him." Grace gives righteousness its power because the penalty I deserve for breaking God's Law has been paid by the Son of God Himself. Satan appeals to my flesh with prideful conceit and vanity, trying to convince me I can be good enough on my own apart from God. The enemy tempts me to sin, then kicks me with the Law for sinning.

In the movie *Patton*, the German general Rommel is drawn into an ambush set by General Patton of the Allied Forces during the North African Campaign of WWII. As the German army is drawn into the trap, Patton turns to one of his aids and colorfully says, "Here's where we grab him by the nose and kick him in the ass." That's exactly what Satan does to me if I follow him.

- The one you obey is your master. – **Romans 6:16**

- You cannot have two masters. – **Matthew 6:24**

- What you take, takes you. – Norman Grubb

Sold to Sin

I think it's important to consider a spiritual principle that serves as the determining factor in blessings or curses.

Romans 7:14 says:

> The Law is spiritual, but I am of the flesh, *sold* under sin. – ESV (*Shank*)

Notice the following examples of being *bought and sold* by God: When Adam disobeyed God and obeyed Satan, all his children were *sold* to sin. There was a change in who was to be his master. Again, sin is the nature of Notgod, Satan. Since Adam had been given dominion over the earth, his domain fell with him into decay and death. All his seed were *sold* to sin with him. This means that all of us who are Adam's descendants were also *sold* to sin. But to our fleshly reasoning, this does not seem fair. Why should I have to suffer bondage to sin because of what Adam did long before I was born? (*You can only ask this question if you do not know yourself or know your master.*)

The mind of the flesh does not understand the things of the spirit. The mindset of the flesh thinks it can do better. But God in His foreknowledge knew each one of us would fall into the power of sin on our own, to become children of wrath. Look at the spiritual principle of the seed revealed in **1 Corinthians 15:42-50**:

> So it is with the resurrection of the dead. What is sown is perishable; what is raised is imperishable. It is sown in dishonor; it is raised in glory. It is sown in weakness; it is raised in power. It is sown a natural body; it is raised a spiritual body. If there is a natural body, there is also a spiritual body. Thus it is written, "The first man Adam became a living being"; the last Adam [*Christ*] became a life-giving Spirit. But it is not the spiritual that came first but the natural, and then the spiritual. The first man was of the earth, a man of dust; the second Man is from heaven. As was the man of dust, [*Adam*] so also are those who are of the dust, and as is the Man of heaven [*Christ*], so also are those who are of heaven. Just as we have borne the image of the man of dust, we shall also bear the image of the Man of heaven. I tell you this, brothers: flesh and blood cannot inherit the kingdom of God, nor does the perishable inherit the imperishable. – ESV (Shank)

So, God is merciful. A fantastic purpose was intended in the creation of man. It has not yet begun. This life is only the qualifying stage for us to choose to be part of that fantastic purpose!

1 Corinthians 15:53-54 says:

> For this perishable body must put on the imperishable, and the mortal body must put on immortality. When the perishable puts on the imperishable, and the mortal puts on immortality, then shall come to pass the saying that is written: (**Isaiah 25:8**) "Death is swallowed up in victory." – ESV (Shank)

Perfect Symmetry
The one-man problem and One-Man solution.
Romans 5:12,15-19 says:

> Therefore, just as sin came into the world through one man, and death through sin, and death spread to all men because all sinned ...

> But the free gift is not like the trespass. For if many died through one-man's trespass, much more have the grace of God and the free gift by the grace of that One-Man Jesus Christ abounded for many. And the free gift is not like the result of that one-man's sin. For the judgment following one trespass brought condemnation, but the free gift following many trespasses brought justification [*salvation*]. For if, because of one-man's trespass, death reigned through that one-man, much more will those who receive the abundance of grace and the free gift of righteousness reign in life through the One-Man Jesus Christ. Therefore, as one trespass led to condemnation for *all* men, so One Act of Righteousness leads to justification and life for *all* men. For as by one-man's disobedience the many were made sinners, so by One-Man's obedience the many will be made righteous. – ESV (*Shank*)

So, if God let sin come into the world by one man, Adam, He could take sin out of the world by One Man, Jesus Christ. We who are the seed of Adam were *sold* to sin by the sin of our natural father. But we who believe and receive the Holy Spirit are the seed of Christ, our new spiritual Father. Born in the natural, we must put on the spiritual by believing in the sacrifice of Christ in our place. The *putting on* of Christ is a repentance that means more than the turning away from our old sins. Ultimately, we must no longer see ourselves as having the nature of the one who had us before. We now have the power of Christ in us to learn how to overcome sin by His power in us to bear His righteous fruit. We are no longer the seed of Adam, but we are the seed of Christ!

As we consider seed, it's interesting to observe in **Hebrews 7:1-10** that Abraham paid tithes to Melchizedek, the King of Salem. The main point of the recounting of this event was to show that Abraham was justified by faith before there was any Law, because the Law of Moses was not given until almost 500 years later. But Moses was a descendant of Levi, a great grandson of Abraham. The Covenant of Faith *preceded* the Covenant of the Law and is therefore greater. But notice what it says in **verse 7:9** regarding the sons of Levi, who were not to be born until 500 years later, to begin serving in the office of the priestly line in Israel:

> One might even say that Levi himself, who [*as a forefather of Moses and Arron's sons, the priests*] receives tithes, paid tithes through Abraham, for he was still in the loins of his ancestor [*as seed*] when Melchizedek met him. –ESV (Shank)

Now if Levi was in Abraham's loins when Abraham believed God, paid tithes and was blessed by God through his great grandfather Abraham's faith, we can also say that we who believe are children of Abraham—and even more in Christ, Who has redeemed us. Christ was also Abraham's descendant through His mother's seed, and He is also one with God His Father. And we who believe are in Christ by the spirit!

More About Being Sold and Bought
In **Genesis 37:28**, Joseph was *sold* by his jealous brothers for twenty shekels of silver. But because he had the favor of the Lord, God's favor went with him. His brothers lost favor with

God, until the same brother they betrayed redeemed (*or bought*) them.

In **Genesis 47:13-22**, all of Egypt became slaves to Pharaoh under the management of Joseph, who sat at the right hand of the king (*like Jesus at the Right Hand of God in* **Ephesians 1:19-23**). When the famine came, the people bought the grain from Joseph until the money was gone. Then they *sold* their livestock to buy grain. The year after that, the Egyptians *sold* themselves to Joseph as his slaves, in order to buy food to survive. As God's agent, Joseph made *all* of Egypt slaves to Pharaoh, just as Adam's descendants were *sold* to Sin and Satan because of their disobedience. In the last days, God will cause all the people of the earth to be *sold* to the Beast because they have rejected Him, persecuted His church and refused to repent.

Israel and Judah were later *sold* for nothing to Babylon for destruction because they valued God as nothing (**Isaiah 50:1**) ... and you will be redeemed (*bought*) without money ... (*only a remnant was saved*). **Isaiah 52:3** says it is because of their rejection of God and His ways. Whatever is no longer valued is sold off by both God and by man.

Jesus was *sold* for thirty pieces of silver (**Matthew 27:9-10**). But His death paid for all our sin. His Blood *bought* us back. Like Joseph, Jesus has God's favor. And like Joseph, He sits at the Right Hand of the Real King, and the whole of creation is under His Feet. We who believe are *bought* with His Blood and get to sit at the Right Hand, in Him.

Romans 11:30-32 says:

> For just as you [*gentiles*] were at one time disobedient to God but now have received mercy because of [*Israel's*] disobedience, [*in the rejection of Christ*] so now they too have been disobedient in order that by the mercy shown to you [*gentiles*] they [*Israel*] may now receive mercy. For God has consigned [*sold*] all to disobedience, that He may have mercy on all. – ESV (Shank)

God's ways are often mysterious and baffling, but the goodness in all His motives will prove out in the end, when we will *know* even as we are *known* by Him. Until then, we know all we need to know to have faith in what He is doing to fulfill the plan and purpose that was laid before the foundation of the earth.

My Flesh Is Mine, But It Is Not Me
Romans 7:15-19 says:

> I do not do what I want, but I do the very thing I hate. Now if I do what I do not want, I agree with the Law that it is good. So now it is no longer **I who** do it, but sin that dwells within **me** [my *members*]. For I know that nothing good dwells in **me**, that is, **my** *flesh*. For I have the desire to do what is right, but not the ability to carry it out. For I do not do the good I want, but the evil I do not want is what I keep on doing. – ESV (Shank)

Sin still takes advantage of the weakness that is in my flesh (**sarx**)—my members (**melesin**)—or body parts. Sin still dwells in my flesh but it is no longer I who do it? How can this be when my old nature has been crucified with Christ? That nature was the character my human spirit had before the in-dwelling of the Holy Spirit, that human heart Jesus described as being desperately wicked. But I now have a new heart. The Word now defines me as a new man in Christ, and the Bible does not lie. This means I can learn to take authority over my flesh with the strength of Christ, Who is joined to me. If I give in to my flesh and sin, I'm still responsible for that sin and its consequences because in unbelief, I have let Satan have his way to bear his fruit in my disobedience. I must repent to restore the favor of God, which is now mine in Christ.

Two Laws at War in Me
Romans 7:20-23 says:

> Now if **I** do what **I** do not want, it is no longer **I who** do it, but sin that dwells within **me** [*my flesh*]. So, **I** find it to be a law that when I want to do right, evil lies close at hand. For I delight in the law of God, in **my** in-ner being [*my spirit*], but I see in **my** *members* another law waging war against the law of **my** mind and mak-

ing **me** captive to the law of sin that dwells in **my** *members.* – ESV (Shank)

The key to understanding this is "if **I** do what **I** do not want" and "**I** delight in the law of God," I am giving evidence to being God's child by *wanting* to be like Him, even though the law condemns me if I give in to sin with willful disobedience. Sin is still close at hand, in that it will always press me through my flesh. But Satan is also proving my sonship of God by regarding both Christ and me as his enemy. The devil testifies that I am no longer his by trying to ruin my testimony and keep me from becoming an overcomer who can do real damage to his king-dom. God allows this vulnerability to persist in me because I must still eat from the Tree of the Knowledge of Good and Evil in this life. That Tree is the Law, and I must chew on that fruit until the next life, when I can eat from the Tree of Life—being part of the spotless Bride.

For now, I must learn to choose righteousness and reject evil by the power of Christ in me. Only in the life to come will I be able to eat from the Tree of Life and live forever without sin or even temptation. Though I am now like Christ in nature, I need to become like Him in deeds as well, by changing the exercise of my free will. God's indwelling Spirit makes me good. But righteousness is now mine by choosing to say no to evil thoughts and deeds. I must choose to produce consistent fruit by living *as if* I have the overcoming life of Christ in me. In this way, faith is mixed with the Word by my making choices *as if* the Word of God is true. This is the only way I will come to know that I am at the Right Hand of God in Christ as de-scribed in **Ephesians 2**. This is the only way I will know that what I bind on earth will be bound in heaven. This is how I will know that Satan will flee me when I tell him to leave in Jesus' Name!

When Shakespeare says in *The Tempest*, "The strongest oaths are but straw for the fires of the blood." He's affirming that my best intentions—my oaths and promises—are futile because of the weakness of my flesh. As long as I believe I am only my flesh, or just a sinner saved by grace, futility will be my fate. But as I learn to unpack the wonderful treasures of Power—

gifts and grace that are now mine because I am in Christ and He is in me—the fruits of faith will most certainly show more and more.

Romans 7:25 describes seeing spirit and flesh:
> Thanks be to God through Jesus Christ our Lord! So then, **I myself** serve the law of God with **my** mind, but with **my** *flesh* I serve the law of sin. – ESV (Shank)

But Paul rejoices in seeing he is not his flesh, with all the condemnation associated with that. He has the mind of Christ. His mind—now knows and wants the will of God, and he no longer wants what his flesh wants. Let me illustrate: Imagine you're watching a bullfight in an arena. The matador is Satan, and the bull is the Christian. The red cape the devil is waving in front of the bull is accusation, condemnation, and temptation. The bull has more strength than he realizes, but the matador distracts him by making him charge a **lie**. Satan knows that once the bull realizes the red cape is not his problem, the powerful bull will come after him! But if the devil can wear out the bull by making him chase futility, the bull can be easily defeated—made ineffective for the kingdom of God.

The big lie Satan uses against me is that I may be forgiven but I still have his old nature—even though the Word clearly says that my old nature, my old self, is **dead**. Satan's argument: "You're just the same person you always were. You love sin. You always give in to it. You don't love righteousness, so God can't use you and He won't even answer your prayers because the scripture says the prayers of the righteous avail much—but you love sin in your heart. Jesus said your anger and lusts are the same as if you committed murder and adultery. You love lust and revenge—you're guilty! All you can do now is grovel for the grace you don't deserve. And God is sick of hearing your apologies and excuses. Who do you think you are? Leave God alone! He won't help you anymore. You have exhausted His grace!" So, who am I going to believe, Christ or Satan?

God's Part & My Part
For a clearer understanding of God's once-and-for-all acts and what man's continuous and perpetual acts are to be, see also

Chapter 12 - The Root of Lawlessness, under The Greek Tenses. Basically, the Greek **aorist** tense refers to *once and for all acts*, and the **present** and future tenses refer to *continuous and perpetual acts*. Got it? When **John 17:17** quotes Jesus' prayer to the Father on our behalf: "Sanctify them in the truth, Your Word is truth"—the **aorist** tense makes it say, *Sanctify them once and for all in Your truth*. This is a *once and forever* thing. When **Romans 6:6** says, "We know that our old self was [*once and for all* crucified...]" the *old self* is really dead. The idea of a Christian's old self eternally battling the new self is a wide spread **error**. The battle is now between the new self and the flesh. The sinful nature of the old man has been put to death *once and for all*.

I battle the devil now only as he can gain advantage of me through the weakness of my flesh. Unbelief and misbelief are his weapons. Therefore, I am to believe *continuously and perpetually* that I have the power to bring my flesh into subjection.

Standing on the *once-and-for-all things* Christ has done; I am to persevere in *continuous and perpetual acts* of obedience. **John 11:25b-26** really says:

> Whoever believes [*continuously and perpetually*] in Me, though he dies, yet shall he live, and everyone who lives and believes [*continuously and perpetually*] in Me shall never die.

In **Romans 1:16** Paul says:

> For I am not ashamed of the gospel, for it is the power of God for salvation to everyone who believes... [*continuously and perpetually*].

Does this mean I am back under salvation by works like the foolish and bewitched in **Galatians 3:1-6**? No. Look at **Joshua 10:24-25**:

> And when they brought those kings out to Joshua, Joshua summoned all the men of Israel and said to the chiefs of the men of war who had gone with him, "Come near; put your feet on the necks of these kings." Then they came near and put their feet on their necks.

> And Joshua said to them, "Do not be afraid or dismayed;
> be strong and courageous. For thus the Lord will do to
> all your enemies against whom you fight." – ESV

If I will resist sin—fight it—the Lord will overpower my enemies. The necks of the kings are like the powers and principalities that God put are under Jesus' Feet in **Ephesians 1:22**; and
in **2:6,** He also raised you and me up to sit with Him in the
heavenly places in Christ Jesus, at the Right Hand of God. If I
will believe, I will fight; if I fight, God will give me the victory.
This is *continuously and perpetually* true if I will *believe* and
act by fighting the enemy. And I will have grace to learn how
to overcome when I make choices *as if* the Word of God is actually true.

The Bride Revisited
Romans 7:2-6

> For a married woman is bound to her husband as long
> as he lives, but if her husband dies, she is released from
> the law of marriage. Accordingly, she will be called an
> adulteress if she lives with another man while her hus-
> band is alive. But if her husband dies, she is free from
> the law, and if she marries another man she is not an
> adulteress.
>
> Likewise, my brothers, you also have died to the law
> through the body of Christ, so that you may belong to
> Another, to Him Who has been raised from the dead, in
> order that we may bear fruit for God. For while we
> were living in the flesh, our sinful passions, aroused by
> the law, were at work in our members to bear the fruit
> of death. But now we are released from the law, having
> died to that which held us captive, so that we serve in
> the new way of the Spirit and not in the old way of the
> written code. – ESV

Death frees me from The Law, because death is the *solution* for
sin. As noted in **Chapter 1,** the wife bears the seed (**sperma**) of
the first husband. If he dies and she remarries, she bears the
seed of the new husband. She never bears seed on her own. The
first husband = the Satan nature, the second husband = the

Christ nature. The first husband bears seed condemned by the Law. The second husband bears the seed of righteousness and freedom from condemnation by the Spirit. If I have the Spirit of Christ, I can now bear His seed in my life.

The human spirit is a receptor meant for the Holy Spirit. This is why we are made in the image of God.

Genesis 1:26, 27 says:
> Let us make man in Our image, after Our likeness.
> So God created man in His own image, in the image of God He created him; male and female He created them.
> – ESV

In **Genesis 2:23**, He created a wife for Adam by taking one of his ribs to make Eve bone of his bone. He created the Church by giving the Spirit of His Son to His Bride, so she could become spirit of His Spirit. The Church is referred to as the Bride of Christ.

John 3:29 says:
> ... the Bride belongs to the Bridegroom.

Ephesians 5:23 says:
> The husband is the head of the wife as Christ is the head of the Church.

And in **Ephesians 5:32** Paul says:
> This mystery is profound, and I am saying that it refers to Christ and the Church.

When we receive the Holy Spirit in our human spirit, that *union* results in a new nature. Women may protest the way God is referred to in the masculine in Scripture, and men may feel strange being part of the Bride of Christ, but this is because the human spirit is *female* in the sense that it receives the Holy Spirit *into itself.* We are transformed by the Holy Spirit into a new creation in Christ, belonging to Him. How else could the Church be a wife fit for Christ? This analogy is further proved by its opposite; the prophets routinely condemned Israel's pursuance of other gods as harlotry and adultery against their

True Husband, God. **Ezekiel 23** is especially graphic in its sexual analogy!

In **Revelation 17**, the great prostitute who rides the beast with seven heads and ten horns is likely the apostate church that has fallen away from the Lord. She is bejeweled with gifts she wears that could represent the honors the world gave her for selling out. But once the beast has finished with her, she will be cast aside, like Israel and Judah in **Ezekiel 23**. The compromised church is the tool of Satan, who always betrays his followers once he has caused them to sin.

Revelation 18:4-7 says:

> Then I heard another voice from heaven saying, "Come out from her, O My people, lest you take part in her sins, lest you take part in her plagues; for her sins are heaped up high as heaven, and God has remembered her iniquities. Pay her back as she herself has paid back others and repay her double for her deeds; mix a double portion for her in the cup she mixed. As she glorified herself and lived in luxury, so give her a like measure of torment and mourning, since in her heart she says, 'I sit as a queen, I am no widow, and mourning I shall never see.' – ESV

Double portion of punishment came to Israel when she rebelled. Double portion of punishment comes to the apostate church as well. They both know better, having begun with God. She says, "I am no widow" (*I am self-sufficient—I am not destitute.*), "and mourning I shall never see" (*she has no need to repent*). If you are a member of a church that is selling out the Word of the Lord, warn them, then, as the angel said "come out from her, O My people lest you take part in her sins, lest you take part in her plagues;"—go find a believing church!

Made to Contain
Romans 7:5,6
Now I am free both from the power of Sin and the power of the Law, by the Body of Christ. In Christ, I no longer live by the letter of the Law, but by the Spirit. – ESV (Shank)

There are only two ways to be. You and I have always been ...

- *Slaves* – either to a Sin owner or to The Righteousness Owner,

- *Branches* – bearing fruit of either the false vine or The True Vine,

- *Wives* – producing the seed of either the Satan husband or The Christ Husband,

- *Vessels* – of either wrath or mercy,

- *A spirit temple* (**naos**) – of either Satan or Christ,

- *A body* – controlled by either a Satan head or a Christ Head,

- *A child* – of either father Satan or of Christ—the Everlasting Father, Prince of Peace, and Almighty God.

Again, you and I have never been self-operated or morally autonomous of either *operator* or *energizer*, the Greek terms for an indwelling deity.

You and I have never been the *originators* of evil or good, but only the expressers of the will of one or the other master. But in Christ, I am capable of expressing the righteousness of His moral nature.

Predestination & Free Will
Ephesians 1:3-14 says,

> Blessed be the God and Father of **my** Lord Jesus Christ, Who has blessed **me** with every spiritual blessing in the heavenly places, even as He chose **me** in Him before the foundation of the world, that **I** should be holy and blameless before Him. In love, He predestined **me** for adoption as a son, [*His child*] through Jesus Christ, according to the purpose of His will, to the praise of His glorious grace, with which He has blessed **me** in the Beloved. In Him **I** have redemption through His Blood,

the forgiveness of **my** trespasses, according to the riches of His grace, which He lavished upon **me**, in all wisdom and insight making known to **me** the mystery of His will, according to the **purpose**, which He set forth in Christ as a **plan** for the fullness of time, to unite all things in Him, things in heaven and things on earth.

In Him **I** have received an inheritance, having been predestined according to the purpose of Him Who works all things according to the counsel of His will, so that **I** who *hope* in Christ might be to the praise of His glory. In Him **I** also, when **I** *heard* the word of truth, the gospel of **my** salvation, and *believed* in Him, was sealed with the promised Holy Spirit, Who is the guarantee of **my** inheritance until **I** acquire possession of it, to the praise of His glory. – ESV (Shank)

A predestined **plan** and a **purpose** were set forth before the foundation of the world—not who is saved and who is not. This is not what election means. Otherwise, what good would it do to *hope* in, or *hear,* or *believe* in, the Word of Truth? As animals live by instinct, shall man, the image of God, live by predestined outcomes? God already **knows** who will believe and who will not. He **sees** the end from the beginning. It's true that He chose Pharaoh to be the instrument of evil, and He chose Moses to be an instrument of good. He even hardened Pharaoh's heart, but that was after Pharaoh hardened his own heart several times.

But the ruling principle is that "many are called but few are chosen" (**Matthew 22:14**). Because God **foreknew** Pharaoh would never repent, He used Pharaoh to make His glory known to both Egypt and Israel. He also **foreknew** Moses would faithfully obey Him. God did not arbitrarily love Jacob and hate Esau when they were born. He **foreknew** what each would be as men and blessed the one He **foreknew** would come to believe. For God to have **foreknowledge** of what people will do is not necessarily to cause them to do it. An all-powerful God can suspend control whenever He wishes. When the Bible says, God will put a hook in the nose of Gog to make him come down and attack Israel, that is the *exception,* not the rule. Again, "many are called but few are chosen." But those whom He chooses, He has first **foreknown**.

God's justice is not in conflict with His sovereignty any more than His love is in conflict with His wrath. Some say that God is not sovereign if He does not control everything. Others argue that God is not just, if some are made for heaven and some are made for hell, making moral choices meaningless. The plan and purpose (**verse 13**) was that all who would *hear* and *believe* in the gospel of Christ would be saved. This is about the free will to choose. Those receiving His Spirit reap the benefit of the predestined **plan** and **purpose** of God, to receive a lavish inheritance in Christ. We who believe are in Him, and He is in us, as Jesus prayed in **John 17:20-22**, that we who have believed should be perfectly one with He and the Father, as They are with each other.

One may ask, what about verses like **Romans 8:28-30?**

> And we know that for those who love God all things work together for good, for those who are called according to His purpose. For those whom He **foreknew** He also predestined to be conformed to the image of His Son, in order that He might be the firstborn among many brothers. And those whom He predestined He also called, and those whom He called He also justified, and those whom He justified He also glorified. – ESV (*Shank*)

And **1 Corinthians 1:27-29?**

> But God chose what is foolish in the world to shame the wise; God chose what is weak in the world to shame the strong; God chose what is low and despised in the world, even things that are not, to bring to nothing things that are, so that no human being might boast in the Presence of God. – ESV

Does this not mean we are all too corrupted by sin to be able to choose God, even more so if we are expressing the will of Satan by our original sin nature? The truth is we were absolutely corrupt, but part of the plan of God is also to reveal the Judgment to come. God mercifully uses the self-interest of our **souls** (*see*

Chapter 5) to motivate us to escape Hell, leading us to repent and then receive the righteous desire for God by His Spirit. The fear of God is the *beginning* of wisdom. (*What's going to happen to me?*) The prodigal son did not repent till circumstances got really bad for him. It was in *his own best interest* to repent and go home in **Luke 15:17**. Notice also Gomer, the unfaithful wife of Hosea, who says to herself when her sins pile up consequences against her in **Hosea 2:7**. I will go and return to my first husband, for it was better for *me* then than now.

Repentance and judgment are meaningless without the power to *choose* what is right and wrong. Fear of consequences provokes faith in the brood of vipers to cry out to God for salvation. John used this phrase when he spoke to the crowds coming to the Jordan to be baptized in **Matthew 3:7-8**:

> But when he saw many of the Pharisees and Sadducees coming to his baptism, he said to them, "You brood of vipers! Who warned you to flee the wrath to come? Bear fruit in keeping with repentance." – ESV

In **Matthew 23:33**, Jesus says the same thing to those who are opposing Him,

> You serpents, you brood of vipers, how are you to escape being sentenced to hell? – ESV

What a perfect picture of the serpent Satan expressing his nature in those who are his brood of vipers, in absolute depravity. But all of us were that way, whether we were subtle or outrageous in our sin. The fear of God's judgment is the beginning of wisdom. We read in the Acts of the Apostles that many who called for Christ's death, even among the priesthood, repented with fear and trembling, when they realized what they had done, after Pentecost. God's Goodness and Power makes all things work together for good to those who will believe. The predestined plan for those who will not believe is to remain the children of wrath. There is no conflict between what is predestined by God and the free will of man. Neither is there a conflict between His Sovereignty and His Justice.

What about **Romans 9:21-23**?

> Has the potter no right over the clay, to make out of the same lump one vessel for honorable use and another for dishonorable use? *What if* God, desiring to show His wrath and to make known His power, has endured with much patience vessels of wrath prepared for destruction in order to make known the riches of His glory for vessels of mercy, which He has prepared beforehand for glory. – ESV (*Shank*)

The key to understanding this passage is the phrase, *What if...*? A Sovereign God can do whatever He wants with what He has made, just like a potter can do whatever he wants with what he makes. Paul's point is about God's absolute authority to do whatever He wants with what is His. He *will* judge the world. But it is not a proof text that God makes some people for hell and some for heaven no matter how they live their lives. We are not predestined for one or the other without a choice! That would make faith, repentance, and judgment meaningless. Why then did Joshua exhort the people of Israel with the command to "choose this day whom you will serve?" Then he declared his own choice to them: "As for me and my house, we will serve the Lord" **(Joshua 24:14-15)**. Without the power to choose, we are saved by predestination, not faith by grace. If that is the truth, why the suffering of Christ on the cross?

The Reformation brought much healing from the damage done by the corrupt doctrines of the past, by re-establishing **Sola Scriptura**. This means the *Scripture alone* is the supreme authority of what is true in all spiritual matters. To the best of our ability, we must be careful that our theology does not overrule what Scripture says, but rather that Scripture must overrule what our theology says, when they conflict. The best teachers of the Word suspend what they think they know about a passage they are preparing, to allow for fresh insight from the Holy Spirit. Then, they consider what they have already come to believe to make modifications, if necessary. Official doctrines of any given denomination must bow in submission wherever they may disagree with the Word. Our spiritual identity is in Christ, not our denominational faction or brand.

The Church of the Middle Ages had allowed great errors of doctrine to warp the truth because of its admittance of pagan doctrines and worldly reasoning. One example of opening a door to worldly reasoning was through Thomas Aquinas (1225-1274) who held that though the will of man was fallen and corrupt, the mind was not. Therefore, it followed that worldly philosophy and reasoning became as valid as scripture, in the apprehension of the truth.

In *HOW SHOULD WE THEN LIVE? The Rise and Decline of Western Thought and Culture* by Francis Schaeffer, the author says the following on page 52, illustrating the extent of the problem:

> "This is well illustrated by a fresco painted in 1365 by Andrea da Firenze, in the Spanish Chapel in Santa Maria Novella in Florence. Thomas Aquinas sits on a throne in the center of the fresco, and on the lower level of the picture are Aristotle, Cicero, Ptolemy, Euclid and Pythagoras, (*pagan philosophers*) all placed in the same category as Augustine. As a result of this emphasis, philosophy was gradually separated from revelation—from the Bible—and philosophers began to act in an increasingly independent, autonomous manner.

> Among the Greek philosophers, Thomas Aquinas relied especially on one of the greatest, Aristotle (384-322 B.C.). In 1263 Pope Urban IV had forbidden the study of Aristotle in the universities. Aquinas managed to have Aristotle accepted, so the ancient non-Christian philosophy was re-enthroned.

> To understand what result this had, it is worthwhile to look at Raphael's (1483-1520) painting *The School of Athens* (c. 1510) to comprehend some of the discussions and influences which followed in the Renaissance period. The fresco is in the Vatican. In *The School of Athens* Raphael painted Plato with one finger pointed upward, which means that he pointed to absolutes or ideals. In contrast, he pictured Aristotle with his fingers spread wide and

thrust down to the earth, which means that he emphasized particulars..."

This error of strengthening the role of pagan *reasoning* caused
an ever-increasing distortion in the thinking of the leaders of
the Roman Church. By the time of the Reformation, Calvin uti-
lized the same kind of Greek metaphysical mechanics of reasoning to say that if God is in control, He must control all, including the will of man, or He is not omnipotent. Therefore,
God *predetermines who will be saved and who will not,* because an omnipotent God must determine all outcomes. This
idea is known as **Double Predestination.**

But to foreknow what men will do is not necessarily to cause
them to do it. To the **Double Predestination** Calvinist, grace
means that in the hopeless corruption of man, God is not
obliged to save anyone, but He chooses to save *some* without
any regard to merit or choice on their part, as His divine pre-
rogative. It may be true that the Lord is not legally obligated to
save us, but in dying for the sins of us all, His Love Nature,
which cannot be denied, saves all who choose to believe and
repent. Those who choose not to believe are lost. It is true that
no one comes to the Son unless the Father draws him, but the
Holy Spirit pursues all with conviction, so all are without excuse for not believing. (**Romans 1:18-19**)

In this **Double Predestination** view, strict Calvinists say the
fact that God damns some hopelessly corrupt people but saves
other hopelessly corrupt people is not in contradiction with
God's justice, but a paradox. When the rigors of their logic
bring them to absurd conclusions, they sneak out the back
door by saying this is something that must be accepted by
faith. But they do not question the presuppositions that im-
prison their logic stream.

Where did this kind of thinking come from? The Calvinist
view of predestination is only 500 years old. It was not the
teaching of the Church before 300 A.D. It was not the teaching
after 300 A.D. either, even though the Church had other doctrinal problems. Calvinists find precedence in Augustine, and
much of what Augustine taught was very good. But, they build

on what were some of Augustine's weaknesses for the worldly assumptions of the day.

Like many of his contemporaries, Augustine was influenced by Neoplatonist *thinking*. This does not mean he believed what Plato believed, but Augustine was influenced by the *way* Plato thought. The Protestant Scholastic thinking that followed after him also approached the Bible from the thinking of Plato and other worldly philosophers. This is where the "omnis" came from: *omnipresence* means God is present everywhere. *Omniscience* means God is all knowing. *Omnipotence* means God is all powerful, and so on. Is God everywhere, all knowing and all powerful? Yes, these are true statements. The faulty thinking comes when forcing the omnipotence of God into *ridged definitions* that scripture does not intend.

Ironically, Calvin himself never advocated this Double Predestination view where man has no choice in his own salvation. But the scholastic thinking that followed him, did.

> "With the death of Calvin, a new phase in the development of Reformed Theology took place, which resulted with the emphasis shifting still further away from justification. The rise of Reformed Scholasticism led to a recognition of predestination as the central dogma of the Reformed Church, even though this emphasis is absent from Calvin's 1559 *Institutio*." – from *IUSTITIA DEI* (*RIGHTEOUSNESS OF GOD*) by **Alister E. McGrath** – page **257**

God is all powerful, but He is also Just. Abraham appealing to the Lord to spare the righteous people of Sodom says: "Shall not the Judge of all the earth, do right?" (*to not destroy the righteous along with the wicked* **Genesis 19**). The Lord delivered Lot and his family out of the city, then He destroyed Sodom.

The Bible clearly says He suspends His controls—holds back His wrath—in order for mercy to allow the free will of man to choose right or wrong—so those who seek Him shall surly find Him. When our ancestors ate from the Tree of the Knowledge of Good and Evil, we eventually got the Law. Why did Jesus fulfill the whole Law so that He could be the Perfect Sacrifice for all the sins of man? Why is that needful, if we are actually saved by God's preselection?

You may be thinking: "I am part of a Calvinist church but I don't hold the hard views you are talking about." Good, and it is only fair to say that there are many who hold modified views on these matters. But Reformed churches pride themselves on the strength of their logical framework and speak despairingly of churches that stress experience over reason. But **Sola Scriptura** must inform both tendencies, whether they be rigid reasoning or unsupported experience—wherever we may be straying.

The Greek philosophers of classical theism ask: "What is God like?" **Sola Scriptura** reveals Who God Is. Few modern Calvinists take his teaching on predestination as far as Calvin's followers did because of the way it undermines God's justice. But, in order to do this, they should also reject the logic they profess, which no longer supports their amended conclusions. But, because one's presuppositions drive one's thinking, they insist on saying this conflict is a paradox of logic which must be accepted by faith. Alas...

Tertullian (155-240 AD) an early church father has said: "What has Athens to do with Jerusalem? What has the Academy to do with the Temple? What has unbelief to do with belief?"

So, what is the larger lesson here? We are all tempted to let the cultural and worldly ideology of our day influence how we interpret the Word. Political correctness, Marxism, fascism, socialism, feminism, capitalism, nationalism, globalism, liberalism, environmentalism, and conservatism, et cetera—all these kinds of ideologies have their place in discussion and debate. But for those of us who believe, vigilance is needed so that our mindset is shaped by the Word above all. The meaning of the Word must not be manipulated to fit the fashion of our times or personal agendas. No "ism" should be permitted to redefine the meanings of the words of Scripture, to promote an ideological agenda. Scripture must inform our ideology, but our ideology must not inform Scripture.

The Lord draws near the humble and the teachable. He resists the proud who refuse to learn. This book took a long time to write and even longer to think through. In numerous re-writes I have made many changes, modifications and corrections— wondering if it will ever be finished. I know it will never be perfect, though I strive for that out of the fear of the Lord. May the Lord make it useful to His purposes. As a man, I am far from perfect, though I strive for it. Many better men than I am have made great mistakes.

Chapter 3 Study Questions

1. Why and how are we sold to sin when we were born?

2. Explain the law powers in **Romans 7:20-23**.

3. How can I possibly say my flesh is not me?

4. Explain God's part and my part as a Christian.

5. How is my human spirit like a bride?

6. Why did God love Jacob and hate Esau even before they were born?

7. What has God predestined, and what has He not predestined?

4

The Law & The Tree

Summary: The Law is the Tree of the Knowledge of Good and Evil, showing the fruit or consequences of each. It is the Tree from which we must eat all the days of this life. It is what Adam and Eve chose against the Will of God. So, God had to remove the Tree of Life from them so mankind would not live forever and thus spoil (*with the corruption of Sin*) the universe and everything else He had made. Their disobedience was what was evil, not the Tree itself. Their obedience to Satan and disobedience to God brought death, as God promised it would. Satan promised their eyes would be opened and they would be like God. They allowed Satan to come between them and God, ironically blocking the truth of God from their eyes by confusing good and evil. Satan lied and did not keep his promise. As it was with them, so it is with us. Death is both the *penalty* and the *cure* for Sin. Death limits the contamination of evil from spreading. Judgment will destroy Sin and all who choose it over the Goodness of God in Christ, because God means to have an eternity undefiled by sin. Jesus took our place with His death, so we who believe will be saved. In the eternity to come, we will be free from sin forever—free to perfectly love and be loved by God and each other. God will not have to withhold blessings from us that might spoil us, because we will no longer spoil.

The children of Adam and Eve did what was right in their own eyes. But this was not what their own eyes saw; it was what Satan wanted them to see, the way *he* sees. This was lawlessness under the power of the lawless one. And the world became overcome with wickedness.

Genesis 6:5-7 says,

> The Lord saw that the wickedness of man was great in the earth, and that every intention of the thoughts of his heart was only evil continually. And the Lord was sorry that He had made man on the earth, and it grieved Him to His Heart. So the Lord said, "I will blot out man whom I have created from the face of the land, man and

animals and creeping things and birds of the heavens, for I am sorry I made them." But Noah found favor in the Eyes of the Lord. – ESV

After destroying the whole world with a flood, the Lord began again with the family of Noah to repopulate the earth. But the family of man fell away again under the power of Satan's evil deception. So God made a people, who would not naturally have been a people since Abraham and Sarah were barren. From them, He made the nation of Israel, who would not have been a nation, and chose to reveal Himself to the world through them. Moses, a descendant of Levi the great grandson of Abraham, was chosen to deliver the house of Israel. Through Moses, they receive the Law of God, so the people would have God's truth about what was right or wrong and what one should or should not do. Blessings and curses followed the choices the people made. When Jesus came, He fulfilled the whole Law and became the perfect sacrifice for sin, since He had no sin of His own. And through Jesus, God made all men; He is therefore worth more than all men put together, because He could make another earth full of men, and another and another. So, His Death value pays for all who will ever be, who choose to believe and receive Him.

The Serpent & Tree of Knowledge
Romans 7:7-14

What then shall we say; that the law is sin? By no means! Yet if it had not been for the law, I would not have known sin. For I would not have known what it is to covet if the law had not said, "You shall not covet." But sin, seizing an opportunity through the commandment, produced in me all kinds of covetousness. For apart from the law, sin lies dead. I was once alive apart from the law, but when the commandment came, sin came alive and I died. The very commandment that promised life [*obey and you will live, disobey and you will die*] proved to be death to me. For sin, seizing the opportunity through the commandment, deceived me and through it killed me. So, the law is holy, and the commandment is holy and righteous and good.

> Did that which is good, then, bring death to me? By no means! It was sin producing death in me through what is good, in order that sin might be shown to be sin, and through the commandment might become sinful beyond measure. For we know that the law is spiritual, but I am of the flesh, sold under sin. - ESV (*Shank*)

How can sin *seize an opportunity*? That phrase makes sin seem more like an active being or an intelligence, than a behavior. The truth is, Sin *is* a person; Satan is Mr. Sin. The Law is Holy, exposing Satan and provoking him to produce sinful desires in my flesh, because that is what is in his nature to do. Even as a Christian, when I buy into the deception that I still want to sin, he gains advantage over me—and I give evidence in sinning. Conversely, if I buy into the deception that I can keep the Law by my own strength apart from God, I sin with pride and soon fail in my deeds. Then Satan condemns me for the sin, and I become ashamed before God. Just as Satan misuses the law, he also tries to use God's Own Justice against me: "see what John just did? He must now be condemned by You because John has broken Your law, and he that breaks any part of Your law, breaks all of it." Not only does my sin bring consequences to others, but also tempts me to hide myself in shame, believing I am beyond hope of being able to change. I do not break that condemnation spell until I repent.

Sin & Sins

Romans 7:14-20 says:

> For, I do not understand **my** own actions. I do not do what I want, but I do the very thing I hate. Now if I do what I do not want, I agree with the law, that it is good. So now it is no longer I who do it, but sin that dwells within **me**. For I know that nothing good dwells in me, that is **my** *flesh*. For I have the desire to do what is right, but not the ability to carry it out. For I do not do the good I want, but the evil I do not want is what I keep on doing. Now if I do what I do not want, it is no longer I who do it, but sin that dwells within **me**. - ESV (Shank)

Look at it this way:
Sin = Satan, the originator and energizer of Sin.
Law = The Tree of the Knowledge of Good and Evil.

Again, it is no longer I that do it, but sin that dwells within me, in my flesh (**sarx**), where no good thing dwells. Sin is coming from **outside** of me now, exploiting the weakness of my flesh. Before I was redeemed, my old man in Satan wanted to bear his fruit and did so. But the new man I am now in Christ wants to bear the fruit of Christ! My true self in Christ does not want to sin. But my flesh, which is mine to inhabit for now, still does. My flesh is mine, but it *is* not me. That's why the flesh cannot be redeemed, but it is under sentence of death. But I am born of the Spirit and will live forever and will be given a new incorruptible body in the life to come. Because I want to be pure like Jesus, I will receive that desire of my heart and be forever like Him in the life to come, with a new incorruptible body!

Before I knew my flesh was not me, I used to get up in the middle of the night, prostrate myself on the floor and revile myself before the Lord. "Why am I still so lustful, so arrogant, so full of envy, and so full of desires for revenge? Shouldn't I be better by now? Why am I still so weak? After being a Christian for years, I am still the beast I was before I was saved." The despair and futility I was feeling represented itself in a number of brutal laminations, including the following, which was written after a fitful dream:

Sanctification Poem
> I drew a razor over my flesh and harvested every hair I could reach with my own hand. I trimmed my nails and the lashes of my eyes, my nose and every orifice, then heaped them on a stone. I set it all alight and sat naked before the stinking twist of smoke that curled up to heaven.

> My vanity was only quenched for a moment as I prostrated myself and prayed. "My sins sprout from me more bountifully than the hairs on my body, which are as natural for my soul to produce. If I had a razor to shave my heart, stubble would reappear momentarily.

> How shall I be holy as You Are? What meaning is there in repentance? What does it profit to cut myself to the quick, to be raw and sore with reproach, to be exhaustive in confession and the master of shame, but still be the slave of myself? How is it that I am dead to sin? Is not the shedding of the Blood for more purpose than just excusing myself from my own life?"

On one of these occasions, the Lord said to me, "You're being honest, but you're not speaking the truth!"

True Self Versus False Self

But I didn't yet know that as long as I allowed myself to measure my spiritual progress by my flesh, I would be forever discouraged. My flesh is hopeless, sold to sin **(Romans 7:14)**. It is irredeemably corrupted. Satan knows this. As long as he can keep me focused on trying to fix an unfixable problem, he will be able to keep me in futility and from seeing the truth.

Galatians 5:16-18 says:

> ... walk by the spirit, and you will not gratify the desires of the flesh, for the desires of the flesh are against the Spirit, and the desires of the Spirit are against the flesh, these are opposed to each other, to keep you from doing the things you want to do. But if you are led by the Spirit, you are not under the Law. - ESV

The flesh is opposed to the spirit to keep me from doing what I want. I am to bring my flesh into subjection, but I will never be able to fix it. My flesh cannot improve. An outrageous thought comes to my mind and my flesh responds favorably to it. Is it sin yet? **No**, it's temptation. Is it coming from my own perversity? **No**, it's from Satan, because I am joined to Christ and have His moral nature. Christ is not perverse; so, the real me, in Him, is no longer perverse. If I am a new creation in Christ, this thought cannot have come from me. But I feel like I really want it; I feel like I really don't want God's will in this. Am I a hypocrite if I say I don't want this sin? **No!** It is just an emotion. It's the other way around. If I do commit the sin, I am a hypocrite because I say I belong to Jesus yet still believe I want to sin!

I am learning to neither make provision for, nor to regard anything that is coming from the flesh. I'm not battling my old nature anymore, because the Bible says it is dead. The battle is between my new nature in Christ and my hopelessly weak flesh. The flesh profits nothing and cannot please God! It will never please me either. If I keep the habit of measuring the authenticity of my intentions by what my flesh wants, I will keep falling into condemnation *because I have not repented of seeing myself as my flesh!*

But we get tired of all this constant battle with temptation from Mr. Sin. When will it ever end? Until the next life, we will just have to continue to chew on this fruit of the Tree of the Knowledge of Good and Evil, until all who have yet to believe in Christ have come to Him. Christ waits patiently for those who are His. So must I. Christ lived under the same constant temptation for 33 years on the earth, but He did not sin.

An Awakened Conscience
Romans 7:9 says:

> I was once alive apart from the Law, but when the commandment came, sin came alive and I died. – ESV

Remember, before the Law, I was free to sin without condemnation in my conscience, even though I was headed for hell because of my sin. But after the Law was made known to me, I was condemned by it. My conscience must be informed by the truth. My conscience is said to be an organ of my human spirit. But I believe a clean heart equals a clean conscience. So, the conscience is corruptible. My human spirit indwelt by the Spirit of God is not corruptible; therefore, I now believe the conscience must be part of the mind of the **soul** (*see* **Chapter 5**). Sin dulls my conscience and hardens my heart, but conviction softens it. My conscience must be informed by the Word, which the Holy Spirit makes alive in me through my spirit union with Him. The Law tells me what is good or evil, removing my excuse for ignorance and disobedience. My conscience must learn to embrace the Law as a loving response to my Lord. This is not the same as trying to justify myself by my own works.

Misplaced Hope
Romans 7:21,22 says:

> So, I find it to be a law that when I want to do right,
> evil lies close at hand. For I delight in the law of God, in
> my inner being, but I see in my members another law
> waging war against the law of my inner being. – ESV

I (*spirit joined to Christ*) delight in the Law of God in my inner being (*my spirit*). I want to do what is right, but evil is
present within **me** (*in my members—part of my flesh*). Under
Satan's lie of an autonomous, self-managed self, Paul was condemned for the sin of coveting, because he believed it was **he**
that wanted it and it was up to **him** in the flesh to overcome it.
But the flesh cannot please God.

As a Christian, I have a new nature that wants to obey and
please the Lord. But if I don't believe I have a *new spirit nature*
in Christ by continuing to let my flesh define me, I will never
be able to overcome condemnation from sinful urges, because
my frustrated hope is misplaced for what I have mistaken for
myself, to be one who is still *separated* from God and must
therefore rely on *self-efforts* to do what is good.

Who Am I in the Flesh?
If I see myself apart from God, I will resort to the lie of self-
effort. If my internal integrity is determined by how things *appear* and *feel* according to the flesh, I will not be able to see
things as they truly are from God's perspective. This is what it
is like to be a carnal Christian. On the other hand, if I allow the
Word to define me—that I am united with Christ—His perspective is now mine, and I can choose against sin by faith and
learn to overcome! I am learning that praying for strength can
sometimes be unbelief, because everything I need to be able to
overcome, has been given to me by the Spirit of Christ in me!

Joined to Righteousness
1 Corinthians 6:17 says:

> He who is joined to the Lord is one spirit with Him.
> – ESV

Conversely, shall we then allow ourselves to be joined to sin any longer? Shall I then allow **myself** to be joined to sin any longer? As a child of God, shall I continue to believe my nature is the same way it was when I was still under the power of sin? This is where the ultimate repentance must come. If I am in Christ, at the Right Hand of God, I will believe what Scripture says is true about me. I will exercise the authority God has already given me, as well as fully embrace His grace to learn how to overcome sin by bringing my flesh into submission by faith in the Truth of the Word, not in the futility of self-effort through my flesh.

Image of God
Genesis 1:26-28 says:

> Let Us make man in Our Image, after Our Likeness. Let them have dominion... over all the earth. So, God created man in His Own Image, in the image of God He created him, male and female He created them. – ESV

Once again, I have *never* been and was *never* meant to be a self-managed person. I was always managed by the will of a master spirit, or operator. This is why I am made in the image of God. And the dominion over the earth was intended to be by God's nature, in His children. Because the one you obey is your master, the Fall affected Adam and his children by allowing Satan to become the master spirit, instead of God.

In the Likeness of Sinful Flesh
Romans 8:1-8 says:

> There is therefore no condemnation for those who are in Christ Jesus. For the law of the Spirit of life has set **me** free from the law of sin and death. For God has done what the law, weakened by **my** flesh, could not do. By sending His Own Son in the likeness of sinful flesh, in order that the righteous requirement of the law might be fulfilled in **me**, I walk not according to the flesh but according to the Spirit. For those who live according to the flesh set their minds on the things of the flesh, but those who live according to the Spirit set their minds on the things of the Spirit. For to set **my** mind on the flesh is death, but to set **my** mind on the

Spirit is life and peace. For the mind that is set on the flesh is hostile to God's law, for it does not submit to God's law; indeed, it **cannot**. Those who are in the flesh **cannot** please God. – ESV (Shank)

God sent His Son in the likeness of sinful flesh and condemned Him in my place. I thank God that I am free in Christ Jesus, where there is now no condemnation. I have His nature in me. I am one spirit with Him. My weak flesh is condemned, but it is not me. To set my mind on the Spirit is to reason according to the Spirit, not the flesh. I am to choose to see myself as the Scripture sees me—as one who is dead to sin and alive to God in Christ—as it says in **Romans 6:11**. God is free to choose, and He made me in His image to be free to choose as well.

I Will Be Bold
Romans 8:28-35 says:

And we know that for those who love God all things work together for good, for those who are called according to His purpose. For those who He foreknew [*would believe*] He also predestined to be conformed to the image of His Son, in order that He [*Jesus*] might be the firstborn among many brothers. And those whom He predestined He also called, and those whom He called He also justified, and those whom He justified He also glorified.

What shall I say to these things? If God is for **me**, who can stand against **me**? He Who did not spare His Own Son but gave Him up for us all, how will He not also with Him graciously give **me** all things? Who shall bring any charge against God's elect (*of whom I am now one*)? It is God Who justifies. Who is to condemn? (*Satan, but so what?*) Christ Jesus is the One Who died—more than that, Who was raised—Who is at the Right Hand of God, Who indeed is interceding for **me** Who shall separate **me** from the love of Christ? Shall tribulation, or distress, or persecution, or famine, or nakedness, or danger, or sword? – ESV (*Shank*)

I will take myself to be blameless as God's chosen one, free of false condemnation, and refined by the conviction of the Holy Spirit whenever necessary. God did not spare His Own Son from suffering, and He will not spare me from suffering. But nothing can separate me from the love of God!

Caution ››› But I must never say I am blameless if known sin and willful disobedience are active in my life. I must call sin what it is when I do it, or I will make a shipwreck of my faith, harm the sincere faith of others, and disgrace the Lord I say I love. Jesus said, "If you love Me, keep My commandments!" I must not allow Satan to deceive me with a conceit that perpetuates sin! Boldness that is also humble knows I will never be perfect in this life, but His grace to me is all I need. I must confess my sin and repent when I know I need to.

Romans 8:37-39 says:

> In all these things, I am more than a conqueror through Him Who loved me. For I am sure that neither death nor life, nor angels nor rulers, nor things present nor things to come, nor powers, nor height nor depth, nor anything else in all creation, will be able to separate me from the love of God in Christ Jesus my Lord.
> – ESV (Shank)

The Carnal Christian
1 Corinthians 3:1-3 says:

> But I, brothers, could not address you as spiritual people, but as people of the flesh, as infants in Christ. I fed you milk, not solid food, for you were not ready for it. And even now you are not ready, for you are still in the flesh. For while there is jealousy and strife among you, are you not of the flesh and behaving only in a human way? – ESV

Hebrews 5:11-14 also says:

> About this we have much to say, and it is hard to explain, since you have become dull of hearing. For though by this time you ought to be teachers, you need someone to teach you again the basic principles of the oracles of God. You need milk, not solid food,

for everyone who lives on milk is unskilled in the word of righteousness, since he is a child. But solid food is for the mature, for those who have their powers of discernment trained by constant practice to distinguish good from evil. – ESV

Alas, let us not find ourselves stuck there. Notice how the immature Christian is described, as one who is saved but still living *as if* they are fleshly (**sarkos**). They are not yet living *as if* they are spiritual (**pneumatikos**). The evidence cited is the presence of jealousy and strife among them. The dullness of their understanding and their need for milk, not being ready for solid food. They are rebuked because they have refused to grow up in their faith. Spiritual passivity causes them to remain dependent on others to see to their spiritual needs. They often do not persevere in prayer or study the Word. They don't have their own motor with the things of God.

Though children of God who should be behaving *as if* they are a new creation, they behave *as if* He is not providing for them, watching over them, or caring. Their assessment of God's presence is limited to the degree to which creaturely comforts are satisfied. They stubbornly cling to the false idea that *if* God loved them, bad things should not be happening to them. When the effects of the fallen world and the attacks of the enemy bruise them, they blame God. When they refuse to understand their own role in their own consequences, they blame God. They often complain about the hypocrisy of the church, but rarely consider their own hypocrisy. They broadcast a terrible testimony to the unbelieving world by making Jesus unattractive. They offend God by constant grumbling and even slander Him.

They are the New Testament equivalent of the Israelites in the wilderness who saw the power and presence of God but still complained and rebelled. New Christians don't know any better. For them, we are to show forbearance in their weakness and ignorance. They need to have their minds renewed, and they need to be discipled. But those of us who have been believers for more than a few years should no longer be weak or irresponsible toward others or unable to wrestle with the deeper truths in the Word in order to overcome. While not all of us are called to be teachers, we are all called to have that level of mature understanding, so that we may make wise and fruitful contributions to the Kingdom of God.

The carnal Christian is a spiritual delinquent. The enemy is still able to manipulate him into being helpless and fruitless at best or disruptive and divisive at worst. If any of us in Christ have besetting sin problems, we need to get help with them, not make a deal to hang on to them. The matters of the heart must be resolved in order to be effective in Christ. The spiritual passivity that sets in when one refuses to grow up and join the battle robs both God and His Church. It also discourages faith in others who refuse to exercise what they already have.

Chapter 4 Study Questions

1. How is the Law related to the Tree of the Knowledge of Good and Evil?

2. Why has God given laws we cannot keep?

3. Why did God make us in His image?

4. Why did Jesus come to us in the likeness of sinful flesh?

5. How am I able to be a conqueror while I am still in the flesh?

5

Soul & Spirit
Trichotomy versus Dichotomy
1 Thessalonians 5:23 says:

> Now may the God of peace Himself sanctify you com-
> pletely, and may your whole spirit, soul and body be
> kept blameless at the coming of our Lord Jesus Christ.
> – ESV

Here, the Greek word **pneuma** means spirit; **psuche** means
soul; and **soma** means body. Scholars who hold the Trichotomy view say that Scripture reveals man to be made up of these
three essential components. Other scholars hold the Dichotomy view, saying there are only two essential components to
man: the visible and the invisible. They would say soul and
spirit seem interchangeable in Scripture and are therefore
equivalent. There are sincere Christians on both sides of the
debate. Neither would exclude the other from fellowship because neither position undermines essential Christian doctrine
regarding salvation. However, I am convinced and have found
useful advantage in holding the Trichotomy view in the practical determination of things like spiritual motivation and mood
bias in behavior. Notice some distinct differences.

Spiritual & Natural Man
1 Corinthians 2:9-16 says:

> But it has been written "What no eye has seen, nor ear
> has heard, nor the heart of man imagined, what God
> has prepared for those who love Him"—these things
> God has revealed to us through the Spirit. For the Spir-
> it searches everything, even the depths of God. For who
> knows a person's thoughts except the spirit of that
> person, which is in him? So also no one comprehends
> the thoughts of God except the Spirit of God. Now we
> have received not the spirit of the world, but the Spirit
> Who is from God, that we might understand the things
> freely given us by God. And we impart this in words
> not taught by human wisdom but taught by the Spirit,
> interpreting spiritual truths to those who are spiritual.

71

The natural person does not accept the things of the Spirit of God, for they are folly to him, and he is not able to understand them because they are spiritually discerned. The spiritual person judges all things but is himself judged by no one. For who has understood the mind of the Lord so as to instruct Him? But we have the mind of Christ. – ESV

The **verse 14** translation reads, "The natural person does not accept the things of the Spirit of God, for they are folly to him, and he is not able to understand them because they are spiritually discerned." But, it is important to note that the word translated for natural person is from the Greek **psychikos**, which does not actually mean natural person, but literally means *soulish person*. If natural man were the intentional meaning of Paul, he would have almost certainly used the word **phusikos**, because that word literally means *natural person*. But he did not! In other words, the one who lives by his soul's subjective perception does not see things by the spirit. There is a real conflict between flesh and spirit, but that is not what is being compared here.

The word for the spiritual person is **pneumatikos**, which is literally accurate in the translation as a *spiritual person*. By contrast, **psychikos** and **pneumatikos** represent different things: *soulish* person and *spiritual* person respectively, not *natural* and *spiritual* persons. Therefore, the correct tension between these contrasting perspectives is spiritual seeing versus soulish seeing, not spiritual seeing versus natural seeing. The significance of this distinction will be developed further.

Obviously from the text, an unbeliever does not comprehend the things of the Spirit if his spirit has not been regenerated. But believers who have not yet learned to walk by the spirit remain soulish in their reasoning and thinking, like the world thinks. They continue to follow their emotions and put their perceived self-interest before all else. Remaining largely indistinguishable from the behavior of the world, they settle for defeat.

But first, **Genesis 2:7** says:

> Then the Lord God formed the man of dust from the ground and breathed into his nostrils the breath of life, and the man became a living creature. – ESV

Adam's body was made of the clay of the earth. Into that body (*Hebrew* 'etsem), God breathed His Spirit (**ruach**); His breath into the man became a living creature (**nephesh**, the Hebrew word for *soul*). The two components—God-made body and God-breathed spirit—combined to make a living man soul.

Sharper Than a Two-edged Sword

Hebrews 4:12 says:

> For the Word of God is living and active, sharper than any two-edged sword, piercing to the division of soul and of spirit, of joints and of marrow, and discerning the thoughts and intentions of the heart. – ESV

The Word is able to pierce the thoughts and intentions of my heart, to distinguish between my perceptions and motives, exposing agendas and self-serving **conceits** that give me permission to sin. The emotion I experience in my soul can also be misinterpreted as discernment in my spirit if I do not understand the self-interests of my soul versus the God-interests of my spirit (*see diagram*). My soul has its affections and my human spirit also has its affections. How am I to know what is going on inside me, if I am unaware of the functional agendas of these two distinct parts of me? Because both are invisible, the Two-edged Sword of the Word of God is necessary to tell them apart. We shall continue to wield the Sword of the Word to that end.

David speaks to his own soul repeatedly in the Psalms. Of note are **Psalm 42:5,11** and **Psalm 43:5**, where he says three times

> Why are you cast down O my *soul*, and why are *you* in turmoil within me? – ESV (*Shank*)

What the spirit and the soul share is invisibility. We all know we can't slice open the brain and find mind or emotions. We cannot see where the spirit or soul of a person is that way either. But they apparently do have subtle boundaries only the sharpness of the Sword of the Word of God can separate. By knowing the piercing Word (**logos**), we know what is of God and what is not, as well as what is spirit and what is soul.

The New Testament refers to the believer as the temple of God (**1 Corinthians 3:16-17**). The temple in Israel described in the Old Testament had three distinct parts:

> 1. The Outer Court had a physical presence all could see; this is like my body, which gives me a presence in the physical world, and enables me to know and experience it in my days under the sun.

> 2. Inside the court was the Holy Place, which was closed off to the outside world—it was lit by the inner lampstand. This is much like the light of my own mind in introspection concerning my feelings, thoughts, and reflexive opinions. This is what my soul does, making it possible for me to know myself.

> 3. Behind that chamber was the Holy of Holies (*the* na-os *discussed earlier*), where the Mercy Seat was placed, separated only by a curtain from the Holy Place. This room was only illuminated inside by the presence of the Lord Himself, corresponding to my spirit as the container of the Holy Spirit, making it possible for me to know God and His ways, as well as myself in relation to Him.

Before the indwelling of the Holy Spirit, making me a child of God in Jesus Christ, my spirit contained the spirit of this world, *the Author of Sin.* At conversion, Satan's slave-to-sin old nature is evicted and my temple was cleansed and restored to the purpose for which it was created, to be the temple and dwelling place of God, *the Author of Righteousness.* I am now a slave to righteousness, but I may not be aware of this at all experientially, if I have not yet believed I am a new creation in Christ, and that my old nature is now dead.

God designed my body to care for itself, to be concerned about my need for physical well-being, safet*y,* and satisfaction. This is a good thing. But Satan corrupts my natural need for rest into laziness; he corrupts my need for food into overeating and drunkenness; he corrupts my drive to reproduce into fornication or pornography. He also misuses the strength of my body—to do work or to protect the weak—into a tool for violence. Every God-designed need and drive is twisted by the devil's evil influence, to take advantage of me. Sin trained my body to expect to get **its** way and to control my choices through my fleshly weakness, in order to do harm.

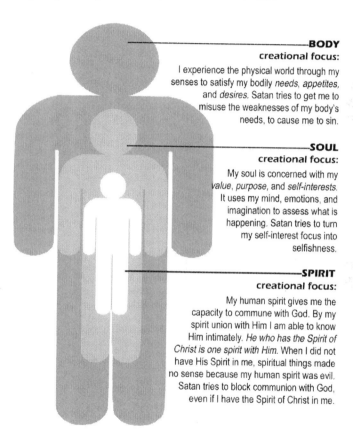

BODY
creational focus:
I experience the physical world through my senses to satisfy my bodily *needs, appetites,* and *desires.* Satan tries to get me to misuse the weaknesses of my body's needs, to cause me to sin.

SOUL
creational focus:
My soul is concerned with my *value, purpose,* and *self-interests.* It uses my mind, emotions, and imagination to assess what is happening. Satan tries to turn my self-interest focus into selfishness.

SPIRIT
creational focus:
My human spirit gives me the capacity to commune with God. By my spirit union with Him I am able to know Him intimately. *He who has the Spirit of Christ is one spirit with Him.* When I did not have His Spirit in me, spiritual things made no sense because my human spirit was evil. Satan tries to block communion with God, even if I have the Spirit of Christ in me.

But if I become a Christian, I must remember that my spirit has changed but my flesh, the natural part of me, will *always oppose* my spirit. I will still feel pulls to pride, lust envy, et cetera. My flesh hates obedience, patience, and self-control. But I am now the master of my flesh and can learn to overcome. In Christ, my flesh is mine, but it is not me.

My soul is focused on my value, my purpose, and my self-interest; and it is designed to see what is in my interest, to feel the meaning and gravity of it in my emotions, and to use the imagination of my mind to interpret opportunities or threats in relation to me and mine. But it is important to remember that my soul is only giving me an opinion based on limited knowledge. Satan wants to corrupt all these God-given abilities, to get the self-interest focus of my soul to act out in *self-ishness*, causing my focus to be exclusively on ME. He wants to bend me away from God's will, so I will do the evil the devil wants me to do.

The devil does not want me to see or feel the effect of my sin on others. He wants me to misremember what happened with a good excuse, so I can have a high reason to do a low thing. He deceives me into believing my faith is subject to my *mood*, so my faithfulness goes up and down by how I feel at the moment. Through this kind of manipulation, I will stay immature and unfruitful. I will not be able to build anything of value because I will start something when I feel inspired, but I leave it unfinished when I feel discouraged. Satan wants me to believe what I *feel* is true, not what the Word of God says is true.

If **my spirit** is not joined to the Holy Spirit, I will not be able to break out of my sin patterns. But if I receive Christ, God puts His Holy Spirit in me and I can begin to use His power, wisdom, and love, to learn how to become a completely different person. He will give me the grace to learn His new ways. His Holy Spirit in me makes me a new creation in Christ. I can now stand before God without shame, because of His forgiveness. I can forgive those who have hurt me. I can show His love to those I have hurt in the past, by making a sincere amends. In Christ, I can now deal with my consequences, the difficulty of my circumstances, and the hopeless feelings in my **soul**. Christ in me will overcome through me. But I must learn to believe and obey Him. My spirit is now empowered by the Holy Spirit, to rightly believe.

My conscience must be guided by my spirit where I can know and experience God, Who is Spirit. He will speak to me. He will hear me. He will show me. I will see what He wants me to see. Without the Holy Spirit in me, my human conscience will default to the selfishness of Satan, to *misuse* my soul to *harm* the bodies and souls of others.

A Definition of The Soul

I see the soul in this way: My soul makes it possible for my spirit to be personally engaged with the world around my body. It tends to be subjective in its response, yet my soul enables the meaning of my circumstances to be experienced. So, I hear someone insult me and it wounds me emotionally. Another may express love to me and I feel elated. I read of dire prospects in the economy in the newspaper, and my mind perceives the gravity of impending possibilities. However, it's very important to understand that my soul is gauging information based on its impact on me, or on others who matter to me, or what would it be like if what happened to you happened to me. This is a good thing to be able to do, because empathy with others is not possible without being able to identify myself with the experiences of others. And if I cannot perceive and experience my own life, I can't relate to God or others in any meaningful way.

If the soul is the result of the union of Adam's clay body and the living breath of God, I believe the soul has an intended function to *link* the body to the spirit. I am one person, not two or three. There is an intended continuity in God's design of me. My soul perceives bodily sensation and translates it into a meaningful experience. It has been helpful to learn to see these perceptions as an *opinion* and not necessarily facts about what is happening. My soul is about my self-interest, what is good for me. Are my needs being met? Am I safe? Am I respected? Am I fulfilled? Is there any danger of losing anything or anyone who belongs to me? I believe Satan works through the weakness of my flesh to bend me toward his ends, by appealing to my soul's self-interested focus. In this way, Satan misuses God's intended design in order to distract me from the will of the Lord.

But my soul needs to take direction from the Spirit of God, if indeed I have the Spirit of God. Often God may want me to go against my self-interest or things I would prefer to do, for the sake of the kingdom and His goodness toward others. I am finite; only God is infinite. I am limited in my perception, but God is eternal and sees all. My mind knows little, but His Mind is universal and knows all, knowing even the end from the beginning.

Imagine a giant ballroom with a plush carpet. God is universal. His mind is as big as the ballroom. In comparison, my mind is a small speck of dust, lost in the strands of the carpet. My little mind may go peep-peep, "Why is God doing that?" peep-peep-peep "Why isn't God doing anything about my problem?" I am completely ignorant of the vast complexity of things God is working together for His good purposes. My speck of understanding cannot begin to comprehend it all; that's why He expects me to have faith in Him for all that is going on around me. Thank God, He didn't make knowledge and understanding the standard of acceptance! The ballroom will never fit inside my speck, but my speck is in Christ at the Right Hand of God. I need only to do what He shows me in His infinite wisdom.

By being reborn in Christ, my spirit is now able to borrow from the Mind of God what I need for the moment I am in. I will never be able to comprehend more than a fraction of what God is doing in the economy of His purposes. I will never know all, but I can trust in the One Who does know all, the One Who loves me. He knows all the hidden factors, circumstances, and agendas of heaven and earth, and He has already taken into consideration my incompetence in His plan for my life. So, God only asks me to *trust* Him and obey what He directs me to do—to live by faith. All that really matters now is that I do the next thing in faith and leave everything that follows for the Lord to manage. In this way, His yoke is light.

Satan didn't want to do that. He wanted to go his own way. And he makes it a point of pride to resist the will of God by urging me to go my own way as well. But if I listen to him, I'm only going his way, not my way. I was made in the image of God, made to be like Jesus and to do the will of the Lord.

Therefore, my soul not only has rapport in its capacity to experience what is happening around me, but it is also aware of the creational needs and appetites of my body. When my spirit was joined to the spirit of the world, Satan was able to take advantage of my weaknesses to gratify the needs of my body *without regard* for its intended use, *without regard* for the hopes and desires of others, and *without regard* for what God wanted. So, the procreative desire intended for marriage becomes fornication. The desire for justice becomes revenge and unforgiveness. Satan appeals to the subjective focus of my soul to entice me to self-gratification at the expense of others. Even when I am a Christian, he tries to get me to believe I can act on behalf of myself *without regard* for what my True Lord wants. Every time I disobey God as a Christian, I obey a **lie**. The more lies I believe, the harder my heart becomes. The harder my heart becomes the more evil fruit I will produce, discrediting my testimony and disgracing the True Lord Who is in me. The eyes of my heart become blind, and my mind is darkened until I repent.

There was a time in my life when I nearly gave up on trying to overcome, because disobedience reduced me to believing "I'm *just* a sinner saved by grace." But this self-serving **conceit** gave me an excuse to sin. The more I gave in to the strong pulls of temptation through my flesh, the more my conscience was bent to believing my flesh was who I really was. Therefore, I became hopeless, and the victory that was supposed to be mine in Christ was impossible. Believing this lie made God seem like the liar!

Before Satan fell, his name was Lucifer, which means Light-bearer. The Bible reveals little of his original purpose, but I think it is reasonable to assume that he was intended to bring light and understanding to man in some way, so he was given access to the thoughts and feelings of man. **Ezekiel 28:11-19** says he was originally "the signet of perfection, blameless in his ways, an anointed guardian cherub," where he saw the Face of God Who had placed him on the holy mountain of God. But with no excuse, he rebelled against the God Whom he knew Face to face and was cast down. In **Ezekiel 28:1-10**, the prince of Tyre is described in all his selfish arrogance. But when the king of Tyre is described, we can see that he is not a man, but an angel (*spirit*) who manifests his evil nature through the prince of Tyre, a man who was *his* slave, reproducing the devil's will.

I believe the reason the prince of Tyre is compared to the king of Tyre is to show the relationship between the root and branch, father and son—the devil being expressed in those who are his. Isaiah 14:12-17 also describes the fall of the illuminator, Lucifer. **Verse 4** compares him to the king of Babylon, who also expresses Satan's evil nature. Though thrown out of heaven, the devil [*the slanderer*] knows the way into you and me by subverting the self-interest focus of the soul and the weakness of the flesh. Once an intended Illuminator, he has now become the Deceiver.

Personal Application

When I resort to fleshly means to control a problem, I'm building my house on sand because my flesh does not want to change. In fact, it cannot change. Using my soul's power to "psyche myself up" lasts only as long as my elevated mood, because self-interest will begin to seek relief from the inevitable return of pain or fear. But withdrawal from sinful habits is survivable—whether chemical or behavioral—in Christ Who is now my Rock. The following very personal example shows how I have learned to process compromising fear with faith.

As a single parent, I raised my teenage son alone. I was ashamed that I had not been able to save the marriage as well as ashamed of all my own sins that contributed to the divorce. I felt guilty that my son didn't have his mother around and that he had to eat my microwave cooking. I was ashamed that I was always without money and couldn't buy him nice things other kids could have. I hated Christmas. Believing I had nothing much left to give him, I became permissive and accommodating to his moods, allowing him to indulge in them and get away with bad behavior. When friends confronted me about spoiling him, I got defensive and angry! I was at a conference at the time and they told me to go to my room and figure it out.

I knew they were right, but I was afraid to dismantle my **conceits**... that my poor son had suffered enough. But I was also afraid that if I stood up to my son, he'd want to go to live with his mother. I was afraid it was too hard for him to receive tough love. He was in so much pain and had no power to stop the breakup of his family. I was also afraid that I would lose the sweetness of his love and affection because I didn't have anything like that with anyone else. I was also afraid I had very little moral authority left in his life. I was afraid I didn't have strength in me to fix this.

Notice how I was seeing myself. I was identifying with the circumstantial fears of my soul, *as if* I was separated from God and had to deal with all of this alone, because that's how I felt. My fear feelings were shaping my thinking, causing my mind to be set on the flesh and the things of the earth. That focus bent my mind to justify selfishness, to find an excuse not to rock the boat with my son because of what trouble it might cost *me*. My self-serving **conceit** gave me a high reason to do a low thing.

When I saw all this in myself, it devastated me. This was never how I meant to treat my son. I had been deceived through my own fear and shame. Satan had taken advantage of our situation to prevent me from being the dad my son desperately needed. I repented. God gives us less painful ways to find wisdom by studying His Word and seeking the counsel of the wise. But many times, wisdom comes from being foolish first, then looking back to find out *why* I was so easily fooled.

I started to set my mind on the things that are above. Would Jesus be afraid to act decisively in a situation like this? **No.** Would He be afraid to call my son up to righteousness? **No.** Would He trust His Father with the outcome of His boldness? **Yes.** Would Jesus be able to suffer loss and the consequences for doing what was right? **Yes.** Does Jesus have any lack of moral authority? **No.**

Then who am I? I am joined to Christ like a branch joined to a vine. The same life and moral power that is in Him is in me. Since He is not hindered by fear to do what is right, *neither am I.* Since He is not afraid to call both my son and me up to righteousness, *neither am I.* Since He is able to suffer loss for righteousness sake, *so can I.* Since He has no lack in moral authority, *neither do I* because of the Blood that was shed for **me** and the Spirit Who is joined to me!

In taking the right view of myself in Christ, I was also able to see the self-centered motives Satan was using to keep me from loving my son selflessly. Not only did I change my parenting, God gave grace to my thirteen-year-old boy to see I was loving him by being a stronger and better father. Perfect love casts out all fears, and the One Who is Perfect loves me, and the One Who is Perfect loves my son. Though I continue to experience fear feelings in my soul, I am learning to see them as not being something I must obey. My flesh will always be weak, my soul will always default to self-interest, but I am a new creation in Christ. **My spirit** is joined to His Holy Spirit, making me a new man! I can take the information my soul sees and feels about what may be in my self-interest and bring it under the spiritual truth for my circumstances. I can make my flesh obey my spirit, but I cannot reform it. My flesh will return to the dust, irredeemable. My spirit will return to the One Who gave it. My flesh is mine, but it is not me.

It is very important to make this truth stick by taking action *as if* the Word of God is true. The old ways must be subverted with acts of radical defiance in obedience to Christ! Satan is no longer my master. I must now disobey him! I cannot have two masters; I must love One and hate the other. Jesus said that if I love Him, I will obey His commandments. So, I must now disobey the devil. And I have the faith charge from the Word, to keep my flesh under control.

Proper Consideration of the Soul

At the Fall of Adam and Eve, the self-interest of the soul was separated from the will of God. The fallen self then became selfish. The death of my old nature in Christ and its replacement by His Spirit in me restores unity with God, while preserving the distinctness of my personal being. My spirit is now in *union* with God. My soul makes me *distinct* from God so I can be in relationship with Him, no longer to be rebellious against Him. I am not dissolved into God like the eastern concept of nirvana, like some anonymous drop of water becoming one with the sea. My new character identity is in Christ because I am one with Him in spirit. But my soul makes me a specific being who can relate to God, person to Person. I now have the "stuff" of God in my spirit to make me like Him in His love nature. And I also experience my relationship with God as an individual soul while being one spirit with Him.

My soul is now intimate with the soul of God. Does God have a Soul? Yes. Does He not say regarding His Son Jesus in **Isaiah 42:1**: "Behold My Servant Whom I uphold, My Chosen in Whom My Soul [nephesh] delights..." God is Spirit and God is love. He loves even the sinner because He cannot deny His Own Nature. But His Soul delights in those who obey and bear His fruit. Therefore, with tears I long for Him to say to me some day, after all He has forgiven me: "Well done good and faithful servant, enter into the joy of your Master." He has loved me through all my treachery and disasters. May He now find some pleasure in me on the last day, in His Soul.

Genesis 2:7, says that man became a living soul [nephesh] by the union of the spirit breath of God [ruach] and the body ['etsem] He had formed from the dust of the ground. - ESV

- Spirit is **ruach** in Hebrew and **pneuma** in Greek.

- Soul is **nephesh** in Hebrew and **psuche** in Greek.

- Body is **'etsem** (*bone*) in Hebrew and **soma** in Greek.

- Flesh is **basar** (*meat*) in Hebrew and **sarx** in Greek.

Soul is the result of the union of body & spirit

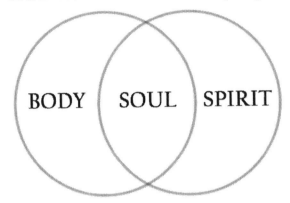

My flesh will always oppose my spirit

Galatians 5:17 says:

> For the desires of the flesh are against the spirit, and the desires of the spirit are against the flesh, for these are opposed to each other, to keep you from doing the things you want to do. – ESV (Shank)

Without getting sidetracked with the many technical applications here, suffice it to say that the New Testament meaning of **sarx** has more to do with sin vulnerability than just the meat of the body or physical weakness. As shown above, the progress of sin corruption that comes with the binding of my heart to temptation draws from both my bodily weakness and my soul's perceived self-interest, through *willful disobedience.*

Romans 8:5-8 says:

> For those who live according to the flesh (**sarx**) set their minds on the things of the flesh, but those who live according to the Spirit set their minds on the things of the Spirit. For to set the mind on the flesh is death, but to set the mind on the Spirit is life and peace. For the mind that is set on the flesh is hostile to God, for it does not submit to God's law; indeed, it cannot. Those who are in the flesh cannot please God. – ESV

Body and flesh are not always equivalent. The context shows how flesh is supposed to be understood. **Genesis 2:23 says** regarding the creation of the body of Eve, "...This at last is bone ('etsem) of my bones and flesh (**basar**) of my flesh..." **John 1:14** says: "And the Word became flesh (**sarx**) and dwelt among us... full of grace and truth." It is saying that the body of Christ, which He got from His mother's DNA, had all the weakness and vulnerability we humans have. But His perfection in His Father's "Spirit DNA" was to never give in to fleshly weakness, by always setting His Mind on the Spirit. **Hebrews 4:15** says Christ was tempted in every way as we are, but He did not sin. He had to suffer the pull of temptation in His flesh, or He would not have been tempted. But His heart did not **bind** with temptation resulting in sin. He did not sin in ignorance or accidentally miss the mark, either. He was the Lamb without blemish for your sin and mine.

Hebrews 2:14-18 says:

> Since therefore the children share in flesh and blood, He Himself likewise partook of the same things, that through death He might destroy the one who has the power of death, that is, the devil, and deliver all those who through fear of death were subject to lifelong slavery. For surely it is not angels that He helps, but He helps the offspring of Abraham. Therefore, He had to be made like His brothers in every respect, so He might become a merciful and faithful High Priest in the service of God, to make propitiation [*purifying sacrifice*] for the sins of the people. For because He Himself has suffered when tempted, He is able to help those who are being tempted. - ESV

In review, look at how the mindset of the flesh operates in the disobedient believer in the diagram below.

Flesh mindset = soul & body ignoring the spirit.

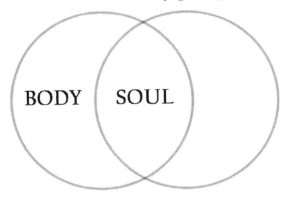

Notice also how obedience works in the mindset of the spirit to overrule the flesh below. Fleshly thinking defaults to body and soulish needs, blocking spirit leading in Christ.

Spirit mindset directs the soul overules the body.

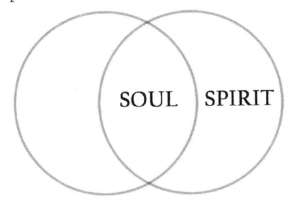

Psalms 51:6 David says of the Lord,
>   Behold, You delight in truth in the inward being, and
>   You teach wisdom in the secret heart. – ESV

One more point about soul and spirit: The soul is reporting its *impression* of my circumstances. While I must recognize its self-interest bias, I should not disregard what it has to say. I must not let it lead, but I should see where it wants to go. Because I see only a fraction of what is really going on around me, my soul's imagination tries to make sense of what is happening by drawing *preliminary conclusions*. Sometimes those conclusions are right, and sometimes they are wrong. Sometimes my thoughts and feelings exaggerate what is there, and sometimes they minimize it. Sometimes my impressions make a thing look too good to be true, and sometimes it makes a thing look too bad to be true. The Bible talks about the mind of the flesh and the mind of the spirit. I have come to understand this to mean *mindset* or *point of view.* The mindset of the flesh is to disobey God. The mindset of my soul is to pursue self-interest. The mindset of my spirit as a Christian is to want to obey the will of my Father. When my circumstances require a moral choice, I'm fully engaged in my options when I see where my soul wants to go with it. The mindset of my flesh is vulnerable to Satan's agenda, which wants to capitalize on my soul's mood or self-interest desire, to bend me toward sin. The mindset of my spirit wants to count the cost of what is at stake, but then choose to do what Christ wants me to do.

After many years of practice, I had learned to block my negative thoughts and feelings because I thought that forgiveness was about minimizing offenses or excusing those who hurt me. I also thought I would be sinning if I let myself feel or understand them, because they often aroused great anger. In blocking my feelings and thoughts, I was fooling myself with a conceit that I didn't have to face the painful realities in my life with others, or a painful truth about myself. In turn, my own wounding of others was either justified or minimized by blocking the way it would feel if they did the same thing to me as I had done to them. This created an extensive network of *internal dishonesty* which blocked empathy and conviction of sin.

I was trying to rebuild my wounded dignity on sand. The way of my flesh was to escape the reality of my problems and circumstances by substituting an alternative reality with my imagination. This blocked taking action by faith. But my problems always found a way to come back to bite me. I could take a vacation from reality but my problems never did. In some ways, even God became a kind of mystical dream, way up there and far away. I thought I needed to lose myself in Him with mystical experiences that would overwhelm my anxiety. I also tried to supplant real faith with magical thinking that everything was going to be all right, without me needing to do anything to change.

When I am in right believing, I am able to express Christ spontaneously. But when I am not seeing the truth about my life and circumstances, I am spontaneously impulsive. I blunder into making foolish decisions expressing destructive anger in unbelief. This occurs when I'm blocking the report of what my soul's self-interest is saying. Yes, I am to take every thought captive in Christ, but that is only possible when I know what my thoughts and feelings actually are. I must reject the old way of thinking that faithless sinful thoughts and desires are originating in me. They always come from Satan, especially since he once made his home in me. But my old nature that used to welcome his counsel is now dead. I must not make the mistake that sick thoughts and feelings are a reflection of my character in Christ. That would be regarding myself according to the flesh. Satan as my operator is sick. Christ as my operator is well. If I believe sin thoughts and feelings originate with me, I fall into despair, or bear sinful fruit in unbelief. The fallen angel of light knows how to make his thoughts *seem like mine*. But I can speak back to those thoughts as mere temptation and do what is right because of the power of the Spirit of Christ in me.

Now I see that faith is being fully engaged with reality by letting my soul's self-interest opinions, apprehend the gravity of my situation, then doing what spiritual faith demands of me. My problems are in reality, but so is God, and He is able to give me solutions that are in reality if I have faith enough to stay in reality with Him! I'm learning not to block my soul impressions anymore, to let myself feel my pain and the gravity of my situation. I'm also learning to let my spirit inform my conscience with the truth of the Word, to let my soul feel the gravity of my sin against another, so I am moved to repent. My flesh does not want to repent.

When my soul is in the service of my spirit, I can't rest until I make things right. This is being honest inside. But I'm learning not to let the enemy use my soul to justify a sinful response. I can identify with Christ by confessing His moral nature is now mine, and I have the power in Him to do what is right. Then I make a faith decision to do what I see as righteous in defiance of sin, trusting God with the consequences. The Bible tells me to rebuke those who are sinning against me, and also to forgive them. I must also repent and make amends where I have hurt others, as well as show generosity to the poor, and long suffering with the weak, as He has always done with me.

Left Hand & Right Hand

1. Let's say that my left hand is my soul with its focus on self-interests, feelings, impressions, desires, et cetera. Also, in my left hand is all that is bothering me, offending me, or intimidating me. I acknowledge what hurts, what angers, what shames... I let myself feel it without trying to block it. I'm honest about what I'm thinking and feeling, because if I minimize the truth of my problem, I will neither be facing it with real faith nor will I be able to see a full answer that is required to fix it. I must let myself know both what is happening as well as the *conclusions* or *opinions* of my soul.

2. Let's say my right hand is my spirit with its focus on doing the will of God, His promises, the Blood of Christ, and my position in Him at His Right Hand— His Spirit being joined to me by indwelling my spirit, my new nature being free from the power of sin and other relevant Scriptures which apply. I set my mind on Biblical truth. Real faith has its eyes open because it believes God is for me and is greater than all that is against me. If there is a solution to my problems, it's in reality where God is, not in unreality where I'm tempted to run and hide. If there is no happy solution, I will still have grace to deal with it. The Word of the Lord does not lie.

3. Now I *defy* the self-interest of my soul and my weak flesh with a choice to do what is right. I place my right hand (*my spirit*) on top of my left hand (*my weak flesh and self-interested soul*) to cover and overrule it in Christ. This illustrates what true walking in the Spirit has become for me. It's not some ecstatic trance state of consciousness I used to seek. It's not getting myself

psyched up to win like an athlete often does. The joy of the Lord, which is my strength, is not about my mood. It comes in believing my spirit, that the love my Father has for me is pleased in seeing the fruit of His Son in me, as I take action in the emphatic belief that what the Bible says is true.

Remembering what **Hebrews 3:19** says again, Israel was not able to enter the Promised Land because of unbelief. **4:2** defines unbelief as *not mixing* faith with the Word they heard. **4:6** says failure to *mix* faith with the Word is disobedience. Christ says if we love Him we will keep His commandments! To feel warmly toward Him is a good thing, but what is pleasing to Him is obedience.

Sin has made my life like a house with holes in the walls. In areas of greater weakness, I have had larger holes for the enemy to break in and steal from me. How can faith fill these holes? Speaking the truth back to the enemy's lies is a good start, but by making a choice *as if* the Word of the Lord is true, has tangible substance. My choice to act in accordance with the truth makes a "brick" I can lay in the hole in my wall, because I have mixed the Word of the Lord with my faith choice. Inversely, if I mix my faith with a lie, *as if* the lie is true, I will widen the hole in my wall. As Norman Grubb says, "what I take takes me." If I give in to temptation, sin "takes me," and I will bear his sinful fruit till I repent. It has been wonderful to find out that when I obey the Lord, His righteousness will "take" me and I will once again bear His fruit—and I will make "bricks" to not only fill in my holes, but I can add other rooms to my house to minister to others.

When trusting God for healing or salvation for a friend, expect that doubting thoughts and despairing feelings will come at you. Don't take condemnation for them because they didn't come from you! They may be experientially intense, but now I treat them as mere temptations. Satan—your adversary, that slandering devil—is lying to you that you don't have the faith to persevere. But feelings are not necessarily facts. If I am in Christ, it is no longer **me** who doubts. Satan is trying to get me to believe him through the weakness of my flesh and the subjective self-interest of my soul. I must press on in faith! My soul must be informed by my spirit, and my flesh must be *overruled.* My flesh is *mine,* but it is not **me**! If I get taken in by the enemy and fall into unbelief, then I just repent by remembering who I really am in Christ, and I get back on track because the Blood covers all sin in me. Remember what Paul says: "It is no longer I who sin, but sin that dwells in my *members.*" (**Romans 7:17**)

In summary, the goal of the body is to satisfy my physical needs in order to move and be in the world. The goal of the soul is to satisfy my self-interest and know myself. The goal of the spirit is to please God, and to know Him and His will.

Chapter 5 Study Questions

1. What is the difference between Trichotomy and Dichotomy?

2. What is the role of the soul in decision-making?

3. What is a self-serving conceit?

4. What are the right and the wrong ways of using my soul's opinion of my circumstances?

5. Where do I need to apply these truths in my life?

6

To Will & To Do

So, I now know I am a new creation in Christ. I know how Satan tries to misuse the appetites and drives of my flesh to get me to sin. I know how he manipulates the subjective opinions and self-interest focus of my soul to try get me to act out in selfish disobedience. I know how he has infected my wounds with the poison of revenge. How he has tempted me with despair over my shameful deeds. How he has tormented me with fear to try to keep me from courageous faith. And I know how to answer these temptations by speaking back to them that the Blood of Christ has paid for my sins, that I am now in Christ and He is in me, I am a new creation who no longer wants what Satan wants, because I'm now one who wants what God wants.

Whenever I stand on the truth and speak back to the lies of the enemy, I defeat him! So why are there still times when I do not choose to stand? Why are there still times when I give in to sin? Why is there still willful selfish disobedience when I know the will of God is good, and the joining of His Holy Spirit to my human spirit makes me holy, and the desire of my new identity in Christ is to please my God?

When I looked at the cost of my sin to those around me, I saw how it gave them cause to turn away from both God and me. My secretiveness was withholding truth and intimacy from others. My gossip betrayed them. My anger flashes frightened them away. My ruthlessness repelled them. My praise seeking manipulated them. My lying undermined trust. My controlling behavior wore them out. My self-pity disgusted them. My insensitivity devalued them. My selfishness ripped them off. My envy made others feel guilty about what they had. My contentiousness provoked arguments. My slander betrayed them. My melancholy shut them out. My conceit presumed and bullied them. My deceit exploited them. My grandiosity created false hope. My escapism abandoned them. My laziness devalued the needs of others. My lust objectified them. My despair drained them ... No wonder God demands all of me.

I knew I had learned these habits of behavior from my old nature. My new nature in Christ did not want them. So, I tried to
sensitize my conscience by reading the scariest parts of the Bible referring to sin consequences, punishment, and judgment.
But that only helped for short periods of time. Then I saw that
a lot of this behavior was rooted in strategies involving a resistance to suffering in submission to Christ.

But **1 Peter 2:21-25** says:

> For *this* I have been called, because Christ also *suffered*
> for **me**, leaving **me** an example, so that **I** might follow in
> His steps. He committed no sin, neither was deceit
> found in His Mouth. When He was reviled, He did not
> revile in return; when He *suffered*, He did not threaten,
> but continued entrusting Himself to Him Who Judges
> justly. He Himself bore **my** sins in His Body on a tree,
> that **I** might die to sin and live to righteousness. By His
> wounds, **I** have been healed. For **I** was straying like a
> sheep, but **I** have now returned to the Shepherd and
> Overseer **of my** soul. – ESV (*Shank*)

And **Romans 8:16-17** says:

> The Spirit Himself bears witness with **my** spirit that **I**
> am a **child** of God, and if **a child**, then **an heir—an heir**
> of God and fellow **heir** with Christ, provided **I** *suffer*
> with Him in order that **I** may also be glorified with
> Him. – ESV (Shank)

No wonder God demands all of me. There is no part of my
life He does not need to be Lord over. I must be willing to share
in Christ's suffering now, that I may share in His glory later.
He rightly demands my absolute surrender, and He also *does
the work* in me to make that happen. God accepts my surrender when it is given, and He builds me up and protects me. He
will surely bless my surrender with favor and fruit.

Psalm 127:1-2 says:

> Unless the Lord builds the house,
> those who build it labor in vain.
> Unless the Lord watches over the city,

the watchman stays awake in vain.
It is vain to rise up early
and go late to rest,
eating the bread of anxious toil;
for He gives to His beloved sleep. – ESV

Andrew Murray wrote a book in 1897 called *Absolute Surren-der*. In it, he points to the Scriptural foundations for an experi-ence with God that shows the way of entering into His rest, in an absolute surrender. His experience harmonizes with other great saints like Jesse Penn-Lewis, Evan Roberts, George Mul-ler, Norman Grubb, and Watchman Nee, to name a few. Murray's book opens with a quote from **1 Kings 20:1-4**:

> Ben-hadad the king of Syria gathered all his army to-gether. Thirty-two kings were with him and horses and chariots. And he went up and closed in on Samaria and fought against it. And he sent messengers into the city to Ahab king of Israel and said to him, "Thus says Ben-hadad: Your silver and your gold are mine; your best wives and children also mine." And the king of Israel answered, "As you say, my lord, O king, I am yours, and all have." The messengers came again and said, "Thus says Ben-hadad: I sent to you saying, Deliver to me your silver and your gold, your wives and your children. Nevertheless, I will send my servants to you tomorrow about this time, and they will search your house and the houses of your servants and lay hands on whatever pleases you and take it away." – ESV

It is interesting that both the Hebrew words in the Old Testa-ment and the Greek words in the New Testament for *messen-ger* can both also mean *angel.* Ben-hadad sending his messen-ger parallels the Devil sending one of his messengers or angels, which are *demons.* Those of us who have been addicted know what it is like to be ruled over by a ruthless spirit who will take everything we love from us. Those of us who have been filled with pride, violence, abusiveness, lust and fear know that spirit too. See Ahab's admission to Ben-hadad, "...As you say, my lord O king, I am yours... my silver and gold, my wives and children. *"*

Why would Ahab say that? Why would he agree to hand over his family and his wealth? It was because he was surrounded by a great army. He could not defeat them in battle, nor could he flee for help. He was trapped. He had to do what was demanded of him. It is the same for those of us who have been become enslaved to addiction—chemical or behavioral. Our very will and dignity are taken away. We are hopeless. All that we love can be taken from us, too. Surely the devil has power over us, he does whatever he pleases with us. How can we ever break loose from his sinful and destructive demands? We have always failed at our best efforts. How can we come to believe in, and even know a God Who is loving and strong, and willing to free us? The devil has power over us in our sin and can only be defeated by One Who is more powerful than he is. Only the One Who is Powerful in Righteousness can make us righteous.

Again, we serve of one or the other of two masters, Christ or Satan. Both of them want all of us. Both of them say, "I am your Master!" Jesus says we cannot have two masters; we will love and serve one but hate and disobey the other. We must do the will of the one to whom we belong. Because of Ahab's wickedness, even though he was king of Israel, his disobedience to God put him under the power of Satan. Ben-hadad acts like Satan because he is reproducing Satan's will. So will it be with the Antichrist when he is permitted to rule the whole earth. Satan has power over a Christian in disobedience who surrenders to his evil will. If we do not repent, his influence will produce more and more evidence that we are hypocrites.

In Old Testament times, Israel was supposed to be God's people. In our time, the church is supposed to be the body of Christ. The more I obey the will of God, the more of His fruit I will bear. But if I disobey God, I can still bear Satan's fruit and discredit my testimony. So how can I as a believer—a son of the Father by the Blood of Jesus and joined to Him the Holy Spirit—disobey God and let Satan bear his fruit in me?

Through deception, the devil makes his appeal to the weakness of my flesh. Masquerading as me, he appeals to the self-focus of my soul to please itself by what falsely appears to be in my own interest, apart from God. When I resort to my own soul-ish willpower for strength, I will frequently give in to sin, even though my spirit does not want to do it. Murray speaks to these same tendencies, we studied in **Chapter 4**:

Romans 7:18b says:

> For I have the desire to do what is right, but not the ability to carry it out. – ESV

Then Murray asks:

> "How is it that God makes a regenerate man utter such a confession, with a right will, with a heart that longs to do good, and longs to do its very utmost to love God?"

Murray says this is powerlessness in a believer in Christ, powerlessness to do the will of God in one who is already regenerated by the Spirit! Murray calls him the *impotent* man. It is because that believer is doing his best to obey the Law of God with his own renewed willpower. Note once again that what is missing in **Romans 7:7-25** "...for I do not do the good I want, but the evil I do not want is what I keep on doing..." is any mention of the Holy Spirit or Christ. But in those same verses, the Law is mentioned 20 times. Put this together with the personal pronouns **I**, **me**, and **my** occurring over 40 times. Murray says we see a believer in self-effort who has not yet come to the end of himself.

But, can anyone come to the end of himself, you may ask? Isn't that process like peeling layers off an onion, always more imperfection to find? When I thought that way, I still believed my problems to be unlimited, and God's ability to help me appeared *limited*. But it is God Who is Unlimited, and I who am limited. Therefore, there is a *limit* to myself—a limit reachable with the help of God.

An interesting verse from **Hebrews 4:11-12** is relevant here:

> Let us therefore *strive* to enter that rest, so that no one may fall by the same disobedience. For the Word of God is living and active, sharper than any two-edged sword, piercing to the division of soul and spirit, of

joints and marrow, and discerning the thoughts and intentions of the heart. – ESV (*Shank*)

I am to *strive* to enter God's rest. I must struggle agains*t* the
weakness of my flesh and the self-serving misuse of my soul, to
do the will of God as He has revealed it to my spirit by His Holy Spirit. I must *wrestle* with the angel of the Lord for the
blessing. But I am saved by grace and not by works, lest any
man should boast. Is it not futile for me to try to make myself
righteous by trying to keep the Law? **Yes.** Does not God give
freely to me out of the goodness of His heart? **Yes.** So why does
He say in the verse above that I must still *strive* in futility,
which seems the opposite of rest?

Murray says God allows believers to fail in their own efforts to
show their own utter impotence. The believer's struggle with
this utter impotence brings him to realize the utter sinfulness
of Sin, which we have been saying is the nature of Satan. This
must be seen before the Utter Righteousness of Christ can be
apprehended and be made manifest in each of us.

When God made Adam and Eve, did He not say they were
good? Yes. They were good, well made, but not yet righteous,
because they were not yet tested. Being able to turn away from
evil and do the good when tempted is being righteous. When I
was saved, was I not made holy by the Blood of Christ and
sealed with His Holy Spirit? **Yes,** but Scripture calls me to
walk in the righteousness I have been freely given, by putting
to death the deeds of the flesh. I am His when I am saved, but I
am unfruitful in all I do outside His will. The struggle proves
and me and proves God, "like silver refined in a furnace of clay,
purified seven times" **(Psalm 12:6).**

Philippians 2:13 says:
> ... for it is God Who works in you, both to *will* and to
> *work* for His good pleasure. – ESV (*Shank*)

God is to do the *willing* in me, through me. He is also to do the
working or *doing* in me, through me, for His good pleasure.
Unless it is Christ *doing* through me, I will sin. If I am absolutely surrendered to Him, He is able to live my life as **me.** Is

97

He not to be the All in all? Is He not to fulfill all? As **Galatians 2:20** clearly states:

> I am crucified with Christ: nevertheless, I live; yet not I, but Christ lives in **me**: and the life which I now live in the flesh I live by the faith **OF** the Son of God, Who loved me, and gave Himself for **me**. (*Only the KJV and the RSV Interlinear Greek-English New Testament get the preposition right here.*)

Therefore, unless the faith **OF** (tou) the Son Himself is keeping me, I shall not stand. Unless Christ is doing the *willing* and the *doing* in me, I shall not overcome. But when Christ is keeping me, willing through me and doing through me, how shall I fail? But how can this be? How can this happen? Let me tell you what I have learned about this from my own experience.

I had reached a point of deep frustration over failures with pride, lust, temper, self-pity, revenge, et cetera. Though much of my outward life had cleaned up and I had received some deep healings inside—even leading others to Christ, a willful selfishness still defeated me. Though everything in my spirit wanted to honor and serve my Lord, Who had done so much for me, I still gave in to selfishness—even though I knew that whenever I would stand on who I am in Christ, I could rebuke the tempter and not fall into sin. Yet there would be those times when I would choose not to take my stand, give in to selfish sin, and afterwards, fall into shame. What was wrong with me? How could I still return to my own vomit (*what I had already confessed with my mouth as sin*) like a dog? I even began to wonder if I had ever been in real repentance from sin. Was I just living life in episodes of binge and purge? Was I, as an alcoholic friend once despairingly described himself, just a man between drinks?

Absolute Surrender

My friend Mark Behlen was raving about a book called *Absolute Surrender* by Andrew Murray. The title was off-putting to me because it seemed to demand of me the very thing I had clearly been unable to deliver. The title was rubbing my many failures in my face. But my friend was a prayer partner and he was beaming with encouragement, so I told him I had better get a copy of the book for myself. He smiled again and said he had already ordered it for me. When it arrived, I suspended my prejudice and ate the book.

By the time I got through Chapter 5, I was strongly convinced of what Murray was saying and got down on my face on the floor. In tears, I prayed that I was without excuse for my sin because of all the Lord had given me but seemed to lack the power in myself to fully obey. I said I was not blaming the Lord for withholding something from me I still needed. I had His Spirit and many years of blessings and fruit. Then I said that I was convinced from Murray's book that the only way I could will and do His good pleasure was if **He** did the willing and the doing in me. I had to give myself completely to Him—*not* for salvation this time, *not* for deliverance this time, *not* for the baptism of the Holy Spirit this time, *not* for gifts of the Spirit this time, but to give completely my willing and doing and let **Him** do the willing and doing, in me. He said, "I've been waiting for you to come to this." He accepted my surrender.

Then a quiet relaxation came into me and I knew I had come to the end of myself. I had finally entered into His rest. Now I have nothing to prove about myself. I am in the Hands of One Who loves me, no matter what happens. I have the same personality. I get all the temptations I did before, but they seem to have lost much of their appeal because I see them for what they are.

I know I don't want them. I still have strong emotions, but they don't rule me like they used to. Am I perfect? No, and that is not for me to care about; My Lord has me and I have Him. We're doing what He wants to do and going where He wants to go. He teaches me, corrects me, leads me, blesses me. I have dreams and ambitions. Some of them we will do and some we won't. We will start what He wants to start, and finish what He wants to finish, and add to whatever He has already going on. So, am I just passively waiting around for orders? **No.** I am surrounded by circumstances, responsibilities, and opportunities that need attention. I am free to obey Him, and all these things are part of His keeping and part of His active plan. He is working in and on me as I am—and pruning me as He wills and works in me.

Rhema and Logos

Matthew 4:4 says,

> ...Man does not live by bread alone, but by every word [rhema] that comes from the Mouth of God. – ESV

It is interesting to note that the Greek word in this verse for what comes from the Mouth of God is **rhema**, not **logos**. **Logos** is used in reference to Scripture, the fixed and unchangeable Word of the Lord. It also refers to Christ in the first chapter of the Gospel of John:

> In the beginning was the **Logos**, and the **Logos** was with God, and the **Logos** was God ... and the **Logos** became flesh and dwelt among us ...

The **logos** of the Scripture is the determiner of whether something is doctrinally true or not. It is also how we know if what is spoken by someone in a meeting or in our own mind in prayer, is from God or not. The **logos** judges if what is spoken is **rhema** or not. If we do not know the **logos** of Scripture, we will not know whether a prophetic word is **rhema**. More of this is discussed in **Chapters 17 and 18**. **Rhema** never contradicts the **logos**. God is not in conflict with Himself. Neither is His Kingdom divided that it might fall. The Scriptural **logos** the prophets of old received and gave to us, came to them first as **rhema**, from the Mouth of God to their hearts and ears. So why is it important to distinguish between these two words if they are in complete harmony with each other?

More and more, I see that the **logos** has to do with objective faith and objective truth. It is what God has revealed in the Bible to all of us concerning everything God wants us to know about Himself: good and evil, history, wisdom and knowledge and so on. The **logos** of God, does not lie.

I also see that **rhema** tends to have to do with the subjective or personal communication from God. Personal commands to me may not be the same for you, but what He says to both of us *never* contradicts the **logos**. You have one calling, I have another. **Rhema** is about my personal relationship and my experience of God. It is also about your personable relationship and experience with God. But it does not mean we are not accountable to others. God's **rhema** to another on my behalf may help me where I am missing the will of God because of some prejudice in my thinking. His keeping of me sometimes comes through others, who will point my prejudice out.

An example of the personal word of God to a believer is in Isaiah 30:20-21:

> And though the Lord give you the bread of adversity and the water of affliction, yet your Teacher will not hide Himself anymore, but your eyes shall see your Teacher. And your ears shall hear a word behind you, saying, "This is the way, walk in it," when you turn to the right or when you turn to the left. – ESV

Rhema *in no way implies moral relativity.* But His command to me may not be the same as His command to you. God guides me with His **rhema** to me. He may also guide one group to go in one direction and another to go another direction, in their ministry roles. God's guidance will never contradict His **logos**, but not all **rhema** is included in the **logos**. If I believe God is calling me to fast and pray for someone, He may not ask you to do the same. He may speak to you about a career change or whom to marry. If so, it would be wise to gain confirmation from others about some of these things, not because these things violate Scripture, but because they might not be the Lord Who is leading. If we are humble, teachable and patient, the will of God will be known by us because God resists the proud but draws near the humble. I have also come to see humility as the grease that helps a heavy stone weight to slide off of me.

The body of Christ, His Church, is meant to live by every **rhema** that comes from the Mouth of God. And the testimony of Jesus Christ is the spirit of prophecy. We are meant to be instruments of God's **rhema** to and from each other, made sharp by knowing His **logos**. I am in Him, He is in me. He is in us, we are in Him. This is all relational. This is all intimate and personal. This is all in God's keeping of us and each other, in His love. This is the fellowship of the true church of Christ! In this sense, Norman Grubb is right in writing that living faith is subjective. Bible faith is essential in revealing what is objectively true, revealing sound doctrine. This is **logos**. The Lord is high and lifted up, far above all else. This is the *transcendent* experience of Him; there is no one Holy like He is. But He is also inside us, in our deepest place, knowing us intimately and wanting us to intimately know Him. This is the *immanent* experience of God. We have both in Christ, if we do not let unrepentant sin harden our hearts.

False prophets can speak falsely, and apparently, an unbeliever can cast out demons in Jesus' Name because of what they know in the Bible alone. In **Matthew 7:21-23** Jesus says:

> Not everyone who says to me, "Lord, Lord," will enter the kingdom of heaven, but the one who does the will of My Father Who is in heaven. On that day, many will say to Me, "Lord, Lord, did we not prophesy in Your Name, and cast out demons in Your Name, and do many mighty works in Your Name?" And then I will declare to them, "I never knew you; depart from Me, you workers of lawlessness." – ESV

Logos is for the renewal of my mind in Christ. **Rhema** is for intimate fellowship with Him, knowing Him personally, by the Spirit. Obedience to Him tunes my heart to hear God's **rhema** and to know what is not rhema. My relationship with God in obedience to Him opens the flow of very personal communication with Him. I know He is in me and I am in Him because the **logos**, does not lie. I know the Lord is my Shepherd because I hear the **rhema** in His Voice, by the Spirit. I can be open and teachable by Him as well, with **rhema** coming through my brothers and sisters.

Disqualifying the Holy Spirit

Recently, a ministry coworker said to me that God had told him to back out of a staff commitment he had made. When one desires to do the will of God, one seeks confirmation with humility. He was not interested in that. He firmly said God told him, so he was leaving. I let him go without objection. Our team needed a willing spirit in each for whatever God would want to show us through each other as well as what the Word says. We needed his participation, and his leaving temporarily hurt the development of the ministry, but when someone plays the "God told me" card without seeking conformation, his heart is *not open.* Better he leaves.

John 13:20 says:

> Truly, truly, I say to you, whoever receives the one
> I send receives Me, and whoever receives Me receives
> the One Who sent Me. – ESV

The reverse of this verse is also true. If you refuse the one whom I send, you have refused Me! **Negative Perfectionism** is the vanity that makes it hard to receive correction from someone I don't respect because they are imperfect. "You can't correct me because you are you have your own problems." Yes, I must strive to remove any stumbling stone that may give another an excuse not to listen. That's why God wants me to walk in integrity, so as not to give someone just cause for the dismissal of what He might want to say through me, on grounds of hypocrisy.

But when God has been dealing with pride and vanity in me, He has often sent correction through others whom my pride considered inferior to me! But this has been a merciful act of pruning. My branch had "dead heads" on it and "fruitless limbs" that needed removal. Shall I reject the truth that comes from another who also has "dead heads" and "fruitless limbs?" No. Then no one can be used by God if each has to be perfect in practice before speaking out for God. Part of the grace extended to me is that He will use even me, as I am now in my current state, wherever He thinks best. He will also use the one I thought in Satan's vanity to be "inferior" to correct me. I must neither barge ahead with pride nor shrink back in self-focused fear from what He sets before me, because I can do all things in Christ Jesus. At the same time, He is using me for another, He is convicting me of where I also need to grow.

Those who are hard of heart will demand that the person bringing correction be perfect before they will listen. But they are dismissing the merit of the truth on the grounds of the weakness of the messenger. There have been times in my life when I have been that hardhearted person. This is extremely dangerous because the conscience becomes seared from re-peated rejection of what is right, whoever the messenger may be. When the Holy Spirit is grieved, the hardhearted perish in their sins. Even Jesus said that the people should do as the Pharisees say, not as they do. One of the consequences of unre-pentant sin is spiritual dullness: eyes that don't see, ears that don't hear, and hard hearts that do not understand. Sin affects our capacity to see, hear, and understand, but God draws near the humble and teachable.

Positive Perfectionism is to say a real Christian does not sin anymore. This disqualifies the Holy Spirit from pointing out real sin when one lies to one's self that sin is not there, when it may well be. **1 John 1:5-10** says:

> This is the message we have heard from Him and pro-claim to you, that God is Light, and in Him is no dark-ness at all. If we say we have fellowship with Him while we walk in darkness, we lie and do not practice the truth. But if we walk in the Light as He is in the Light, we have fellowship with one another, and the Blood of Jesus His Son cleanses us from all sin. If we say we have no sin, we deceive ourselves, and the truth is not in us. If we confess our sins, He is faithful and just to forgive us our sins and to cleanse us from all unright-eousness. If we say we have not sinned, we make Him a liar, and His Word in not in us. – ESV

It is extremely important that I don't block, minimize, or in any way suppress the gravity of my circumstances, as per-ceived by my soul. Fears, offenses, consequences, and other stresses—with their attendant temptations and agendas—must be acknowledged for what they are before real faith ac-tion can be taken. Real faith comes from facing the subjective truth of my soul's opinions and imaginations formed from ap-pearances. I must then answer them with the objective Biblical Truth wherever it may apply. My spirit is joined to the Spirit of Christ and wants to do my Father's will.

To this end, I'd like to say a bit about the problems of the **Sin-less-Perfection** doctrine and the ironic way in which it can produce spiritual dishonesty—that is to say as a real Christian,

I can receive from the Holy Spirit a state where I sin no more in this life. Those who believe this way will quote **1 John 3:9**:

> Whosoever is born of God doth not commit sin; for His seed remains in him: and he cannot sin, because he is born of God. – RSV

But this is not a proof text to be taken by itself. We see a contradiction if we compare it to **1 John 1:8**:

> If we say we have no sin, we deceive ourselves, and the truth is not in us. – RSV

The Word holds paradox at some points, but it does not contradict itself. One must look at the tension in a paradox to find the qualifying principles. It's also important to make sure the translation is accurate by testing it against other versions. I believe the ESV translation of **1 John 3:9** is more accurate with the verb tenses in the Greek:

> No one born of God *makes a practice of* sinning, for God's seed abides in him, and he cannot [*habitually*] keep on sinning because he is born of God. – ESV (*Shank*)

When I lie to myself about myself, I can't have an honest relationship with God. When I lie to myself about myself, I will lie to my friends, too. If I base my standing with Christ on sinless perfection, then *any* sinful disobedience breaks my relationship with Him, because sinless perfection testifies against me being in Christ. In this view, where sin has in fact occurred, Christ is no longer with me, or maybe has never really been in me; so, I become reluctant to admit I have sinned. I am likely to either rationalize my sin or even justify it. The point is that I am in darkness with unconfessed sin because my holding onto it lets sin hold onto me. But I am not cancelled out as a child of God unless there is a refusal to repent. That means resisting all the efforts of the Holy Spirit to be restored. It is a bitter irony that those who advocate sinless perfection might unwittingly blaspheme the Holy Spirit, the unpardonable sin, by denying their need to confess and repent.

Internal honesty is the only way of real righteousness. When I had a season lost in bitterness and unforgiveness, the Lord never gave up on me. That bitterness was a powerful **conceit** that justified the production of many sins. But the Lord disciplines those whom He loves and also shows mercy. He gave grace to me until I repented, first from individual sins. The fact that I kept repeating them again, over and over, led me to examine the **conceits** and selfish desires that empowered them. Those entitling **conceits** and desires drew their justification from my root of bitterness. And my root of bitterness got its power from the futility of my efforts to forgive and change because I regarded myself according to the flesh and thought I couldn't—or really didn't want to—change. Then I saw the reason I believed I couldn't change myself was because I was hopelessly flawed and corrupt, thus denying my new nature in Christ!

I was seeing myself according to the flesh only, the way Satan wanted me to see. I finally saw that my repentance had to reach all the way down to no longer seeing myself apart from Christ. I was *joined* to Him by the indwelling of the Holy Spirit, instilled with His desire to please God. My fleshly weakness still whines for satisfaction and contends with my spirit. But so what? I know the truth, so I can be honest about what is going on inside me. I must embrace the conviction of the Holy Spirit when I am in the wrong because sin is inconsistent with my new nature. Satan wants me to believe I am not a new creation in Christ. That is condemnation.

Romans 8:1-2 says:

> There is therefore now no condemnation for those who are in Christ Jesus. For the Law of the Spirit of life has set you free in Christ Jesus from the law of sin and death. – ESV

This means I must embrace that truth as aggressively as I once embraced the lies of sin. When Satan is able to deceive me, his agenda is to clobber me with condemnation afterward, so I will no longer feel worthy to stand in faith for myself or anyone else. He attacks my identity with condemnation, which is morbid shame. On the other hand, when the Holy Spirit convicts me of sin, His agenda is to build me up. He says, "John, why did you do *that*? You're in Christ now—you're better than that! Don't be a hypocrite! Get back to where you belong, bearing the fruit of Christ!" See the difference?

But my subject here is spiritual dishonesty. Sound doctrine should reach all the way from my head to the ground. It should touch my relationships with the Life of God. It enables me to perform my ministry of reconciliation, which is our purpose with one another. Much of Holiness Theology is wonderful, but sinless perfection has many casualties when internal honesty is suppressed. God is real to those who are real.

Spiritual Laws, Principles & Proverbs

- The golden rule says: *Do unto others, as you would have them*
  do to unto you.

- The law of judgment is: *As you judge, so shall you be judged.*

- The command of forgiveness is: *Forgive others or you will not be forgiven.*

- The principle of reaping says: *Whatever you sow, you will also reap.*

- The directive of spirit is: *What you take, takes you, and what*
  you fight, fights you.

- The rule of symmetry says: *The wound you have received is the wound you will give to others, but the healing you have received is the healing you will give to others.*

- The power of nurturing is: *In nurturing others, you will nurture yourself. We comfort others in the same way the God of all comfort, has comforted us.*

- The power of keeping is: *God has already taken into consideration my incompetence in fulfilling His plan for my life.*

These are lyrics to a song I wrote inspired by **Psalm 18 &
2 Samuel 22**. It's called *No Fool*

He reached down and took a hold of me,
Drew me out of the deep, deep waters,
He rescued me from my enemies,
They were too strong for me.

To the faithful He shows Himself faithful.
To the blameless He shows Himself blameless.
To the pure He shows Himself to be pure.
But to the crooked He shows Himself to be shrewd.
He is no fool!

He saves the humble and the lowly,
But His Eyes are on the proud to bring them low.
The fool says in his heart, "there is no God."
The wicked say, "God does not see."

But to the faithful He shows Himself faithful.
To the blameless He shows Himself blameless.
To the pure He shows Himself pure.
And to the crooked He shows Himself to be shrewd.
He is no fool; God is no fool!

Chapter 6 Study Questions

1. What is the *impotent* man, according to Andrew Murray?

2. How can one enter absolute surrender?

3. What is the difference between *logos* and *rhema*?

4. What is sinless perfection and how does it hinder internal honesty?

5. Why must I listen to the message even if the messenger is weak?

7

Faith, Heart, Will and Conscience

My will is my chooser, and I am free to choose because God is free to choose and I am in His image. He made me for eternal relationship with Him in righteousness. I do not live like an animal, which follows the narrow parameters of instinct in what it does. My chooser is commanded by God to follow the mind of the spirit, not the mind of the flesh. As mentioned earlier, I have found it helpful to see mind in this case as the *mindset* of the spirit or the flesh. A mindset is a perspective that has the components of desire, motive, and attitude. **Galatians 5:16-17** says the desire of my flesh is opposed to the desires of my spirit when my spirit is joined to the Spirit of God. When my spirit was not joined to God it cooperated with the flesh, as my old nature. The desire of my soul is focused on my self-interest, but my soul has only a subjective perception of what that actually is. (*See* **A definition of the soul** in **Chapter 5**)

Romans 10:8-11 says:

> But what does it say? "The Word is near you, in your mouth and in your heart" (that is, the word of faith we proclaim); because if you confess with your mouth that Jesus is Lord and believe in your heart that God raised Him from the dead, you will be saved. For with the heart one believes and is justified, and with the mouth one confesses and is saved. Everyone who believes will not be put to shame. – ESV

The Greek word for heart in this passage is **kardia**, from which the English gets the word *cardiac* referring to things relating to the physical heart. The New Testament also uses **kardia** when referring to the physical heart, but many other verses use **kardia** to mean something more than the blood pump in our bodies. Jesus says: "...out of the abundance of the heart the mouth speaks" (**Luke 6:45**) In those cases, the heart is playing a vital role in expressing or suppressing right believing. My understanding of this is shown in the following diagram:

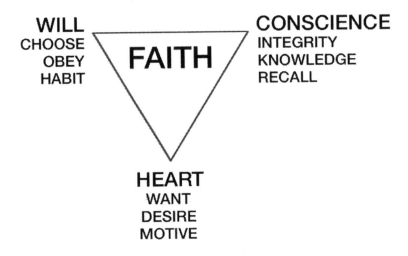

Some say the heart of a person is the spirit of the person, but I don't think that holds up consistently in Scripture. It is true that God gives me a new heart when I receive the Holy Spirit, but it makes more sense to me to see this as a purifying of my desire and motives due to the fact that my old self has been crucified and I have received a new nature—Christ in me. The union of the Spirit of God with my human spirit makes a new me. The indwelling of the Spirit also changes the orientation of my heart, as well as stimulating my will, and enlightening my conscience. It is a reset of my faith clock, if you will. But my heart, my conscience, and my will must be cleansed whenever they are contaminated by sin. My human spirit does not need further cleansing because it is now indwelt with the Spirit of God.

The Faith Process
The heart seems to be one of three components in the determination of my faith or faithless choices. My heart has to do with what I deeply want, what I desire or treasure, and what motivates me. It is the place where I *believe.* It is also the place where I am wounded—where I must heal. My heart can become hard or soft. My heart can be either wicked or righteous in response to my circumstance or situation. The root of bitterness can grow there. My heart can be cleansed and it must be renewed.

"The *Word* that is near you, in your mouth and in your heart," quoted above, is the Greek word **rhema** which is the personal Word of God to my heart and conscience. As explained in **Chapter 6**, logos is the Greek word referring to Scripture and makes the same appeals to everyone who will read it. But, the word **rhema** in this verse expresses an intimate and personal appeal to the integrity of my conscience as a child of God—to Christ in me, that brings revelation knowledge to my mind and motivation to my heart. The Holy Spirit is convincing me of what is right in my conscience, to bring me into integrity in my believing. The Holy Spirit is also inspiring the desires of my heart to change, so that my will would choose to obey.

Matthew 4:4 says:
> "Man shall not live by bread alone, but by every word [rhema] that comes from the mouth of God."

The Word is near. The Spirit is deeply involved with me. If I am not a believer, He is urging me to repent and be saved by the confession of faith, in taking action with my will—with the lips of my mouth—that the Holy Spirit may come into me. If I am already a believer, He is urging me to act like one by confessing who I am in Christ, and by acting in accordance with that truth—to make decisions to *act as if* the Word of God is true, not from how things may seem or feel.

The evil one is also near. If I am not a believer, he is making his appeals to bend the integrity of my conscience away from God. He is bending the desires of my heart away from God's desires, that my will would choose to disobey, confess lies with my lips and remain under his evil power. If I am a believer, Satan wants to discredit the integrity of my conscience and the integrity of my testimony, with sin and a moral collapse. Then in disgrace, I will not be able to bring hope to others in Christ because my testimony is ruined. Satan wants to bend my actions to *look as if* the Word of God is *not* true.

All this is most dramatically displayed in relapse—when coming out of addiction or other besetting sin behaviors—if I fall back into the old ways. But sin consequences can bring pain that speaks louder than the words the Spirit has been trying to tell me if I have been resistant to hear Him. So, when I finally break down and repent and give myself completely to the Lord, He fills me with His Spirit and I am now a new person in Christ. I testify to my skeptical family and friends that I am born again. I have a wonderful season of sobriety. Some of those who know me even start to trust me again. Then, if I relapse, what happened? What is wrong with me? Did God fail me?

Am I a hopeless fraud? **Romans 7:16,17** says:

> For I do not understand my own actions. For I do not do what I want, but I do the very thing I hate. (see **Chapter 3: My Nature Is in My Spirit** page 31)

What then is faith? The Spirit of Christ and Satan both contend for my faith. Shall my faith be in the service of good or evil? One could say faith is the trajectory of a life lived, my spiritual history. What treasures in my heart will I give up to receive the treasures of heaven?

The Progress of Corruption:

> 1. Temptation pulls at the weakness of my body and appeals to the self-interest of my soul, apart from my spirit. I should not take condemnation for that struggle, but let my spirit take the lead in what I choose to do. This condition is not yet sin. My flesh will always be whining and fussing to get its way.

> 2. As Norman Grubb has said, "what you take, takes you." When I choose to allow my heart motivation to bind with temptation, a perverse corruption begins to contaminate my conscience with a mindset to rationalize evil deeds. I am now in sin.

> 3. This heart-motive binding brings me under the power of lies. What is wrong starts to seem right or at least justifiable. Jesus said that if I am angry with someone, I have committed murder in my heart. If I am lustful, I have committed adultery in my heart, even if I redirect myself so I do not actually commit murder or adultery, but still harbor the desire. Out of the abundance of the

heart, the mouth speaks. In the binding of my heart's motive to hold on to sin, I have deceived myself and my heart is now wicked. The longer I go without repenting, the longer I am deceived.

4. The longer I am deceived the more I will rationalize my behavior with more lies. Spiritual blindness, deafness, and hard-heartedness will then block the voice of God as well as the appeals to conscience from other believers. My faith can become increasingly subverted and misdirected, and my attitude can become more and more hostile to God.

5. Willful disobedience unchecked by repentance can make a shipwreck of my faith. Without deep repentance, I can even be led to falling away from faith, trampling on the Blood of Christ, outraging the Holy Spirit, and potentially becoming impossible to be restored! **(Hebrews 6:4-8)** I have security in the goodness of Christ my keeper, but His keeping is not unconditional. I must persevere in faith and not reject repentance out of contempt towards my Lord.

What I have been describing as stages of corruption through a hardening of heart should provoke fear. The fear of the Lord is clean. **(Psalm 19:6)** The fear of the Lord is the beginning of wisdom. **(Proverbs 1:7)** Mercifully, God disciplines me with the correction of consequences. Since a wicked heart can no longer be appealed to with the higher motives of spirit or the love of God—because I am living like one who has never believed—the Lord starts to use consequences to appeal to the self-interest of my soul. This is intended to cause me want to change my heart, at first only for the sake of myself. (*Aw Lord God, my pleasure seeking has caused me to miss true rewards... my bitterness has caused me to lose friends... my fears have caused me to miss great opportunities...*)

At this stage, I have become like an unbeliever who only wants to save himself from his circumstances. The prodigal son first saw it was not in the self-interest of his body and soul to feed pigs for strangers who hardly fed him. He went back home for the food and shelter. His father took it from there. Most of us came to God to escape the consequences of hell, or to seek healing or deliverance. God knows the old sinful nature is not capable of more than enlightened self-interest. (*You do this for me and I will do that for you.*) He gives a whole new nature to those who receive His Holy Spirit and are saved. But willful disobedience makes a believer produce the fruit of an unbeliever. In disobedience I will have allowed my conscience to be numbed with rationalizations, excuses, and even doctrinal perversity about the character of God. A hardened heart seeks doctrines that give permission to sin in areas I do not want to give up. I become blind until I repent and once again return to the Lord. In repentance, what I have now retaken, also takes me back.

To maintain a clean heart, I must have a clean conscience. My conscience must be informed by the **logos** of Scripture as to what is true, or the Holy Spirit's personal **rhema** Voice as to what specifics I must do. If there is any conflict between what I believe to be **rhema** and **logos**, Scripture always rules. As we have just seen, my human conscience can be corrupted and the subjective perception of my soul can be deceived.

In my circumstances, faith must be protected with integrity. Otherwise a deceitful heart and a corrupted conscience will misuse my faith by causing me to trust in lies. The following disciplines of repentance must be rigorously practiced:

> 1. Internal honesty about sinful desires, motives and attitudes, must be seen and humbly confessed to the Lord, Who loves me and already sees what is in me. It is also good to make a habit of regular mutual confession of sins with a believing friend. The Lord has forgiven me and given me grace to grow. This is the maintenance of my repentance.

> 2. He wants me to forgive those who have hurt me, so that no root of bitterness will bind me with *soul-ties* through my wounds, to the one who has caused them. I must release him or her from the judgment they deserve for what they did to me, as the Lord has forgiven

me and released me from the judgment I deserve. Only then will I begin to heal, because I am back in alignment with the will of God.

Forgiveness must be given to those who have hurt me, but trust must be earned. God does not want me to open myself to further abuse if my abuser refuses to change. Boundaries may still be appropriate with those I have forgiven.

A Guide for Forgiving

Lord, I release _____ in Jesus' Name. Hold no sin or offense against _____ on my behalf, forever. Open the way of healing, revelation, salvation and blessing to _____ because I plead the Blood of Jesus for _____ sins. Show _____ the same mercy You showed me. May _____ now be able see, hear and be healed in Jesus' Name, as You have so graciously done for me.

Then when painful recall arises in me to tempt me with anger and the desire for revenge, I must speak back to the devil like this:

It's no longer *me* who wants revenge. That desire is coming from Satan, who is trying to get me back into condemnation and unbelief. I refuse condemnation for those thoughts and feelings because they are no longer coming from me, and **God is my witness** that I have released _____ from judgment as far as I am concerned. My soul's emotions are something I am experiencing but they are no longer my desire. I repent of measuring myself by what my soul's emotions want to do. I also **repent** of justifying and entitling myself to more sin because of my pain.

3. The Lord wants me to make amends to those I have hurt, to remove stumbling stones from the faith of those I have harmed, and to break any soul-ties leading to a root of bitterness through the wounds I have caused. When I humbly own my part without excuses and ask for forgiveness, I can help restore dignity to the one I have harmed, because my offense has been

acknowledged. I want to make it easier for those whom I have hurt to be able to forgive me, that they may also become free from bitterness and begin to heal.

For many smaller offences, a humble apology will do, as long as it does not use language that says: "I'm sorry **if** I hurt you..." Using the word "**if**" implies my offence is not necessarily real or true, or it is not as important to me as it is to you. But for larger offences and breakdowns in relationship, an amends can be a real help. I must be sure **not** to include any excuses for myself for what the one I harmed may have done to provoke me, when I make an amends. I must address only my part; otherwise my amends will backfire and become another argument. My amends must show that I "get it." I must humbly ask the one I have harmed to forgive me.

A Guide for Making Amends

I have been thinking a lot about you and, as well as how much I have hurt you. I have been very upset with myself for how _____ (*Be specific, you know what they are angry about.*) I have been. I am appalled at how you were treated by me. I don't blame you for being angry and disappointed with me. I understand how you may not feel safe to trust me right now. You did not deserve this from me, and I understand that you don't want to be hurt by me anymore. I am so sorry.

I know I can't change what happened, and I can't repay the harm I have done to you. I can only hope you will someday be able to forgive me, not because I deserve it, but so God can bring healing to your heart for the pain I have caused you.

I want to be a better person, and better at showing love. I want to be involved with your life in a way that will show how much I love you—if you will let me. I want to help you in any way I can, as soon as I am able, as much or as little as is comfortable to you.

Notice what is going on here. I know that when someone has really hurt my soul with a deep wound, I feel like my dignity, rights, value, and power have been gouged out of me. I'm left feeling weak, small, dishonored and abused in my heart. Then the enemy comes to sow seeds of bitterness into that wound. Those bitter seeds charge my legitimate anger to feel like I have power and rights to revenge. I will try to build protective walls against the one who hurt me, to safely keep them out. Then, what I call a *frustration feedback loop* gets set up in me with memories and revenge fantasies recycling over and over in my soul. Pain and obsession become like a microphone mistakenly placed in front of a speaker on stage that shrieks louder and louder UUUOOOOEEEEEEEEEEEEEEE... inside me!

When I have really wounded the soul of another, I must remember that the same crippling gouge and revenge response is happening inside the one I have harmed. I have created a *frustration feedback loop* in them too! That's why I recommend language that acknowledges the rights of the one I have harmed to feel angry, robbed of dignity, safety or power. My amends should focus on giving back the power I took away, so they might once again be able to rebuild trust with me. I must show that I "get it" by humbling myself in genuine remorse. I must lovingly show empathy with the one I hurt, to give them grace to be able to receive healing through my amends.

Going forward, I must rigorously live a life of repentance, with honest confession of sin. I must always forgive those who have hurt me. By making amends, I can help those whom I have hurt, to begin to heal. All of this can be done through Christ Who lives out through me. We all fall short of the glory of God and miss the mark in ignorance or immaturity. Some of my sins have been deliberate and with malice. I must never make excuses for them.

Willful disobedience harms my conscience by disregarding what I know God wants me to do. Through deceitful lies to myself, I can build self-justifying conceits. My heart will surly become poisoned again if I push the Lord away for a while so I can disobey. If I do, His voice will become less clear, and I will miss knowing the guidance of His will because of my willful disobedience. My sense of security in Him will be eroded, and shame will wither my faith. If poisonous **conceits** are mixed with the truth, I will make a shipwreck of my faith, unless I repent.

WHO AM I?
Personal meditations on the Word
As I mentioned, I have I found it extremely helpful to make the revelation of these verses real by personalizing them—by inserting myself where appropriate. This makes them more chewable in feeding my faith. Read these out loud to yourself with your mouth, chew and swallow. They are for your nourishment!

Galatians 2:20 My identity is in Christ
> I have been crucified with Christ. It is no longer **I** who live, but Christ Who lives in **me**. And the life **I** now live in the flesh, **I** live by the faith [of] the Son of God, Who loved **me**, and gave Himself for **me**. – ESV (*Shank*)

Father, I choose to take hold of this truth and apply it as I go forward in faith. I thank You that the faith of Christ Himself upholds my faith! In my new nature, I can stand on the Rock that cannot be moved. He upholds me. My "I" has changed completely. I am now the expression of Christ in **me**. I am no longer who I was before. My old nature is dead, and I am no longer who I thought I was. I am now Christ in my form—a Christ-*ian*. Let me know the full meaning of this truth as I learn to walk in it.

The Naos of God
1 Corinthians 3:16,17 says:
> I know that I am God's temple and that God's Spirit dwells in **me**. If anyone destroys God's temple, God will destroy him. For God's temple is holy, and I am that temple." – ESV (Shank)

The word translated from the Greek as temple is **naos** (*also see* Chapter 1). When Paul says, "I am the **naos** of Christ," I am where the Spirit of Christ is, because His Spirit indwells me. He makes me holy because I contain His Spirit. Father, forgive me for trusting my soul's feelings and impressions instead of trusting in Your Word. There are times when I feel as if You are far from me, but Your Word says Christ is in me and I am in Him. Your Word does not lie, so You are never apart from me.

An Ambassador

2 Corinthians 5:17, 20b, 21 says:

> I once regarded myself according to the flesh, but I do so no longer. Because I am in Christ, I am a new creation. **My** old nature has passed away and a new nature is now the real **me**... God is now making His appeal through **me** for others around **me**. On behalf of Christ, I implore others to be reconciled to God. For their sake as well as **mine**, God made Christ to be sin, though He never sinned, so that in Christ I might become the righteousness of God. –ESV (Shank)

Lord, I must see and stand on the truth that the indwelling and joining of the Spirit of Christ to my human spirit is the *core* of who I really am. He is the source of power to overcome the old ways I learned when I had the old sinful nature, which is now dead. My flesh will always resist You. It is hopeless, but in union with You, my flesh is mine but it is *not* me. I can learn to control it by Your power.

A Branch

John 15:1-7

> Jesus is the Vine and God the Father is the Vinedresser. Every branch in Jesus that does not bear fruit, He takes away, and every branch that does bear fruit God will prune that it might bear more fruit. Already I am clean because of the word [logos] Jesus has spoken to **me**.
>
> I abide in Jesus and He abides in **me**. Because a branch cannot bear fruit by itself, I cannot bear fruit apart from Christ. The same life that flows in the Vine now flows in **me**. If I do not abide in Jesus, I will be thrown away like a branch that withers; and will be gathered with other dry branches and thrown into the fire and burned. Because **I** abide in Christ and His Words live in **me**, Jesus says I may ask whatever I wish and it will be done for **me**. – ESV (Shank)

To abide in Christ is to live in Christ; I am in *union* with Christ. That union does not make me God, but it makes me godly. I have Christ's Life flowing in me and nourishing me. His fruit is born on my branch as I believe by obeying this truth in choosing to do my Father's will, as Jesus did.

Heavenly Favor
Ephesians 1:3-10 says:

> Blessed be the God of my Lord Jesus Christ, Who has blessed **me** in Christ with every spiritual blessing in the heavenly places, even as He chose **me** in Him before the foundation of the world, that I should be holy and blameless before Him. In love, He predestined **me** for adoption as His child through Jesus Christ, according to the *purpose* of His will, to the praise of His glorious grace, with which He has blessed **me** in the Beloved. In Him I have redemption through His Blood, the forgiveness of **my** trespasses, according to the riches of His grace, which He lavished upon **me**, in all wisdom and insight making known to **me** the mystery of His will, according to His purpose which He set forth in Christ as a *plan* for the fullness of time, to unite all things in Him, things in heaven and things on earth.
> – ESV (Shank)

I have privilege as Your child because You foresaw that I would believe before the earth was made. It was always Your plan for me before I was even born. This news is too wonderful for me, But in You, I am learning to become the child You had in mind when You made me. Wonderful blessings and favor are covering me for this life as well as the next, because You are the One Who *promised* and You are Wonderful promise *keeper!*

Lifted to the Right Hand
Ephesians 2:1-10 says:

> I was dead in the trespasses and the sins in which I once walked, following the course of the world, following the prince of the power of the air, the spirit that is now at work in the sons of disobedience—among whom I once lived in the passions of my flesh, carrying out the desires of **my** body and mind, and I was by na-

ture a child of wrath, like the rest of mankind. But God, rich in mercy because of the great love with which He loved **me**, even when I was dead in **my** trespasses, made **me** alive together with Christ—by grace I have been saved—and raised **me** up with Him and seated **me** with Him in the heavenly places in Christ Jesus. In grace, I have been saved through faith. And this is not **my** own doing; it is a gift of God, not as a result of **my** works, so that I may not be able to boast. For I am His workmanship, created in Christ Jesus for good works, which God prepared beforehand, that I should walk in them.
– ESV (Shank)

Lord, You keep me from presumption by declaring I am at Your Right Hand in Jesus. This privilege and authority gives me boldness to pray for others because all powers and principalities are under His Feet and I am in Him. My understanding cannot fathom this; it is too wonderful for me. But because Your love wants me beside You There, I will have faith to pray *as if* this is true, because Your words are faithful and true

The Oneness of The Father and The Son

John 17:1-5 says:

When Jesus had spoken these words, He lifted up His eyes to heaven, and said, Father, the hour has come; glorify Your Son that the Son may glorify You, since You have given Him authority over all flesh, to give eternal life to all whom You have given Him. And this is eternal life, that they may know You the Only True God, and Jesus Christ Whom You have sent. I glorified You on earth, having accomplished the work that You gave Me to do. And now, Father, glorify Me in Your Presence with the Glory that I had with You before the world existed. – ESV

Jesus, You were praying for the restoration of Your Glory when You returned to Your Father. Your Father was pleased in all You did to fulfill His Law and commandments, even to the death. Therefore, I am confident Your Father restored the Glory You set aside when You came down to us to die for all our sins. Your Father has said **Yes** to Your prayer!

Extending the oneness of the Father and the Son to the disciples.

John 17:10,11 says:

> ...All Mine are Yours, and Yours are Mine, and I am glorified in them. And I am no longer in the world, but they [*the disciples*] are in the world, and I am coming to You, Holy Father, keep them in Your Name, which You have given to Me, that they may be one, even as We are one... – ESV (Shank)

Jesus, You prayed that the disciples would share in the unity You have with Your Father and Your Father has with You. All the Father has the Son has. All the Son has the Father has! Your Father has even given You *His Own Name!*

Isaiah 9:6 says:

> For to us a Child is born, to us a Son is given; and the government shall be upon His shoulder, and His Name shall be called Wonderful Counselor, *Mighty God, Everlasting Father,* Prince of peace. – ESV

Praise God, the Father has granted Your request for the disciples to share in the unity the Father and the Son have with each other, Your Father has said **Yes** to Your prayer!

We Also Are One with Him

John 17:20-26 Now Jesus prays for you and me who have believed in Him through the work of the disciples:

> I do not pray for these only [*the disciples*], but also for those who will believe in Me through their word, that they [you *and* I] may be one, just as You, Father, are in Me, and I in You, that they [you *and* I] may also be in Us, so that the world may believe that You have sent Me... The glory that You have given Me I have given to them, [you *and* I] that they may be one even as We are one, I in them [you *and* I] and You in Me, they [you *and* I] may become perfectly one ... Father I desire that they also [you *and* I] whom You have given Me, may be with Me where I am, to see My glory that You have given Me before the foundation of the world. – ESV (Shank)

Jesus, after living Your entire life, never ever disobeying Your Heavenly Father, *never saying no* to Him, You have fulfilled the whole Law. *Will God in heaven not agree to do what You have asked of Him?* YES, He Will! Since You have asked that I would be one with the Father as You are one with Him, *will the Father grant the request of His perfectly obedient Son?* YES, He Will! Thank You Father that You have said YES! Therefore, I will believe and receive this truth, that through Christ, I am spiritually one with the Father and the Son.

Hebrews 4:14-16 says:

> Since then I have a great High Priest Who has passed through the heavens, Jesus, the Son of God, I hold fast to **my** confession. For I do not have a High Priest Who is unable to sympathize with **my** weakness, but One Who in every respect has been tempted as I am, yet without sin. – ESV (Shank)

Being born like me in the flesh, You felt the pull of every temptation I feel, but You did not sin. Feeling the pull of temptation is not sin. My flesh will always want to have its way. But I am learning to believe my flesh is mine to control, but it is not me. If I obey the pull and sin, I sin and am responsible for it, as well as for whatever consequences may happen. Sin will have power over me, until I repent. When I repent, I thank You that I am immediately restored because of the sacrifice of my High Priest Jesus.

Philippians 4:12b-13, 19 says:

> In any and every circumstance, I have learned the secret of facing plenty and hungry, abundance and need. I can do all things through Him Who strengthens **me** ... And **my** God will supply every need of **mine** according to His riches in glory in Christ Jesus. – ESV (Shank)

I am no longer compelled to resort to sinful measures to meet my needs. You, O God, will provide what I need and give me grace to endure until my need is met. As I walk in this truth, I will soon find out what I really need as opposed to what I think I need.

Christ in Me Is to be my Aroma
2 Corinthians 2:15-16 says:

> For I am the aroma of Christ to God among those who are being saved and among those who are perishing, to one a fragrance from death to death, to the other a fragrance from life to life. – ESV (Shank)

To those who want You and Your righteousness, I will have a pleasing aroma. To those who don't want You and Your righteousness, I will stink. It was the same for You Lord when You were on the earth. So will it be with me because I am Yours, and I am still in the earth. My life is no longer about my reputation, and I do not need the approval of those who hate You. Forgive me when I get fooled into desiring the approval of men. Thank You that You have accepted me forever.

Grace Not Perfection
Philippians 3:12 says:

> Not that I have already obtained this or am already perfect, but I press on to make it **my** own. – ESV (Shank)

Though I will never be perfect in the execution of my faith, I thank You Lord that You regard my faith as perfect, because I trust the Perfect One Who upholds me. I will not outlive my need to grow or to be pruned. I must always remain teachable. You resist the proud but draw near to the humble. Lord, keep me humble.

Favor in All Circumstances
Romans 5:1-5 says:

> Therefore, since I have been justified by faith, I have peace with God through **my** Lord Jesus Christ. Through Him I have also obtained access by faith into this grace in which I stand, and I rejoice in hope of the glory of God. More than that, I rejoice in **my** sufferings, knowing that suffering produces endurance, and endurance produces character, and character produces hope, and hope does not put **me** to shame, because God's love has been poured into **my heart** through the Holy Spirit Who has been given to me. – ESV (Shank)

My life is no longer about me but what You, Lord, and what You want to accomplish through me. Suffering from my sinful consequences motivates and refines me in my faith. Suffering the resistance of the world, the flesh, and the devil makes me strong. Suffering unjustly for Righteousness sake gives me rewards in heaven, with You, Jesus, forever. My suffering is revealing to me the value of those whom have I hurt, and my value through those who have hurt me, and the value of the Righteousness and Person of God. Choices *matter* because God and those who He has made, *matter*!

Romans 13:14 says:

> I put on the Lord Jesus Christ, and make no provision for the flesh, to gratify its desires. – ESV

Lord, I no longer want to keep a stash for my flesh to feed on. I will deny my flesh and feed my spirit with the Body and Blood of Christ, Who loves me.

Transformed to Be Like Christ

2 Corinthians 3:17 says:

> Now the Lord is the Spirit, and where the Spirit of the Lord is, there is freedom. And I, with unveiled face, beholding the glory of the Lord, am being transformed into the same image from one degree of glory to another. For this comes from the Lord Who is the Spirit. – ESV (Shank)

As I walk in obedience, You, Lord give me freedom. I want to see more and more of Your Glory and be transformed more and more by You.

Galatians 3:26-27 says:

> ...for in Christ Jesus I am a child of God, through faith. For I am baptized into Christ and I have put on Christ. – ESV (Shank)

Lord, my flesh will always make me feel like I'm doing something strange when I turn away from it. Putting on Christ sometimes seems like a costume to my flesh. But putting on Christ just means choosing to walk in the Spirit of Christ by making choices against what my flesh wants to do. You Lord are my new Master and You want me to act like You!

Grace to Me
Ephesians 1:3-14

> Blessed be the God and Father of **my** Lord Jesus Christ, Who has blessed **me** with every spiritual blessing in the heavenly places, even as He chose **me** in Him before the foundation of the world, that I should be holy and blameless before Him. In love, He predestined **me** for adoption as a son [*His child*], through Jesus Christ, according to the purpose of His will, to the praise of His glorious grace, with which He has blessed **me** in the Beloved. In Him I have redemption through His Blood, the forgiveness of **my** trespasses, according to the riches of His grace, which He lavished upon **me**, in all wisdom and insight making known to **me** the mystery of His will, according to the purpose, which He set forth in Christ as a plan for the fullness of time, to unite all things in Him, things in heaven and things on earth.
>
> In Him I have received an inheritance, having been predestined according to the purpose of Him Who works all things according to the counsel of His will, so that I who hope in Christ might be to the praise of His glory. In Him I also, when I heard the word of truth, the gospel of **my** salvation, and believed in Him, was sealed with the promised Holy Spirit, Who is the guarantee of **my** inheritance until I acquire possession of it, to the praise of His glory. – ESV (Shank)

What Satan means for evil, You Lord use for good for all those who believe in You. May my old wounds and sinful pathways no longer drive me to make excuses for more sin. My wounds have been transformed into opportunities for me to reach out to others with the wisdom You have taught me, to help them overcome as well. No matter how bad it has been, no matter how long it's lasted, You can redeem me and bear fruit through me, if I repent and obey You.

Your Word says in **Joel 2:25,26**:

> I will restore to you the years the swarming locust has eaten, the hopper, the destroyer, and the cutter, My great army, which I sent among you. You shall eat in plenty and be satisfied, and praise the Name of the Lord your God, Who has dealt wondrously with you. – ESV

I Will Change Your Name

The following is a wonderful prophetic song, filled with the truth we have been discussing. It seems to recall **Genesis 35:9-15**, where God gave Jacob a new name and affirmed him in the blessings and promises of Abraham. In **Genesis 32:28**, God said Jacob's name—which means *he deceives*—was to change. He would now be called Israel because he *strived* with God and man for blessing and has *prevailed*. This is what the Lord is calling us to do: to believe the blessings of God above all opposition and become overcomers like Jacob.

In **Revelation, Chapters 2-3**, the seven churches are affirmed for what they are doing right and warned about what they are doing wrong. Then the encouraging phrase is repeated to each, "The one who conquers..." (*overcomes*) will receive many wonderful blessings and rewards, among them is a new name written on a stone fixed forever.

I WILL CHANGE YOUR NAME - by J.D. Butler
Intro. 3/4 time. D// G// A/////   D// G// A/////
```
D              G            A
I WILL CHANGE YOUR NAME.
D                  G         A
YOU SHALL NO LONGER BE CALLED
D      G    A  F#m  G      D   A
WOUNDED, OUTCAST, LONELY OR AFRAID.

D              G            A
I WILL CHANGE YOUR NAME.
D              G            A
YOUR NEW NAME SHALL BE
D      G    A    F#m  G    D       A
CONFIDENCE, JOYFULNESS, OVERCOMING ONE;
D          G       A       F#m
```

FAITHFULNESS, FRIEND OF GOD,
     G   A   D
AND ONE WHO SEEKS MY FACE.

(Response)
D   G   A
LORD YOU HAVE CHANGED MY NAME.
D   G   A
MY NEW NAME SHALL BE
D   G   A   F#m   G   D   A
CONFIDENCE, JOYFULNESS, OVERCOMING ONE;
D   G   A   F#m
FAITHFULNESS, FRIEND OF GOD,
     G   A   D
AND ONE WHO SEEKS YOUR FACE.

II: The Passionate Breaking of My Fallow Ground

8

The Role of Suffering & Rewards

That you may know the love of God: know love has gravity, and our choices matter. We are not living in a video game. Real people have lives that matter. Know that suffering and rewards are measures of the value of God, His creation, you and me. My sins have meaning and so my being forgiven does also. My pain matters because I have value and purpose. If I hurt you, it matters because you are a valuable person in the Eyes of God. Because life has value and our choices matter, we are meant to experience that gravity in real suffering and real joy. God is love, and He wants to lavish His love on you and me. God is love, and He cannot deny Himself. He loves me in spite of myself, so I can learn to love others in spite of themselves, knowing the gravity and meaning of the life to which God has called you and me.

If I do not comprehend the meaning of my choices, I will continue to be a blundering beast, trampling everyone around me. But in seeing as He sees, I will know what needs to change in myself, because my spirit will want to live like Him. Anyone who has the Spirit of God is one spirit with Him. His Spirit living in me will motivate and empower me to want to change. I now see that when God seems to wound me, He is pruning me to make me more able to bear His fruit. He is also enlarging my capacity to receive blessing from Him, by the stretching. He has the right to discipline me. I am His child.

Gravity from my pain builds empathy with others, if I let it be transformed by forgiving those who have hurt me. Gravity from the pain I have inflicted on others creates empathy with them through my conscience, because I know how it feels when someone has hurt me. And I will want to repent and make a healing amends to them as soon as possible. The Lord is lavishing His grace on me to forgive the most outrageous offenses, because I am now like Him—not returning evil for evil, but by learning to return good for evil. I will suffer now as He has suffered, because the world is evil; but later I will enter into the joy of my Master forever in a paradise, because pain will have served its purpose and will be no more, forever. And the Law—that Tree of the Knowledge of Good and Evil which is fulfilled in Christ, will be exchanged for the Tree of Life!

We need that kind of love from Him. Nothing less will do. Our need may seem bottomless, but His fulfillment is greater. How else could a man like me be changed, who has been so ruthlessly selfish? How else could a man so treacherous, vengeful, fearful, shameful, ruthless, lustful, devious, willfully rebellious, and self-deceived for so long, begin to turn all that around? Do I exaggerate my sin? No. I see it as it truly has been, with all its painful gravity, that I may also experience the gravity of God's grace and loving-kindness. I now see my sin to be utterly sinful (**Romans 7:13**). The love I desperately need from God is now mine to give away to others in this life and the next.

Bad choices matter. My bad choices hurt me and others. And the bad choices of others hurt me. Some of that damage cannot be repaired, even when forgiven. Good choices matter too. They bless me and others. When good choices cost me, God will remember me, even if others reject me. Just as I need God's loving grace for myself, others around me need that same loving grace from Him, too. If Christ lives in me by the Spirit, I am now able to be Christ to others. He has reconciled each of us to Himself so we can now be reconciled to others—if they are willing to be reconciled. God's creation matters. He had to withhold the Tree of Life from Adam and Eve, so their sinful nature would not eventually spread to contaminate the whole universe—as it surely would have if we all had lived forever in their sinful state. God did not let that happen. He wants His creation to be restored to the paradise He originally intended. And He will have what He wants as soon as sees His Book of Life is filled.

> 1. If death was not introduced to quarantine sin, all creation would eventually become a hell. For this reason, even the evil angels will be destroyed.

2. If painful consequences were not introduced, I would have no reason to change, let alone have my conscience sensitized. If I have blocked my conscience with self-deception or medication, it will hurt while I detox and begin to feel the painful gravity of my sin. Whenever I am convinced of evil in me, I know my desperate need for God to change me. Jesus went through tremendous pain Himself for the gravity of my sin and yours, that both of us might be saved. His empathy with us stirs His compassion for us.

3. If rewards were not given for goodness, I would have no incentive to be good or be able to endure those who hurt me. For the joy that was set before Him, Jesus endured the cross (Hebrews 12:2). So must I. In His favor, I can stand before God without shame and know I have favor when I pray. My heart will not condemn me, and I will rejoice in Him without hiding in shame.

4. If grace was not given to me, I would have no chance to learn from my errors or learn how to overcome. His love for me wants me to persevere in faith and learn the wisdom of good and the folly of evil.

5. If death was not the solution for sinners who will not believe, repent, and receive the Spirit of Christ, there would be no paradise. God would not be able to give without restraint to us, in heaven. And I would not be able to give back without restraint, either. In the paradise to come, I will no longer be corruptible. The Tempter will be gone forever, and his sinful power to corrupt will also be dead. My corruptible body will be replaced by an incorruptible new one. I will be fully new in Christ. In the glorified body He will give me, I will have rest from the temptations and ravages of sin. We will all be safe.

6. If evil is not punished with destruction, there would be no justice in the Kingdom of God. Judgment Day has great gravity because life with or without God, has great gravity.

7. If I am not transformed into being the righteousness of God, why was I be made in His image? Relationship with Him is my purpose and fulfillment.

1 Corinthians 2:9 says:

> ...no eye has seen nor ear heard or even the heart of man imagined the good things God has prepared for those who love Him... – ESV

God will *not* let what is *not* good be in the eternal paradise forever with Him. This must be believed. *Notgod* will not be there either, and the kingdom of *Notgood* will be destroyed.

Romans 8:31-39 says:

> What then shall we say to these things? If God is for us, who can be against us? He Who did not spare His Own Son but gave Him up for us all, how will He not also with Him graciously give us all things? Who shall bring any charges against God's elect? It is God Who justifies. Who is to condemn? Christ Jesus is the One Who died—more than that, Who was raised—Who is at the Right Hand of God, Who is interceding for us. Who shall separate us from the Love of Christ? Shall tribulation, or distress, or persecution, or famine, or nakedness, or danger, or sword? As it is written, "For Your sake, we are being killed all the day long; we are regarded as sheep to be slaughtered." (Psalm 44:22)
>
> No, in all things we are more than conquerors through Him Who loved us. For I am sure that neither death nor life, nor angels nor rulers, nor things present nor things to come, nor powers, nor height nor depth, nor anything else in creation, will be able to separate us from the love of God in Christ Jesus our Lord. – ESV

None of these beings, things, circumstances, or even our sins can separate us from the Love of God! But one thing is missing from this list: active unbelief from my past. Do I know my sins have been forgiven? **Yes.** But my old habits of believing need to be brought into alignment with my new reality in Christ, in order to experience the Love of God, which is already there. We also have old wounds that trigger reflexive responses that contaminate our expression of Christ. These issues need to be addressed and healed. God is Love, and He cannot deny His Own Nature. To whatever extent I find that Biblical Truth is difficult to believe, I may have active unbelief that needs plowing, so my fallow ground will bring forth good fruit.

My Loaded History

I've put **Hosea 10:11–12 & 11:3–4** to music and recorded it with some good friends. The chorus is a word of encouragement by the Spirit.

Fallow Ground AcousticNerve / *Lord of Love* – iTunes
Ephraim's a trained heifer, she loves to thresh,
So I will put a yoke upon her tender neck.
I will drive Ephraim and Judah will plow,
For Jacob must break up all of his fallow ground.
Jacob must break up all of his fallow ground.

> Sow righteousness to yourself,
> You will reap my unfailing love,
> Break up your fallow ground,
> Seek the Lord till He comes
> To shower righteousness on you,
> Rain down His righteousness on you.

I will teach you to walk with me,
Take you by the hand,
Lead you with My cords of kindness
—My loving bands.
Then you will put down your roots,
Your green shoots will grow,
Because you're breaking up all of your fallow ground;
Because you're breaking up all of your fallow ground.

> Sow righteousness to yourself,
> You will reap my unfailing love,
> Break up your fallow ground,
> Seek the Lord until He comes
> To shower righteousness on you,
> Rain down His righteousness on you.

Having hopefully laid a Biblical foundation for our identity in Christ, we must now keep our past from spoiling our future. Let's move on by putting up the truth against the storehouse of energy still bound up in memories, habits, and attitudes of our life experiences. This is the still active unbelief underneath our fallow ground. Many of us are driven by obsessions and compulsions we do not fully understand. They can seem like huge immovable obstacles that severely hinder us, or powerful unmanageable forces that seem to ignite destructive energy.

Outbursts of rage, incapacitating fear and anxiety, flights of grandiosity, and self-loathing shame are common among us. Some struggle with overbearing control in the micromanagement of others; some have emotional shutdowns that isolate. Irritating touchiness, perfectionism, relationship sabotage, ruthless pettiness, bullying, vengeful slander and gossip, a bottomless need for affirmation, or manipulative self-pity all destroy what we try to build for others and ourselves. The list is endless. We may have tried to manage these sinful tendencies with some success, but their inevitable reoccurrence provokes discouragement. Some of us have chosen ways of medicating our pain with behavioral and/or chemical addictions.

When we begin to realize that these dispositional behaviors are part of a larger system of wounds, weakness, lies and false conclusions, we begin to see a pressing need to go deeper to find inner healing. If I am in Christ, why are all these things still happening? Let's revisit a scripture we read earlier.

1 Corinthians 15:42-49 says:
> So is it with the resurrection of the dead. What is sown is perishable; what is raised is imperishable. It is sown in dishonor; it is raised in glory. It is sown in weakness; it is raised in power. It is sown a natural body; it is raised a spiritual body. If there is a natural body, there is also a spiritual body. Thus it is written, 'The first man Adam became a living being;' the last Adam became a life-giving spirit. But it is not the spiritual that is first but the natural, and then the spiritual. The first man was from the earth, a man of dust; the second Man

is from heaven. As was the man of dust, so are those who are of the dust, and as is the Man of heaven, so also are those who are of heaven. Just as we have borne the image of the man of dust, we shall also bear the image of the Man of heaven. – ESV

If I believe I am a new creation in Christ, I can boldly say, my flesh is mine, but it is not me. And I can now fearlessly examine the dark pathways and prison walls that sin still tries to make for me, with the bright light of the Word of God and the healing Hand of The Holy Spirit, without condemnation or fear. The deeper I'm willing to plow the fallow ground where old lies lay buried, the deeper my healing will be. I have put off the old man, my Satan-self with his sinful nature and put on the new nature of Christ. My sin is not bottomless, but the love of God IS! My old habits and reflexes built in wrong believing can now be uprooted. My old man is now dead, but sin remains in my flesh. The new me can now fearlessly rebuild righteous ways and deeds through Christ, in a whole new season of life.

Ecclesiastes 3:1-8 says:

> For everything there is a season, and a time for every
> matter under heaven:
> a time to be born, and a time to die;
> a time to plant, and a time to pluck up what is planted;
> a time to kill, a time to heal;
> a time to break down, and a time to build up;
> a time to weep, a time to laugh;
> a time to mourn and a time to dance:
> a time to cast away stones, and a time to gather stones
> together;
> a time to embrace, and a time to refrain from embrac-
> ing;
> a time to seek, and a time to lose;
> a time to keep, and a time to cast away;
> a time to tear and a time to sew;
> a time to keep silence and a time to speak;
> a time to love and a time to hate;
> a time for war and a time for peace. – ESV

Consider these verses in the context of what we are saying:
There's a time to be born—for new beginnings in Christ; *and a time to die*—a time to put to death the old life in Satan.

There's a time to plant—new ways in faith *and pluck up* by the roots what was planted without faith.

There's a time to kill—to put to death the deeds of my flesh. *and a time to heal*—from old wounds.

There's a time to break down—the prideful agendas I built in Satan *and to build up*—in humility new ways that are like Christ.

There's a time to weep—over my sins and what they have done to others, *and a time to laugh*—for joy over how God is restoring me and making me a blessing to others.

There's a time to mourn—for the lost and for my own sin, and there's *a time to dance* for those who have found salvation and for my own forgiveness and healing.

There's a time to cast away—old foundation stones, wrong assumptions, lies, and conceits, *and a time for gathering*—and laying new foundations in the truth.

There's a time for an encouraging *embrace,* and *a time to refrain from embracing*—so as not to take the edge of conviction off someone who needs to repent, or disrespect personal boundaries.

There's a time to seek—the Lord for something diligently, *and a time to lose*—gracefully when He says no to my requests.

There's a time to keep—what is good, *and a time to cast away*—what is evil.

There's a time to tear away—or break off from sinful associations that make me stumble, *and a time to sew*—myself into righteous associations in the Body of Christ.

There's a time for me to keep silence—and listen to the Spirit, *and a time for me to speak*—when the Spirit of the Lord tells me to be bold.

There's a time to love—Jesus and His will, *and a time to hate*—Satan and his will.

I am a soldier in a War between good and evil. My Prince of Peace is coming to win the victory!

Ancestral Curses and the Demonic
Exodus 34:6-7 says:

> The Lord passed before them and proclaimed, "The Lord, the Lord, a God merciful and gracious, slow to anger, and abounding in steadfast love and faithfulness, keeping steadfast love for thousands, forgiving iniquity and transgression and sin, but Who will by no means clear the guilty, visiting the iniquity of the fathers on the children and the children's children, to the third and the fourth generation." – ESV

These words are repeated in **Exodus 20:25** and **Numbers 14:18**. This curse that befalls the wicked—and is extended to their children's children—is often cited as a cause of besetting sin in a person. In counseling, one often hears a justification such as, "My father was immoral and my mother was a drunk, so I can't help the way I am!" It certainly is observable that the sins of the children are like the sins of the parents in many cases. There also seems to be dispositional weaknesses passed on through both heredity and family cultural habits. Much of this is from the Fall of Adam in general, but specific sinful behaviors in families seem to mark them as family traits. Certainly, a family that has rejected God will pass on the curse of the first Adam, who did the will of Satan. In deliverance meetings, where prayer is sought to break demonic strongholds, generational curses are often cut off in Jesus' Name.

But for those who have turned away from following the Lord after even many years of knowing Him, there is the fearful prospect of **Hebrews 10:26-31**:

> For if we go on sinning deliberately after receiving the knowledge of the truth, there no longer remains a sacri-

fice for sins, but a fearful expectation of judgment, and a fury of fire that will consume the adversaries. Anyone who has set aside the law of Moses dies without mercy on the evidence of two or three witnesses. How much worse punishment, do you think, will be deserved by the one who has spurned the Son of God, and profaned the Blood of the covenant by which he was sanctified, and has outraged the Spirit of Grace? For we know Him Who said, "Vengeance is Mine; I will repay." And again, "The Lord will judge His people." It is a fearful thing to fall into the Hands of the Living God. - ESV (*Shank*)

Notice the charge in **Ezekiel 18:1-4**:

The Word of the Lord came to me: "What do you mean by repeating this proverb concerning the land of Israel, 'The fathers have eaten sour grapes, and the children's teeth are set on edge?' (*This is a reference to generational curses, as an excuse*). As I live, declares the Lord God, this proverb shall no more be used in Israel. Behold, all souls are Mine: the soul who sins shall die..." – ESV (*Shank*)

Then the Lord clarifies what He means in the rest of the chapter, with generational scenarios in **Ezekiel 18:5-20**, summarized here:

If a man is righteous and does what is just and right... he shall surly live, declares the Lord. If he fathers a son who is violent, a shedder of blood... he [*the wicked son*] shall surely die.

Now suppose this man [*the wicked son*] fathers a son who sees all the sins that his father has done; and does not do likewise... he shall surely live. As for his father... he shall die for his iniquity.

Yet you say, "Why should not the son suffer for the iniquity of the father?" [*A question rooted in the generational curse written by Moses, referenced above.*] The Lord answers: "...The son shall not suffer the iniquity of the father, nor (*shall*) the father suffer for the iniquity of the son. The righteousness of the righteous shall be

138

upon himself, and the wickedness of the wicked shall be upon himself. – ESV (Shank)

Continuing in **verse 21,**

But if the wicked person turns away from all his sins... and does what is just and right, he shall surely live; he shall not die. None of his transgressions shall be remembered against him; for the righteousness that he has done he shall live. Have I any pleasure in the death of the wicked, declares the Lord God, and not rather he should turn from his way and live? But when a righteous man turns away from his righteousness... shall he live? None of the righteous deeds he has done shall be remembered... he shall die. – ESV

The people question the justice of what The Lord has just said; they think the good man who went bad should be justified by the good deeds he did before. But God does not count good and evil like karma, where the bigger pile of good or bad deeds determine one's fate in the next life. We all sin, so we must all repent! Even the most wretched among us, like the guilty thief on the cross, can be saved if we have a good finish in faith with repentance.

In **Ezekiel 18: 30-32** The Lord replies:

Therefore I will judge you, O house of Israel, everyone according to his ways, declares the Lord God. Repent and turn from all your transgressions, lest iniquity be your ruin. Cast away from you all the transgressions that you committed and make [*bring forth in*] yourselves a new heart and a new spirit! Why will you die, O house of Israel? For I have no pleasure in the death of anyone, declares the Lord God; so turn, and live.
– ESV (Shank)

What can we conclude from this? Even while under the Law in the Old Testament days, the generational curses from Moses were clarified, to put the emphasis on repentance, not on a fate determined through one's family history. "As I live, declares the Lord God, this proverb shall no more be used in Israel." Because of the atonement of Christ, I have the transforming power of the Holy Spirit in my spirit making me a new creation in

Him. Because the curse of the Fall is cancelled in Christ, ancestral curses are valid only for the unsaved who are still living in the old nature of the first Adam. But, if I am a Christian who has no idea I have another way to live, I can be easily deceived through my ignorance of the overcoming power of the Spirit of Christ Who is joined to me. I think it is better to inform fellow Christians who believe they are under ancestral curses that all curses are broken by the Blood of Christ. If a person has difficulty believing this and still insists on deliverance prayer, I ask them to repeat after me that Satan's power has already been broken in Christ and they are free to learn to overcome in Jesus' Name. They are no longer under the power of a lie. If they will not believe me then, what more can be done for them?

I have seen abuse of the issue of ancestral curses when sympathetic counselors say in ignorance that a Christian in besetting or chronic sin is still under a family curse. This takes personal responsibility for sinful behavior away from the believer by making the problem someone else's fault. It also shows that the profound truth of who we are in Christ is lost on those who still believe like this. Either we believe we are at the Right Hand in Christ—with all powers and principalities under our feet, and His Holy Spirit is in us to empower us to learn to say no to our flesh—or we do not believe it. Praise God that longstanding old habits of unbelief can be overcome in Christ!

The Christian & Demonic Possession

I believe the Bible is clear that once I am saved, I have a new nature in Christ and my old nature is dead. I am now free to grow in grace and learn to overcome. There is grace for me when I stumble, but then repent. But if I do not repent, I begin to have problems. If I have not been taught that I now live from the Right Hand of God, or if I don't believe it because I have not grown beyond the immaturity of soulish mood faith, I will have problems. These problems add to and draw from that loaded history buried in my fallow ground.

When I pray with someone to become a Christian, I try to be thorough. I ask that person to repeat after me in prayer and answer my questions truthfully as we pray. If they don't understand what I'm saying, they are encouraged to ask me what I mean. If they agree with the explanation, we go on.

If they do not agree with the answer in this step of the process, we stop. I will not contribute to an illusion that someone is saved if they are not yet ready to believe. But those who are ready are encouraged to repeat after me, or read aloud as follows:

> Father God in heaven, I believe Jesus is Your only begotten Son, Who was born in the flesh like me, was tempted in every way as I am, but without sinning, and that He suffered and died in my place to pay for all my sin. Then He rose from the dead and is now seated at Your Right Hand, in heaven.

> I freely confess to being a sinner who desperately needs the Blood of Jesus to be saved. I agree with You Lord, that I am guilty of all the sins Your Holy Spirit has shown me to be wrong.

> I renounce Satan and all his works in my life, and I turn away from him to serve my new Master, the Lord Jesus Christ. I renounce the lies from Satan that I have believed. I renounce my bitterness and rights to revenge, which I have held against You and those who have harmed me. I renounce my fears that Satan has used to cause me to suppress my conscience, steal my boldness, and withhold love from You and those around me. I renounce my shame that Satan has used to make me a liar, a deceiver, and one who tries to hide from Your Goodness, O Lord.

> Father, I do not deserve Your mercy, but please be merciful to me and forgive me all my sins, because of what Your Righteous Son has done in love for me. Teach me what You are really like by showing me Your Truth and Your Lovingkindness.

> Please fill me with Your Holy Spirit that I may be born again as a new man in Christ, with the power to repent and follow You faithfully, and to bear Your fruit of righteousness in my life. Open Your Word to me that I may learn Your living wisdom. Heal my bitterness as I

learn to forgive those who harm me, that I may become sweet. May Your Word fill me with faith to face all my fears with righteous courage, and may You help me to be quick to confess and repent when I have sinned. Please clothe the nakedness of my shame. And please deliver me from habits of willful disobedience.

Receive me now into Your keeping and lead me to a strong Bible believing church where I may be baptized and become a disciple. I thank You Lord and trust that You will give me the grace I need for my weaknesses, so I may be able to follow You faithfully, in Jesus' Wonderful Name, amen

Then I lay my hand on my friend's shoulder and pray that my friend be filled with the Holy Spirit. Rejoicing follows, sometimes tears, sometimes speaking in tongues, sometimes a quiet smile. I give the following blessing to the one who just prayed the prayer above:

May the Lord anoint you with His Holy Spirit because you have believed. May His Spirit fill you and lift your spirit with the power to overcome evil. May the eyes of your heart be opened to His Wonders and His Lovingkindness. May He open His Word to you with wisdom and understanding. And may the Lord refresh you, heal you, and keep you in Jesus' Wonderful Name, amen.

So, if one has received Christ and rejected Satan, why do Christians still seem to have problems with being overpowered by demons? If Satan is out, how can he get back in? The answer is that real Christians are harassed but not possessed. So, what about the house swept clean, how can seven more unclean spirits come back and make things even worse?

In **Matthew 12:43-45**, look at what Jesus says:
When the unclean spirit has gone out of a person, it passes through waterless places seeking rest, but finds none. Then it says, "I will return to my house from which I came." And when it comes, it finds the house empty, swept, and put in order. Then it goes and brings with it seven other spirits more evil than itself, and

they enter in and dwell there, and the last state of that person is worse than the first. So also will it be with this evil generation. – ESV

The answer from the verse is that the house was empty not occupied. When Jesus explained this phenomenon, He was not yet crucified or resurrected. Exorcism was not uncommon in those times, but the Holy Spirit did not yet indwell believers as He does now. Holy Spirit indwelling was not possible until after the Resurrection and Ascension of Christ. New Testament living did not begin until Pentecost in **Acts 2**. Also, unclean spirits require a host to have influence in the physical world. They are parasitical thieves, who must climb over the wall to steal and kill. They do not enter the physical world by the lawful gate of birth, as Jesus Himself did by being born as humans are. Living things also contain water; non-living things are dry and waterless. Demons get no parasitical pleasure from being inside things that are dry and *waterless*. They love to ride on the pleasures of sins they induce in the living. Idols are not where demons reside, but in the people who disgrace themselves by bowing before them. (*For more on this subject see* Chapter 16 *on* **True and False Spirituality**.)

Some think they are Christians when they are not. Some are merely cultural, philosophical, or traditional in their beliefs. They are not like the woman who washed Jesus' feet with her own hair and tears. They stand next to Christ like a colleague (!), like the Pharisee in **Luke 7:38-50**, not realizing the Person to Whom he is speaking.

Some start but do not stay in faith. They have a specific agenda they want God to fix, but nothing more. If we say we believe in Jesus because He got us out of a jam, but don't begin to live the way He wants us to live, our house remains empty. Worse jams will keep coming until we repent and believe. Remember what I quoted from Norman Grubb: "What you take takes you." The opposite is also true: What you reject cannot take you.

Proverbs 26:2 reminds us:
Like a fluttering sparrow or a darting swallow, an undeserved curse does not rest. – NIV

I have also seen abuse by counselors in regard to the demonic. Evil spirits attack wherever we are vulnerable to temptation. Some people have a false and unbiblical idea that sins are spirits. For example, this personification takes the form of a "spirit of nicotine" that needs to be exorcised for a person to quit smoking, or a spirit of lust that must be cast out because of problems of unclean thoughts. There is no precedent in Scripture for this foolishness. In fact, a sick dependence is created between the counselor and the one counseled. The one seeking freedom now becomes the slave of the special leader who repeatedly gives them one-on-one attention over and over again. The leader may well be satisfying his own personal need to be needed, as well.

Maybe you can quit smoking because you believe from the deliverance prayer that a spirit of nicotine has left you. But then, when the urge to smoke returns, must you go to the leader and have the demon kicked out again? The urge to sin is temptation, and we will *always* be tempted. Sins are acts of disobedience to God and obedience to Satan, in motives and in deeds. Temptation is not sin but acting on it is sin. Feeling the urge is just the flesh wanting something it is used to having. There may be withdrawal discomfort. So what? Aren't you seated in Christ at the Right Hand of the Father?

A widespread **conceit** held by many is to believe that Christians should not have to suffer if God loves us, or if we do everything right we should have a smooth life. Then, when life gets hard, we have an excuse to disobey because God didn't come through for us in the way we expected in our misbelief.

Hebrews 2:18 says about Jesus:
> For because He Himself has suffered when tempted, He is able to help **me** when I am being tempted. – ESV (Shank)

1 Peter 4:1-2 says:
> Since therefore Christ suffered in the flesh, I arm **my-self** with the same way of thinking, for whoever has suffered in the flesh has ceased from sin, so as to live for

the rest of this time in the flesh no longer for human passions but for the will of God. – ESV (Shank)

Romans 8:16-17 says:

> The Spirit Himself bears witness with **my** spirit that I am a child of God and a fellow heir with Christ, provided I suffer with Him in order that I may also be glorified with Him. – ESV (Shank)

When poor understanding of what the Bible teaches about the demonic is mixed with emotional soulish believing (*see* **Chapter 5 Soul & Spirit**) and an incorrect understanding of temptation is believed, great confusion can result. I've known many who repeatedly went back for re-deliverance because they believed the demon had come back. They began to seriously doubt the power of God or even their salvation. One very bright young man had serious depression as a result of going from one church or one pastor to another, for deliverance. But he said the demon always came back to torment him. He was scaring his friends away with bizarre manifestations, couldn't study at school, or keep a job.

I said I would pray for deliverance once, but then he needed to learn how to properly defend himself with right believing. After a series of personal conversations, it all became apparent. He was trusting in his feelings and racing thoughts, believing them to be true above what the Word says is true. Though a Christian, he still defaulted to defining himself according to the flesh and the learned behavior of manifesting symptoms he had before his deliverance. I insisted he believe he was harassed, not possessed. In Christ, his old nature that wanted to sin is now DEAD!

One night he growled and cursed in defiance. I told him to stop acting that way anymore in Jesus' Name because Satan was now under his feet. I said he could control himself now. He stopped manifesting. Later, there were times when he got angry when I appeared to be uninterested when he thought he was in a crisis, but I just kept reminding him he was free, and gradually he began to believe it as he learned to take authority over his flesh. By faith, he has now learned a new behavior.

Now he sees temptation for what it is, a doorway he no longer needs to enter. He has been able to get good grades in school, as well as hold a job. He now teaches others by putting his active mind to better use. Is everything easy now? No, but he is learning he is free from demonic possession. His flesh will always want to sin, but so what? He must no longer regard himself according to the flesh. He can now say, my flesh is mine, but it is not me.

This habit of believing reminds me of a childhood memory. As a small boy, I liked to catch bees and wasps. They fascinated me. One day I caught a bumblebee in a glass jar with air holes driven through the thin brass lid. I put some grass and leaves along with a dandelion blossom in the jar because I thought the bee might want to eat them. The bee was enraged and beat against the glass walls of his prison, but he could not escape. The next morning, I went out to look in the jar. The bee was still alive but the jar was frosted from the dew. I felt sorry for it and decided to let it go, but because I didn't want to get stung, I carefully loosened the lid and let the bundle of grass with the bee in it slowly slide out onto the ground in one piece.

For a short while, the bee thought it was still in the confines of the glass jar that had imprisoned it because the bundle still kind of held the form it had inside the jar. As the bee crawled over it, the bundle fell apart. The bee still thought it was trapped inside its invisible prison, so it didn't try to fly away. Instead, it seemed to stumble out of the grass bundle onto the ground. It seemed confused at first that the jar was gone; then it flew away. Like the bee, we can continue to believe we are still prisoners of Satan out of habit. Though free in Christ, we stick to old ways we were never able to change when we still had the old nature. But we have been delivered. When we see ourselves as free, because those whom the Son set free are free indeed, we can fly away!

Accountability & Discipleship

To begin breaking up fallow ground, it's a good idea to make a list of significant life events, both positive and negative. I don't mean writing a life story; instead list in summarized paragraphs the circumstances and culture of your family of origin, along with the impact those events had on you. You should also list significant choices you have made, both wise and foolish. It's also very important for you to be in fellowship with the Body of Christ, in a local church. You must come to know them and let yourself be known by them. Find someone with spiritual maturity of the same gender.

A husband and wife need to have open and trusting communication, but there are some things only a woman can fully understand about a woman—about which she can only speak frankly to another woman. Likewise, there are some things only a man can understand about a man and communicate frankly to another man. There are also some things both men and women don't even want to know about each other! Note this is not to be a loyalty-pact where I try to find someone who will agree with me in everything, or else he can no longer be my friend! This must be a relationship of mutual submission. I may need to submit to Christ in my friend when the case is made that I must change a destructive pattern. The same must be true of my accountability partner. Both of us must have faith and be able to submit.

We also need to trust God with our submission. We need to trust God that He will speak through our accountability partner. We need to trust God that we will be able to speak His truth to our accountability partners, too. We must trust God that if one or both of us is off track, God will set it right. Faith is a *choice* to believe by taking action *as if* God rewards those who seek Him!

James 5:16 says:

> Therefore, confess your sins to one another and pray for one another, that you may be healed. – ESV

I can receive even painful observations from someone who cares about me, especially if my friend allows me the same candor. But I must be careful whom I allow into my inner circle of trust. We are not obligated to pour out problems to anyone who asks just because they have the Spirit of Christ. They may be well meaning, but if they have not yet begun to plow their own fallow ground, or are not a recognized counselor, they may not yet be safe or wise enough to help us. We must save the deep things for those who are deep, who have proven themselves trustworthy and mature. We must take a little time in faith to find the right person. We must not confide in a gossip or someone who is arrogant or vengeful; their fallow ground has not yet been plowed. We must choose someone who is humble about their own weakness, but who has found faith to overcome at least some of their sins.

If we have begun to date someone with the intent of marriage, we must be careful. Certainly, there must eventually be a deeper mutual exchange of faults for emotional and spiritual intimacy to grow, but we shouldn't go too fast. We may not marry, and if the other person is not the right mate, and we must break it off, we may find our trusted confidences shot back at us in fiery arrows of revenge. If on the other hand, we have gone through this process with a same-sex accountability partner, we may receive wise counsel as to when to go to a deeper level of exposure to our intended. Our accountability partner has more objectivity—not having stars in their eyes. This subject will be explored further in **Chapter 16 True & False Intimacy**.

Matthew 28:19-20 says:
Go therefore and make disciples of all nations, baptizing them in the Name of the Father and of the Son and of the Holy Spirit, teaching them to observe all that I have commanded you. And behold, I am with you always, to the end of the age. – ESV

Discipleship is largely absent in most churches today. Of those who do practice it, many limit discipleship to doctrinal instruction. People float from church to church without taking root or submitting to anyone. Others stay in dead churches because their **conceits** are never challenged and they are not expected to grow. I believe accountability partners help make real Biblical ways of living possible, if each one spurs the other on to bear more fruit in Christ and to outdo each other in love.

Chapter 8 Study Questions

1. What is the Biblical definition of fallow ground?

2. What are ancestral curses and in what way might they be relevant today?

3. What kind of power can demons have over a real Christian?

4. How can one find an accountability partner?

5. What are my strong influences, difficult problems, life-changing events, important achievements and failures, tragedies and wounds? Write a summary of them and begin to see from where you've come.

NOTE: **Chapters 9-12** present four different inventories: The Root of Bitterness, The Root of Fear, The Root of Shame, and The Root of Lawlessness (*which could be called The Root of Shamelessness*). Do not feel compelled to do all of them at once. After you have read through them, pick one and be thorough. Later, as you grow, do another to gain more perspective. For example, for years I thought my root issue was resentment. Recent events have led me to see shame was the deeper root. Each of us will have different findings.

9

The Root of Bitterness

Again, just as a branch bears good fruit if it's rooted in Christ, sin also has roots and branches—in the sense that bad behavior is founded on reasoning and energy from Satan through sinful assumptions, in the mindset of the flesh. In Christ, Satan is no longer our root, but we may still have some of his old behavior habits from deeply rooted **conceits** that need to be cut out.

I look at the problem this way: The brain stores facts, memories, assumptions, and conclusions. It is also designed to have reflexive responses to similar life situations. Learned behaviors tend to form habits for the sake of mental efficiency. Like an app on a smart phone, my mind makes a shortcut so I don't have to think through what I should do over and over again, in similar circumstances. This mental efficiency is not evil; it's designed by God. Satan misuses that design capacity to imbed his agendas as habits in me, like bad code. Many of these habitual responses were formed when I was still a child, with immature childish reasoning, and with false or mistaken assumptions to justify them. Other reflexive responses were intentionally formed as I became wise in my own willful deceitfulness.

Hebrews 12:15 says:
> See to it that no one fails to obtain the grace of God; that no root of bitterness springs up and causes trouble; and by it become defiled. – ESV

Amos 5:7 says:
O you who turn justice into wormwood [*bitterness*] and cast down righteousness to the earth! – ESV (Shank)

A root of bitterness causes resentments that justify a multitude of sins one would not ordinarily commit. Bitterness justifies a sense of entitlement that overrules righteousness and creates a Royal Victim Mentality that manipulates sympathy and demands allegiance from others, while granting permission to personally indulge in ruthless acts of selfishness. The ruthless always want mercy for themselves, even though they will often withhold it from others. But the Lord says if we do not forgive, we will not be forgiven. This brings on powerful conviction if we let ourselves believe this truth and feel the gravity of its ramifications.

If we refuse to change, we become entangled further in more acts of ruthless behavior. Rage is the engine of this destructive machine, but it is not always expressed with violent tempers. Depression that is not the result of brain chemistry imbalance can be compressed rage. Some suppress their pain with chemical and behavioral addictions. Some don't get angry; they just get even—with cold revenge in passive-aggressive behavior. Some use control, slander, sabotage, arrogance, withholding affections, cheating, chronic lying, and denial.

This is not like Christ, so why do Christians still have problems with things like this? Where is the fruit of the Spirit—the love, joy, peace, long-suffering, and gentleness? Where is the goodness, meekness, temperance, and faith, against which there is no law of **Galatians 5:22-23**? In a season of bitterness 30 years ago, I had to ask myself why I was like that. Yes, my painful circumstances were a factor, but it was also because I needed to plow my fallow ground. So how do we plow fallow ground to remove the root of bitterness?

There are different strategies. Counseling, accountability partners, and prayer are all helpful. The Alcoholics Anonymous Big Book teaches very effective steps that have formed a basic approach for many other recovery programs. You don't have to be an alcoholic to use them. Consequences are a humbling motivator. When God gave Israel the Promised Land, they had to

take it city by city and region by region. It did not come all at
once or without setbacks. When we receive the overcoming
nature of Jesus Christ, we have the power to overcome, but we
need to exercise faith consistently as we learn to use that power. The important thing to realize is that we already have the
power necessary for everything we need to overcome in the
Holy Spirit.

Recall **2 Peter 1:3-4**:

> His Divine power has granted me all things that pertain
> to life and godliness, through the knowledge of Him
> Who called me to His own glory and excellence, by
> which He has granted to me His precious and very
> great promises, so that through them I may [*once for all
> time*] become a partaker in the Divine Nature, having
> escaped from the corruption that is in the world be-
> cause of sinful desire [*lust corruption*]. – ESV (Shank)

This means I have first been made instantaneously holy in my
human spirit by the indwelling of the Holy Spirit. Then, because of that indwelling nature and power, I can learn by grace
to bring my habitual thoughts and actions into conformity
with the thoughts and actions of Christ. This does *not* mean I
am becoming more and more holy, it means I am becoming
more consistent with Christ's holiness in me.

I have already been made holy in Christ and now have the
power to claim the victorious promises of Scripture, by the
obedience of faith. This is not earning favor by keeping the
Law. It is the power of Christ in me to fulfill the moral Law as
the *fruit* of faith. I am free to plow my fallow ground without
fear of condemnation. What I am now digging up is what Satan planted through the old me—who is now dead! Yes, it's
painful to look at it. Yes, it's repulsive to see it as it really is. It
provokes embarrassment, remorse, shame, and a strong desire
to make amends.

But this is good because my conscience is beginning to recover—and with it the incentive to change my ways. If I remind
myself that what I once believed and did were done by the old
me who is now dead, I am free to go as deep as my need for
healing will take me. I can examine my sins from the safe view

of my new reality as a child of God, in order to discover what hidden unbelief may still remain. I have been forgiven, saved and made holy—in an instant in my spirit! What pleases Christ is not for me to wallow in what I *did* but embrace what I will now learn to *do* by His power in me.

Processing Resentment

When my root of bitterness grew bitter consequences as fruit, God mercifully used my consequences—and my new spirit nature—to motivate my soul's self-interest focus, to change. (See **Chapter 5 Soul & Spirit**.) As I began to change, I began to recover my conscience. This recovery was painful, but it destroyed many of my **conceits**, which had previously enabled me to disregard the pain I was causing others. I believed I deserved compensation for what I didn't have or what had been taken from me. The ruthlessness I saw in everyone else was now plain to be seen in me. It hurt, but that began to kill my **conceits**. I was powerless to change what others had done to me. I was also ungrateful for what others had done for me because that would obliterate my excuse to continue to allow my sin-serving **conceits** and **agendas** to drive my behavior.

I began to see that I was as evil in my doing as the evil that was being done to me. No wonder those who hurt me were the way they were. They had the same fallow ground justifying their conceits that I did. If I wanted mercy for myself, I had to show mercy to them, even though most of them hadn't changed yet. Because Christ showed mercy to me before I had changed, that same mercy was available to them, from both Christ and me.

There are no longer fixed good people or bad people in my mind, because we're all vessels of either Christ or Satan. We express the will of One or the other. We humans express the will of the one we obey and bear the fruit of the vine to which we are attached. My enemies have the potential to become wonderful friends in Christ if they will also repent and believe. Christians who have hurt me can also be forgiven for being deceived by Satan, just as I have been. Who do I think I am if I don't forgive?

2 Corinthians 5:16-21 reminds me:

> From now on I regard no one according to the flesh.
> Even though I once regarded Christ according to the
> flesh, I regard Him in this way no longer. Therefore,
> since I am in Christ, I am a new creation. The old **me**
> has passed away; I now see the new **me** has come. All
> this is from God, Who through Christ reconciled **me** to
> Himself and gave **me** a ministry of reconciliation; that
> is, in Christ God was reconciling the world to Himself,
> not counting the world's trespasses or **mine** against
> **me**, and entrusting to **me**, together with **my** brethren in
> Christ, the message of reconciliation. Therefore, I am an
> ambassador for Christ, God making His appeal through
> **me**. So I implore others on behalf of Christ, to be recon-
> ciled to God. For **my** sake, God made His Son to be sin
> Who knew no sin, so that in Christ I might become the
> righteousness of God. – (Shank)

My wounds are changing from being something I once used as
a **conceit** to justify my sin. Now my wounds are transformed
into being an instrument of empathy with the sin and sufferings of others. In bitterness, my hand was a fist. In healing, my
hand is now opened up to others because my pain has been
redeemed, becoming a means to identify with others who are
suffering in bitterness, as I have. I can now offer them more
than pity. I can help them heal the same way I was healed, because the Lord has shown me the way out through the release
of forgiveness.

But what if I say I don't want to forgive what was done to me?
I want the one who did *that* to me to burn in hell forever! To
this question I must ask myself, from where does my "not
wanting to forgive" come from? Does Christ want to forgive
sinners? **Yes**. Who wants sinners to remain in their sins? Satan.
Who deserves the allegiance of my will, Christ or Satan? To
whom will I demonstrate that I belong by my actions? But for a
long time I had said I just hurt too much to be able to forgive.

I say again, I must begin to break that evil power in me
through real forgiveness. What God commands is **fixed**: the
one who sins shall **die**. Satan uses that as leverage against me

before God, to block blessings from the Lord if I refuse to repent. The devil can stand before God and say: "Do not answer this man's prayer or show him mercy, because he does not show mercy and forgive others. This man disobeys Your fixed command. You, O God, must not go against Your Own Holy Words to even hear his prayer!"

Understanding this, I used to say I forgave those who hurt me, but when painful memories came up, I'd get mad again. And then I would condemn myself because I thought I must not have forgiven them after all. Because my pain and desire for revenge was still there, I thought I must be unable to forgive. Then a wise older man set me straight. I was believing what my emotions said, not what my spirit said. He said forgiveness was a spiritual transaction with God, not an emotional one. If I had *done* it, I must *believe* it and *stand* on it, just like when I gave myself to the Lord and He *took* me. So, what is real forgiveness? See the guidelines to forgiveness on **page 116.**

Only God can forgive all the other sins the one who hurt me has done to other people. Those sins remain between God and the one who hurt me. Satan was using others to harm me. Now I must let Christ use me to forgive them. I must give forgiveness to those people, but their trustworthiness must be earned, not the other way around. God did not wait for me to prove I was trustworthy to earn His forgiveness. But I am not commanded to be around someone who may seriously harm me again—unless they also change and become safe. But I must forgive.

Over the years, I have been amazed to find that my emotions are healing. My pain from others in the past is now almost completely gone. When forgiveness is given to others, the healing begins. I only have the authority to forgive what they did to me. They must deal with God for the rest of their sins as I must deal with God for mine. My wounds and consequences are real. I remember them. But now, I am more and more free from the evil power that came from the pain others have caused me. My old wounds no longer have the power they once had warp my judgment and response. I can continue to heal and grow more and more each day, in the grace God has given me.

If you've seen the movie *The Passion of the Christ* directed by **Mel Gibson**, you will likely remember a scene that powerfully affected me. Jesus has just had an obscenely cruel beating with rods and barb-tailed whips. His Blood is all over Himself and on the ground. He'd been up all night, enduring mockery and slanderous accusations. It's so bad, His friends hide themselves. On His way to Calvary, He is dragging the spar of His cross and falls down in exhaustion, as the crowd now pours wrathful insults all over Him.

At that point in the movie, I had a surge of rage as I marveled at His determination to go all the way. I thought to myself, if I were Jesus there, taking all that horrendous abuse, I would have thrown down my cross and shouted for God to send a legion of angels to blast them all. Send all these wicked people to hell, they're not worth all this torture, I've had it, I quit! But He did not quit, even though He had obviously had it to the full. Because of what He did, I'm not only forgiven, but He has given me His Holy Spirit to be in my spirit, so I can be like Him. I have His nature in me now. I have no excuse for withholding forgiveness from another who has wronged me. I must take up my cross and do likewise.

Processing What You Did & What I Did
What we are doing involves more than just psychology (*knowledge of the soul*); it's also pneumatology (*knowledge of the spirit*). The Holy Spirit reveals the way to liberation from bondage, reveals moral healing, and reveals the ability to bear fruit where there has been no fruit before. Looking over our resentment inventory, we can group similar responses with similar provocations. There is probably a humiliation group, an abandonment group, a rejection group, an abuse group, a loss group, a betrayal group, et cetera.

To begin to plow my fallow ground, I follow a variation of the method the Big Book recommends in Step Four.

I started by making a list of everyone I resented and why. I even included people on the list I had suspicions about but could not prove. I included larger categories like institutions, race, and gender resentments. I even included God, because as one counselor said to me at the time, "You're mad at God too, and He knows it!" I do not recommend sitting down and making the list all at once. That may actually stress you and you probably won't want to work at it. Instead, carry around a pocket notebook and ask the Spirit to bring to mind a memory to write down. Then write it and put the book away till another one comes. This way the Lord will bring the most helpful examples to mind for you to process. In a week, you will easily have plenty.

When I got to **30 or 40 examples**, I wrote down how each one hurt me in each case and what each one had cost me—physical and emotional abuse, destruction of my reputation, cruel insults, abandonment, rejection, humiliation, hardships, betrayal, et cetera.

Then after each example in the list, I wrote the ways I got revenge or how I comforted myself, followed by what I learned to do to protect myself from further pain. For revenge, did I do the same things to others that were done to me? Did I become judgmental, cynical, disrespectful of authority, or shut down? Was I back-stabbing, passive-aggressive, acting out sexually, withholding intimacy from my spouse, escaping through chemicals, lying, cheating, stealing, over eating, over spending? Did I give up on people too easily? Did I hold on to people too long? Did I look for other people to save me from my troubles? Did I become grandiose about my dignity and importance?

Then I listed the messages I got about my value and the value I gave to others from what happened. Did I think of myself as a victim who is entitled to special privilege, or am I nothing? Am I the judge, the executioner, the controller of others, the fool, the loser who throws himself away, the freak no one wants to be with, or do I think I'm terminally unique?

I also looked at the way my wounds corrupted my beliefs about God since He had allowed these things to happen. Did I doubt there was a God, or believe Him to be neither good nor just, or that He didn't care about me, or He hated me? Perhaps He's too strict, or He can't be trusted? Perhaps He doesn't want me to have any fun? Or am I convinced that my way is better than His?

I took stock of what responsibility I might have had in what happened to me, which ranged from complete innocence in some cases to full responsibility in others. Did I provoke this, or was I naïve or not thinking ahead in my expectations? Did I set up the one who hurt me to make him/her look bad? Was I argumentative or insulting, careless, reckless, believing I was exceptional and could escape the consequences other people with similar behavior normally get? Did I act crazy to make others think I didn't have to be responsible?

In my list, I began to notice recurring patterns of behavior that exposed ruthless tactics and false pay-offs, producing painful consequences as well as permissive **conceits** that justified the pursuit of sinful agendas.

THE BITTERNESS INVENTORY

WHO HURT ME?	HOW WAS I HURT & WHAT DID IT COST ME?	HOW DID I GET REVENGE OR COMFORT?	HOW DID MY RESPONSE MAKE ME SEE MYSELF?	HOW WAS MY BELIEF IN GOD EFFECTED?	IS ANY PART OF THIS MY FAULT?
1					
2					
3-40					

I shared my findings with my accountability partner and submitted to his advice in what I needed to do. The goal is not to vent my frustrations about what was done to me or to punish myself with humiliating memories and responses. If I am a new creation in Christ, I can be bold with these things. What was done before I was born again were things done by and to a man who is now dead. My old self was crucified with Christ. Certainly, the effects of those things may have consequences with my life now, but God has forgiven my part in what happened. All those things that were done to me can be forgiven by me. Those old ways I learned in the flesh—to either block or retaliate—can now be changed. I can forgive all who have hurt me, as Christ has forgiven me for all those I have hurt.

Chapter 9 Study Questions

1. What is a root of bitterness?

2. What role do soul and spirit play in breaking **conceits**?

3. According to **page 116**, how do I deal with painful recall after I have forgiven my enemy?

4. What have I learned about myself from applying the questions from the Resentment Chart?

5. What reoccurring behavior patterns do I see?

6. What tactics and justifying conceits keep coming up?

7. What observations does my accountability partner see?

10

The Root of Fear

When discussing the soul in **Chapter 5**, I said the soul has self-interest as its focus. It's supposed to be that way. It's designed to weigh and assess my circumstances, and then to offer an opinion from the perspective of what is good or bad for me and mine. Moral choice is not possible without assessing value or danger to me, or to the interests of those about whom I care. What if what happens to you should happen to me? Or, will I hurt you if I satisfy myself?

Counting the cost of a choice is then to be brought into submission to my spirit, where the Holy Spirit dwells. My soul gives its opinion but must not lead. Sometimes my soul is right and sometimes my soul is wrong in its opinion. It has a limited perception from one point of view. God's Mind is universal and sees All. His Holy Spirit now indwells my human spirit. My born-again human spirit wants to do the will of God. It wants first to seek the Kingdom of God and His Righteousness; all other things are added on after that. But my human spirit is finite and does not see All. The Holy Spirit tells my conscience what is right by His Word in the Bible (**logos**) or by His Word (**rhema**), which is the witness of the Spirit as a personal command or insight to my dilemma. This does not mean my circumstances determine what is moral. Rhema never contradicts the logos. When in doubt, logos must rule.

Isaiah 30:21 describes how rhema works:
And your ears shall hear a Word behind you, saying, "This is the way, walk in it." When you turn to the right or when you turn to the left. – ESV

In **Matthew 4:4** Jesus rebukes Satan quoting **Deuteronomy 8:3** saying:
> It is written [*in the* **logos**], "Man does not live by bread alone, but by every Word [**rhema**] that comes from the Mouth of God." – ESV

The more I disobey the Word of the Lord, whether it comes as **logos** or **rhema**, the harder it becomes for me to see or hear

Him, and the harder my heart becomes to understand Him. But the more I obey the Word of the Lord, the clearer it becomes for me to see and hear Him, and my heart becomes more and more tuned to respond to Him. My heart is the attitude and will of my desire. If Christ is in me, how can my heart become hard? Can a husband and a wife sleep in the same bed and not want to speak or hear from each other? As it should not be with a husband and a wife, so should it not be between Christ and His Bride. In a dispute between a husband and a wife, sometimes the husband is right and sometimes the wife is right. There is often a mix of right and wrong in both. But in any dispute I may have with God, He is always right. All I try to accomplish apart from Him comes to nothing. I am fruitful only when I obey Him.

Healthy & Toxic Fear

There are healthy fears, which are wise. When I was still in my corruption, incapable of motives that were pure because I was still Satan-operated, I feared the hellfire of judgment. I feared what would happen to me if I didn't deal with God and give Him what He wanted. This fear was used by God to energize the self-interest of my soul to pursue Him, lest sin and damnation destroy my life. It was only after He forgave me and joined His Holy Spirit to my spirit that I became able to even care about righteousness. Healthy fear—that God sees all—provoked faith in me to keep and protect what is sacred, to help and protect the vulnerable, the lost, the poor, and the little ones (**fetus** – *Latin*) because their angels in heaven have the ear of God and see His Face. (**Matthew 18:10**)

The fear of God is the beginning of wisdom, but it is not the end of it. There is infinitely more wisdom to be found in obeying His Word, because in obeying Him we learn His wise ways. The more we grow in His wisdom, the more love becomes our motivation to obey. The fear of God confronts my sin against Him and against others; it confronts my fear of the opinions of man. Healthy fear also protects me. It keeps me from putting my hand on a hot stove, jumping off a cliff, or crossing the street without looking both ways.

There are also toxic fears, which are foolish. Those fears energize faithlessness, cowardice, moral weakness, and allow Satan to plunder me and others. Faithless fear cannot enter into God's rest or reap His rewards.

Luke 19:20-26 says:

> Then another came, saying, "Lord, here is Your mina, which I kept hidden away in a handkerchief; for I was afraid of You because You are a severe man. You take what You did not deposit, and You reap what You did not sow." He [*the Lord*] said to him, "I will condemn you with your own words, you wicked servant! You knew that I was a severe man, taking what I did not deposit and reaping what I did not sow? Why then did you not put My money in the bank, and at My coming I might have collected it with interest?" And He said to those who stood close by, "Take the mina from him, and give it to the one who has ten minas." And they said to Him, "Lord, he has ten minas!" [*Then the Lord says*] "I tell you that to everyone who has, more will be given, but from the one who has not, even what he has will be taken away. But as for these enemies on mine, who do not want Me to rule over them, bring them here and slaughter them before Me." – ESV (Shank)

Notice that the Lord does not challenge the wicked servant's soul assumption that the He is a severe man worthy of fear, but He condemns him with his own words. "So, you know I am a severe man? If so, why didn't your fear of My severity cause you to make sure you took measures to make Me happy and escape My wrath?" Then the Lord pointed out that the money the servant was given, belonged to the Lord. "Why didn't you take *My* money and deposit it in a bank and make interest?" The money is the life God gives into my keeping. I will be held accountable for how I spend it, how I invest or waste it. Do I fear God and let His life shine out through me as a light to others, or do I fear man and hide it under a bushel? If I am a branch that bears no fruit, I might be cut from the vine and burned in the fire.

Revelation 21:7-8 says:

> The one who conquers will have this heritage, and I
> will be his God and he will be My son. But as for the
> *cowardly*, the faithless, the detestable, as for murderers,
> the sexually immoral, sorcerers, idolaters, and all liars,
> their portion will be in the lake that burns with fire
> and sulfur, which is the second death. – ESV (*Shank*)

Among murderers and sorcerers who are justly condemned,
why are mere *cowards* also condemned? Cowardice is the result of a systematic choice to obey toxic fear. It quenches and
grieves the Holy Spirit. It defeats faith and bears no fruit—
producing no interest from the life God entrusted to me. My
life is ruthlessly more concerned with myself, to the point of
not giving a damn about you, let alone the will of God! Toxic
fear is an evil attitude, not just an emotional weakness! It must
be overcome by repentance that includes building new faith
habits and identifying and dismantling faithless habits of believing. As was well-illustrated in Germany before World War
II, great evil was allowed to prevail when good men refused to
stand up for what was right.

Make no mistake: there is no condemnation for fear *feelings* as
such. The soul's emotions are intended by God's design to be
part of my response to my situation, that I might apprehend
the personal gravity of it. But in my spirit, I must not let fear
rule my attitude to opposes what is right, any more than I am
to give in to any unclean urges that misuse the legitimate created needs and desires of my flesh.

1 John 4:18 says:

> There is no fear in love, but perfect love casts out all
> fear. For fear has to do with punishment, and whoever
> fears has not been perfected in love. – ESV

Once again, the Perfect Lover is God. Faith is deciding to trust
Him by making a choice to obey Him, *as if* what He says is
true, though there may be some personal risk. Are fear feelings
wrong—are they supposed to go away? No. We should never
take condemnation for fear feelings. As we have been saying
regarding the soul and its self-interest or self-preservation fo-

cus, the soul's opinion needs to be part of the consideration process, but it must be overruled when it wants to resist faith. Jesus saw fully what being arrested was going to cost Him.

The fear He felt as He prayed to His Father made the sweat fall from Him like drops of blood. Jesus has a soul as well because He is fully man as He is fully God. He was in full realization of what His obedience was going to cost Him. That's why He saw Peter's rebuke in **Mark 8:31-33** as being temptation from Satan, even though Peter didn't know Satan was using him at the time. Jesus gets no condemnation for courageously feeling His fear. Neither should I. If Jesus can feel His fear but still obey what His Father was commanding He do, so can I. The Spirit of Christ in me also wants to do the will of God. And the Word of God does not lie.

I manifest faith after counting the cost and making the choice to do what my Father wants me to do, *as if* He has already empowered me to do it. I will have fear-feelings, but I am not to be ruled by those feelings, because I believe I am no longer under death or judgment. Even if my choice costs me my life, the Spirit of Christ in me, perfects me in the Perfect Lover's love.

Processing My Fears

Begin by making an honest and probing list of recurring fears. Choose to reject condemnation for what you find; the Lord is healing you. If you have experienced serious trauma in your life, you may be tempted to hide from remembering painful details. There may be a lot of defensive behaviors and attitudes around trauma that you have constructed to protect yourself from ever experiencing anything like it again. Include even embarrassing fears that you may believe in your mind as unlikely to happen. Remember that anxiety is stressed fear that manifests itself in obsessive thoughts. After you've listed around **30 to 40**, notice recurring categories and patterns, as you process them across the chart below.

If you have trouble getting enough fears on your list, you are blocking your memory. Blocking is a defensive tactic we use when we believe we're not safe to open ourselves to ourselves, or to others. We misbelieve we have to maintain control over the truth. We're acting *as if* we are separate from God in these areas and must take back the control we never really had in the first place. Only God is autonomous. We will always be dependent. Self-effort is a lie from Satan who misbelieves he can do what he pleases, without God. Even if we now know our dependence on God is real, our actions may still have the habit of unbelief, choosing the futility of blocking the truth.

When I was first confronted with what was being exposed deep inside me, I experienced almost catatonic shutdowns that sometimes took several days for me to recover. I turned to stone inside. I was numb. I felt my body encased in rubber or injected with Novocain. I was afraid the truly awful truth about my interior was about to be shouted from the rooftops! An accountability partner can be of great service here. I had friends who were able to help me out of it by reminding me of who I am in Christ. As a man in Christ who is joined to Christ, I was already forgiven and was free to see the evil Satan had used to deceive me. Having already confessed my sins, I was now beginning to discover the pathways sin had made in me. The enemy wanted to continue to misuse me, to disgrace my testimony, and to continue to use me to hurt others. It was now a matter of exposing how his evil still worked in my members. I was experiencing Satan's fear through my emotions, because he was the one being exposed and his influence was being broken! My flesh is mine, but it is not me.

I was asked to describe what was happening before I locked myself up. Little by little, I was able to retrace my steps. Confessions I made in the context of being in Christ helped me to lay aside the debris of lies under which I was hiding, so I could stand again in faith and press on to freedom. My foundation of unbelief was being destroyed so a foundation of faith could be rebuilt in its place.

My Fear Inventory
The following are a few examples of recurring patterns from my personal fear inventory that are common to us all. The processing pattern is similar to what I used for my resentment inventory. First, I listed my fears. When I got **30 to 40** of them, I had a large enough sample to start looking for recurrent categories that could be grouped together. In what follows, I'm

processing the same five categories through each stage of ex-
amination for your benefit. You can treat other categories from
your own list in a similar manner. When I saw the list of the
crazy ways I was often thinking, I was embarrassed. I didn't
want to see myself in this raw, unguarded way without any
rationalizing filters. But then I realized that this was the old
way of reasoning from my soul's self-protection. I needed to
answer it with the spiritual truth.

Without my union in Christ, my fears were threatening. Thank
God I now have the mind of Christ! What I was processing
were the old lie stumps, the habit stones and the poisonous
salts that were keeping my ground fallow. Now, I am letting
the plow of the Holy Spirit do His work in me—letting the
Vinedresser prune me. Since all my sins have already been forgiven, and I am safe at the Right Hand. I can now tear down
the old altars from the old high places and burn the old idols.

THE FEAR INVENTORY

WHAT DO I FEAR?	WHY DO I FEAR IT?	WHAT ARE MY DEFENSE TACTICS?	WHAT DOES MY DEFENSE COST ME?	HOW DO MY FEARS MAKE ME SEE GOD?	WHAT IS THE TRUTH ABOUT GOD?
1					
2					
3					
4-40					

I've picked out five fear groups that were part of my larger fear
inventory, as they were processed through the categories in
this fear chart. These were groupings that had similar wounds,
resulting in fears of rejection, exposure, intimacy, lack of intimacy and decision-making. I carried them through for your
benefit, to show how I processed them. These would be common to many of us. Some, however, were caused by some dev-

astating traumas in my life, which provoked over vigilant defensiveness and warping distortions in my view of God.

Five Examples of What I Fear & Why

1. Fear of Rejection – I'll lose a relationship if I speak up about my faith. Fear of giving helpful advice that may offend. Fear of stepping up to take responsibility and take reasonable risks because I believe I'm defective. I'm in fear of being unsatisfied in giving up sinful pleasures because God won't satisfy my needs.

2. Fear of Exposure – If the real me shows, I'll be perceived as unsafe, ugly, and unworthy of love. I'll lose trust and respect from others.

3. Fear of Intimacy – I can't let myself be known by you with personal knowledge of my needs, wounds, secrets, and weaknesses.

4. Fear of a Lack of Intimacy – I will have no meaningful relationships because no one will really want to trust me with knowledge of their needs, wounds, secrets, and weaknesses.

5. Fear of Decision-making – I won't be able to choose the right strategy. My foolishness will find me out. I have negative ESP, always making the wrong plan or picking the wrong option.

My Five Defense Tactics with These Five Fears

Fear of Rejection – I compromise my values through people-pleasing, projecting an image I think will be more acceptable to keep friends. Trying to engender a sense of obligation with someone so they will need me. Making myself important to someone or trying to buy acceptance with favors. Trying to make myself appear to be valuable or at least amusing.

Fear of Exposure – I conceal parts of me, avoid accountability, and project a false self.

Fear of Intimacy – I test others. I sabotage. I hold my cards close to the chest. I lie, or I escape into fantasy.

Fear of Lack of Intimacy – I sometimes over-steer into inappropriate internal exposure of myself. I can behave manipulatively or seductively, and act obsessively in pursuit of others by not respecting or being aware of their boundaries.

Fear of Decision-making – I make impulsive choices without careful consideration, using procrastination and magical thinking that things will work out even if I do nothing, and consoling myself with an imagined future when I finally do what I want, without ever putting my goals to the test by taking action.

What Does My Defense Cost Me?
Fear of Rejection – My people-pleasing breaks down; my unhappiness shows; I lose friends from painful outbursts. I am found out.

Fear of Exposure – My loss of respect can happen anyway, and my mistrust of others leads to more rejection.

Fear of Intimacy – I'm not liked or trusted by those who matter to me. I have no warm relationships or have clumsy, combative relationships, often feeling alone.

Fear of Lack of intimacy – I'm too forward, scaring people off and drive others away. I am treated with suspicion, not having meaningful rapport or warmth from others.

Fear of Decision-making – I always seem to have an empty checkbook, missed opportunities, reckless lifestyle, depreciated self-confidence, and choose frequent irresponsible behavior that creates pain for those I love.

How Do My Fears Affect How I See God?
Fear of Rejection – God is critical, hostile, and looking for a reason to blast me to hell.

Fear of Exposure – God is going to hate me and make me stand naked in front of everyone, to be mocked and jeered.

Fear of Intimacy – God is not worthy of my trust, is dangerous, and must be avoided. He will get me in trouble with people, and I won't have any fun.

Fear of Lack of Intimacy – God does not want to know me, and I'm afraid I won't really know Him.

Fear of Decision-making – God does not or will not guide me. I'm living in a world without order or purpose. God made me defective, and He doesn't care what happens to me.

What Is the Truth About God?
Fear of Rejection – Ephesians 2:4-10,

> But God, rich in mercy because of the great love with which He loved **me**, even when I was dead in **my** trespasses, made **me** alive together with Christ—by grace I have been saved—and raised **me** up with Him and seated **me** with Him in the heavenly places in Christ Jesus. In grace, I have been saved through faith. And this is not **my** own doing; it is a gift of God, not as a result of **my** works, so that I may not be able to boast. For I am His workmanship, created in Christ Jesus for good works, which God prepared beforehand, that I should walk in them. - ESV (Shank)

Fear of Exposure – Proverbs 18:10,

> The Name of the Lord is a strong tower; the righteous man runs into it and is safe. - ESV

Proverbs 29:25,

> The fear of man is a snare, but whoever trusts in the Lord is safe. - ESV

Fear of Intimacy – Hebrews 4:14-16,

> Since I have a Great High Priest Who has passed through the heavens, Jesus the Son of God, I will hold fast to **my** confession. For I do not have a high priest who is unable to sympathize with **my** weakness, but One Who in every respect has been tempted as I am, yet without Himself sinning. So, it is with confidence that I draw near to the Throne of Grace, that I may re-

ceive mercy and find grace to help in my times of need.
– ESV (Shank)

Fear of the Lack of intimacy – **From Psalm 139:**

You Know Me
You have searched me and known me,
You know where I sit down and where I lie.
You discern my thoughts from far away,
You see my path and my resting place
with Your Eyes

    You are acquainted with all of my ways.
    You know my words before I even speak.
    You beset me behind and before,
    And You lay Your Hand upon me,
    And You lay Your Hand upon me.

    Such knowledge is just too wonderful,
    Too wonderful indeed for me.
    It is high, I cannot attain it.
    So high I cannot see.

Whither shall I go from Thy Spirit?
Whither shall I flee from Thee?
If I should ascend to the heavens,
Or make my bed in Sheol, Thou art still
with me.

    And if I should take the wings of the morning,
    To dwell in the outermost part of the sea,
    Even there Thy Hand shall before me,
    And Thy Right Hand shall hold onto me,
    And Thy Right Hand shall hold onto me.

    And if I say, "Let the darkness cover me,
    And the light about me be as black as night."
    Even the darkness to Thee is bright,
    Darkness is day in Your sight.

For You did form my inner parts,
Knit me together in my mother's womb.

I will praise Thee, You're fearful and
You're wonderful,
Wonderful Your handiwork, too.

> You know me right well,
> My frame was never hidden for Thee,
> When I was being made in secret;
> Fearfully fashioned beneath.

> Your Eyes beheld my unformed substance,
> And in Your Book were numbered all of my days
> Before they were even lived, they were known to You;
> How precious are Your thoughts and Your ways,
> How precious are Your thoughts and Your ways.

Search me, know my heart.
Try me, know my thoughts.
See where there be some wicked way in me,
Lead me in Thy ways everlasting.

You Know Me / *Yeshua* /Peniel Music / johnbyronshank.com

Fear of Decision-making – **John 16:13-15,**

> When the Spirit of Truth comes, He will guide you into all truth, for He will not speak on His own authority, but whatever He hears He will speak, and He will declare it to you. All that the Father has is Mine; therefore, I said that He will take what is Mine and declare it to you. –ESV

Chapter 10 Study Questions

1. What is the difference between healthy and toxic fear?

2. Why is cowardice such a serious sin?

3. How does perfect love cast out all fear?

4. Process your own fear inventory in the way outlined in the chart on page 131. My list was much longer. So will yours be.

11

The Root of Shame

The Vine

When I was sixteen
I wanted to ditch myself
Down by the side of the road,
Leave myself behind by the side of the road.
Tried on so many other faces
But I never could find one that I could call my own.
Tried on so many other faces
But I never could find one that I could call my own.

There was a twig at the end
Of a long spreading branch
That was my family tree,
And I knew that twig was me.
I thought no matter how hard I try
There was nobody else that I could be.
I thought no matter how hard I try
There was nobody else that I could be.

But there's a knowledge that comes
In the delay of an answer
And a wisdom that comes,
Comes in the delay of relief,
And a truth that can be heard while waiting in the si-
        lence
For that still, small Voice to speak.
Yes, a truth that can be heard while waiting in the si-
        lence
For that still, small Voice to speak.

The Words of the Lord are flawless
Like silver refined in a furnace of clay
Purified seven times,
Refined in a furnace seven times.
They say my life is in the Vine,
My spirit is His and His Spirit is mine.
They say my life is in the Vine,

172

> My spirit is His and His Spirit is mine.
> – *River of Delights* / Peniel Music / johnbyronshank.com

Shame is self-loathing with severity. It can be the result of an outrage to my body or my vanity or dignity by someone else. It can also be caused by my own ruthlessly sinful behaviors. It's often hidden by emotional blocking or with secrets to avoid painful exposure. It plays a major part in the avoidance of God in prayer, in the fruitful expectation of faith, and in hindering intimate fellowship with others. Unbroken by repentance, self-loathing leads to downward spirals of thinking and behavior that make problems worse and worse. After Adam and Eve disobeyed God by eating from the Tree of the Knowledge of Good and Evil, they saw they were naked and covered themselves, in shame.

Genesis 3:8-13 says:

> And they heard the sound of the Lord God walking in the garden in the cool of the day, and the man and his wife hid themselves from the presence of the Lord God among the trees of the garden. But the Lord God called to the man and said to him "Where are you?" And the man said, "I heard the sound of You in the garden, and I was afraid, because I was naked, and hid myself." The Lord said, "Who told you that you were naked? Have you eaten of the Tree of which I commanded you not to eat?" The man said, "The woman whom You gave to be with me, she gave me fruit of the tree, and I ate." Then the Lord God said to the woman, "What is this that you have done?" The woman said, "The serpent deceived me, and I ate." - ESV

Notice that the disobedience of Adam and Eve made them see themselves as naked, as exposed in the painful light of Truth. Adam and Eve were ashamed in the presence of Christ in the Garden of Eden. This made them try to hide from the All-seeing and All-knowing God Who made them. Christ, the Word of the Lord, called to the man, "Where are you?" not because He didn't know where they were, but because He wanted them to stand before Him and tell the truth with their own lips. Adam's confession was cowardly and insulting because he implicitly blamed God by inference: "The woman whom You gave to be with me, she gave me fruit of the tree, and I ate." The implication here is that God had given him someone who was flawed to be his companion, so he was not entirely at fault for what he did. Never mind that he knew better and put her above the command of the Lord so he could have what she now had—and be able to know what she now knew. Eve rightly blamed Satan for deceiving her, but she did not acknowledge that she also became an instrument of corruption in drawing Adam into her sin. She wanted what Satan wanted—to grab more power by willful disobedience, which the Most High had withheld. She was quick to pull her husband into her sin.

Philippians 2:5-8 says:

> Have this mind among yourselves, which is yours in Christ Jesus, Who, though He was in the form of God, did not count equality with God a thing to be grasped, but made Himself nothing, taking the form of a servant, being born in the likeness of men. And being found in human form, He humbled Himself by becoming obedient to the point of death, even death on a cross. - ESV

Shame Versus Conviction

Shame is different than conviction. Shame condemns who I am; conviction condemns what I have done. Satan takes advantage of us when we sin, by using the Law against us for condemnation. He wants us to hate ourselves to the point of despair. He is *Notgod* the *Unmaker* and wants to draw us into morbid shame if he can, to make us believe we are hopeless. Jesus says that he who hates his life will keep it, and he who loses his life will find it. The Lord also says that we should agree with our accuser on the way to the judge, so the court will not condemn us (**Matthew 5:25**). If Satan is the accuser, under what circumstances can we agree with him? Jesus also says to the Pharisees, "Your accuser is Moses" (**John 5:45**).

Romans 7:12 says:

> So, the Law is holy, and the commandment is holy and righteous and good. - ESV

Ironically, both Moses and Satan use the Law against us: Satan to condemn us for sin; but Moses to convict us of sin.

Romans 8:1-2 says:

> There is therefore now no condemnation for those who are in Christ Jesus. For the Law of the Spirit of life has set **me** free in Christ Jesus from the Law of sin and death. – ESV (Shank)

So, what conclusions should we draw? Let's review the difference between condemnation and shame. When I sin, Satan condemns me saying, "You're worthless, you're hopelessly corrupt, you can't do right, just give up!" But the Holy Spirit convicts me saying, "Why did you do *that?* You're better than *that,* you're a child of God, get back on track!" The Holy Spirit actually affirms me by saying the thing I did was wrong. Sin is no longer your master. Make it right; repent because in Christ you have a nature like Christ. Condemnation to the Christian is *never* from the Holy Spirit.

I'm learning to reject condemnation in Jesus' Name and to agree with the conviction of whoever is right in accusing me of sin. I just need to confess, change, and move on in faith. Regarding shame, it's important to realize that the enemy may be right in pointing out that what I did was terrible, but my acknowledgement of my sin does not mean I must also take on his condemning conclusion about who I am. I must reject that condemnation! But I must never minimize or deny what I have done if it is wrong.

I am free to confess my sin because of the power of the Blood that has cleansed me. I have grace from God to get up and press on in faith once I have dealt with my sin. Lingering in condemnation produces morbid shame that keeps me in a pit of despair and is spiritually unproductive. Shame as an emotion is helpful for remorse, that I may appreciate the gravity of my sin's effect on another. But when shame is not answered and becomes a way of life, it turns morbid, distorting the character of God as well as my own.

To give an example of the effects of morbid shame in my own life, let me share a picture the Spirit gave me about how I once saw the Lord and myself:

There was a very wealthy man who came down to the pier where a large ship was docked. He wanted to buy the ship, the cargo, the company, and everything. In acquiring everything he wanted, he also bought a rat that was living in the bottom of the cargo hold. The rat was me. I was purchased along with the boat, but I was *not* what he desired. I was now his, only because I was hidden among the other things the buyer *really* wanted. This is how I viewed my being bought by the Blood of Christ!

What's wrong with this picture? First of all, I had a **conceit** that in order to be loved by God, I had to be someone He desired for some value I had in myself. He would only love those who fulfilled some self-interest He had, or whose personality He enjoyed being around. God was just like everybody else. Second, because I was a hopelessly corrupt person, I would never find a way to be loved by God. So, I had another **conceit** that I might as well keep on sinning because I couldn't win God's affection anyway. I wrung my hands with self-pity and consoled myself with more sin. This kind of thinking followed me after my conversion, even though I knew better. I excused myself from difficult stands of faith because I continued in the **conceit** of believing I didn't matter.

The truth is that God Is Love. He loves the worthless in spite of themselves—and I am made in His image. While we were still sinners, Jesus died for us all. God cannot deny His Own Nature, which is to love. I was not just allowed in on the deal because He loved everyone else. This is reverse grandiosity—that I'm exceptional in some negative way.

I was also thinking I was capable of exhausting God's grace, until He said to me, "Do you think the suffering and Blood of My Son were NOT enough for YOU? Something MORE than the Blood is needed to make YOU acceptable?"

Shame Sources
Shame becomes rooted in me through sinful acts that were done to me *by* others, as well as sinful acts I have done *to* oth-

ers. These humiliating events and experiences are numerous in their expression. They are wounds that need healing. Some may even be traumatic. A partial list would include rape, incest, abortion, betrayal, beatings, maiming, abandonment, rejection, divorce, excessive control, bullying, promiscuity, adultery, pornography, prostitution, addiction, slander, anger storms, passive-aggressive behavior, theft, murder, degrading assessments, violation of intimacy, lies, emotional blackmail, withheld affection...

These kinds of wounds to ourselves can make us victims, and victims have great potential to become the victimizers of others. Shame is a reflexive response to hide what has happened, and through shame, we can deprive ourselves of help. We also want to hide what we have done. Some of us block the significance of the painful truth with shutdowns, or minimize the true significance with rationalization, or justify it with excuses. Some of us resort to medicating ourselves with chemicals or other compulsive behaviors. Some of us artfully redesign our memories to create something completely false. Some of us go on a rampage of self-entitled revenge, creating more to be ashamed of, when we come to our senses.

To break the power of shame, we must break the system of **lies, false payoffs,** and **conceits** that have been woven into our beliefs, attitudes, and behavior. I found the following inventory process to be very helpful and healing. There are seven steps in it. Begin by listing shameful memories in step 1. Once you have 30–40 examples, you have a large enough sample to expose patterns of thinking and behavior. Then do step 2 for each example. After you have worked through the whole list, do step 3, and so on. I strongly urge against taking one shame example and processing all seven steps at once. The greatest benefit comes from doing one number column at a time, moving down through the whole list sequentially. Be patient with yourself and trust God for breakthroughs. You will experience some painful recall in the process, but joy and freedom will follow if you persevere in faith. God means this process for healing, not condemnation or to provoke relapse.

I found my own shame inventory to be very revealing. Through my wounds, I saw much more clearly the embedded shame that was corrupting my faith, my perceptions, and my behaviors:

1. I saw how a man-who-hurts, hurts others and continues to hurt himself.

2. Shame gave me an excuse to act out to comfort myself, to sell out to protect my selfish agendas, and to procrastinate in order to delay being responsible.

3. My shame caused me to attach my self-worth to my personal circumstances, not to Jesus. Real cause and effect was confused and distorted. Small criticisms seemed like attacks on my value as a person, when they were sometimes given as helpful, candid advice. Shame was an automatic interpreter that made things *mean* something that was not necessarily true. My shame was unable to distinguish between what was an insult and what was not.

4. My shame made chronic self-mockery and even self-curses a reflexive response to even the most trivial mistakes I made. My sudden flashes of anger were often out of proportion to my circumstances. My outraged *vanity* expected perfection. Shame triggered grandiosity as a false compensation... I am supposed to be *Great!*

5. My shame gave me frequent irrational nightmares, unfounded insecurities, and profound self-hatred. It reinterpreted many of my weaknesses as occasions to despise myself in comparison to others; it made me jealous of them and ungrateful to God about how I was made.

THE SHAME INVENTORY

MY SHAMEFUL MEMORIES 30-40 EXAMPLES	HOW WAS I HURT?	HOW DID I HURT OTHERS?	WHAT WAS MY REVENGE?	WHAT DID I WRONGLY BELIEVE ABOUT ME?	HOW WAS GOD'S TRUTH CORRUPTED?	WHAT IS THE BIBLICAL TRUTH?
1						
2-40						

My Shame Inventory

It is a holy thing to confront my unholiness. To do this honestly, I must know I am under the Blood, know I am forgiven, and know who I am in Christ and know Christ is in me. This inventory should begin as a black and white self-analysis, raw and unbalanced, without justifications or excuses. Balance will return in the later steps of this process, but first, the sin must be fearlessly exposed for what it is. This is about finding Satan's ways in me from my past, so I will not be fooled again by his lies to my soul. If I am born again, all these things have been forgiven.

1. SHAMEFUL MEMORIES. List any shameful act that becomes a trigger for shame in me and provokes painful recall when it comes to mind. It can be either something that was done to me or something I did to others, or something I did to disgrace myself even if no one else appeared to be harmed. (*Don't stop collecting examples until you have at least 30-40.*)

2. HOW WAS I HURT? How was my value and dignity stripped from me? What loss did I suffer? In what ways did I lose my sense of confidence? In what ways did I lose the capacity to trust? How did I lose the respect or my reputation with people who know me? How was I betrayed...? This is important even in cases where the greater part of my shame was in what I did to someone else. (*Apply these kinds of conclusions to each of your examples.*)

3. HOW DID I HURT OTHERS? How was value and dignity stripped from the one I harmed? What loss did the one I harmed suffer? In what ways did the one I hurt lose self-confidence? In what ways did the one I hurt lose the capacity to trust? How did what I have done cause others to lose respect or reputation with those around them? How were they betrayed by me? In what ways were others provoked to sin because of what I did...? (*Summarize how others were hurt by me where it applies.*)

4. WHAT WAS MY REVENGE? How did I get even or console myself with revenge—theft, slander, lying, temper, violence, control, vandalism, cutting people off...?

What **conceits** gave me permission to act in those sinful ways—I deserve this, you deserve this, you owe me, this is payback, life is not fair...?

How did I overcompensate for my shame—medicating, binging, controlling people, blaming them, being irresponsible, impulsive self-indulgence, holding judgmental contempt, self-absorption, hiding, shutting down, sabotage, undermining authority, withholding love or help or support...?

What *false payoff* was I looking for in my actions? In what ways did my sinful response change me from being a wounded victim into someone who wounds and makes victims of others? (*Apply your responses to each example.*)

5. WHAT DID I WRONGLY BELIEVE ABOUT ME? I'm the one who should be in charge. I am a misunderstood genius. No one understands my special circumstances. I am worthless. I am the greatest. I am the worst. I am helpless and should be excused from responsibility. I am bottomless in my need. I am hopelessly corrupt or defective. I cannot change. (*Take no-*

tice where some these conclusions are repeated in your list.)

6. HOW WAS GOD'S TRUTH CORRUPTED? What lies about God's character and motives were given plausibility by sinful deception? God is against me. God is too strict and unfair. God is not there. God does not love me. I am beyond God's forgiveness. God does not see or care what I am doing. God does not care what other people are doing to me...

How did I blaspheme God with my deeds as well as my words? It is all God's fault. God made me defective. The Blood is not enough for me. God doesn't keep His promises. God is not worthy of my worship or obedience. Faith in God is foolish and without joy...

7. WHAT IS THE BIBLICAL TRUTH? Answer the lies in steps 5 and 6 with scripture verses that give a new foundation for truth.

In Summary
Record any patterns you see emerging from
your inventory.

1. What have been my shame payoffs from my sinful responses? What did I think I was avoiding by doing what I did?

2. What lies have I repeatedly misbelieved? What self-serving **conceits** gave me permission to believe what I did was justifiable?

3. What have been my reflexive responses? What do I always seem to go back to in response to shame triggers that cause painful recall in similar situations?

4. What are my continuing problems? What has will-power not been able to fix me?

5. Where do I go from here? Who do I need to forgive? Who do I need to make amends to and ask for forgiveness? What does the Lord want me to do for change and healing?

12

The Root of Lawlessness (The Root of Shamelessness)
2 Thessalonians 2:1-12 says:

> Now concerning the coming of our Lord Jesus Christ and our being gathered together to Him, we ask you, brothers, not to be quickly shaken in mind or alarmed, either by a spirit or a spoken word, or a letter seeming to be from us, to the effect that the Day of the Lord has come. Let no one deceive you in any way. For that day will not come, unless the rebellion comes first, and the man of lawlessness is revealed, the son of destruction, who opposes and exalts himself against every so-called god or object of worship, so that he takes his seat in the temple of God, proclaiming himself to be God. Do you not remember that when I was still with you I told you these things? And you know what is restraining him now so that he [*the lawless one*] may be revealed in his time. For the mystery of lawlessness is already at work. Only He Who now restrains it will do so until He is out of the way. And then the lawless one will be revealed, whom the Lord Jesus Christ will kill with the Breath of His Mouth and bring to nothing by the appearance of His coming. The coming of the lawless one is by the activity of Satan with all power and false signs and wonders, and with all wicked deception for those who are perishing because they refused to love the truth and so be saved. Therefore, God sends them a strong delusion, so that they may believe what is false, in order that all may be condemned who did not believe the truth but had pleasure in unrighteousness. – ESV (Shank)

Those who are lawless will embrace the lawless one. They will express the same nature of Satan the lawless one expresses. When the light of the Holy Spirit is taken out of the world with the rapture of the church, darkness will be unopposed for a season. Even now, the lawless are increasing in their influence. They are happy to hold Christians to the laws of God to gain advantage over them, but the lawless will not hold themselves to those same laws. They will not obey. They will take advantage of those who follow Christ, whom they believe to be fools and sheep to be slaughtered.

They are like those described in **Psalm 2**:
[*First David speaks.*]

> Why do the nations rage and the peoples plot in vain? The kings of the earth set themselves, and the rulers take counsel together, against the Lord and against His Anointed, saying, "Let us burst Their bonds apart and cast away Their cords from us." He Who sits in the heavens laughs; the Lord holds them in derision. Then He will speak to them in His wrath, and terrify them in His fury, saying, "As for Me, I have set My King on Zion, My Holy Hill."

[*Then His Anointed King Jesus speaks:*]

> I will tell of the decree: The Lord said to Me, "You are My Son; today have I begotten You. Ask of Me, and I will make the nations Your heritage, and the ends of the earth Your possession. You shall break them with a rod of iron and dash them in pieces like a potter's vessel."

[*Then David speaks again:*]

> Now therefore, O kings, be wise; be warned, O rulers of the earth. Serve the Lord with fear and rejoice with trembling. Kiss the Son, lest He be angry, and you perish in the way, for His wrath is quickly kindled. Blessed are all who take refuge in Him. – ESV (*Shank*)

There are many more verses that refer to what will happen to those who reject Christ and follow the antichrist. But my purpose in writing this chapter is to warn *believers* about being deceived by the root sin of lawlessness. When I say root, I'm not saying real Christians are still rooted in Satan. A real Christian is joined to Christ by the Holy Spirit. We now have the new nature of Christ—the old nature is dead. The point of the inventories I've offered is to provide some effective tools for breaking up our fallow ground, by exposing patterns of behavioral response to temptation that lead us into sin. Many of these were formed before we were children of God, when we had the old nature of Satan. We will remain unfruitful in areas of life where the Plow of the Holy Spirit has not yet been invited to turn over the soil. Those places will be where seeds of the Word just lie on the hard ground and the birds will carry them off before they can germinate, or the seeds of the Spirit that will be choked out by cares of the world.

In **Psalm 2**, this phrase is key: "Let us burst Their bonds apart and cast away Their cords from us." In other words, "Let's cut free from the moral restraints of God and His Son, that hold us back from what we want to do. We will not have Them rule over us." This sort of thing is to be expected from those who are still vessels of Satan. But great evil is still possible for Christians who are willfully rebellious in their ways.

1 Timothy 1:18-20 says:
> This charge I entrust to you, Timothy, my child, in accordance with the prophecies previously made about you, that by them you may wage the good warfare, holding faith in good conscience. By rejecting this, some have made shipwreck of their faith, among whom are Hymenaeus and Alexander, whom I have handed over to Satan that they may learn not to blaspheme.
> – ESV (Shank)

We will study prophetic utterance and individual callings in the body of Christ later (in **Chapter 18 - Personal Gifts of the Spirit** and in **Chapter 19 - Motivational and Office Gifts of the Spirit**). But what is more relevant to our discussion here is the harm to one's faith and conscience as a result of willfully disobeying the Holy Spirit.

I believe the conscience is a component of our human spirit. It helps us maintain integrity with what we know is right. But what the conscience knows is right, must be informed by the Word of God, just as it had previously been misinformed by the lies of Satan. When I obey the Word of God, I bear His righteous fruit. This is a willful disobedience of what Satan wants me to do. On the other hand, if I willfully disobey the Word of God and obey Satan's call to rebel, I will bear the fruit of sin even if I am a Christian. I get fooled sometimes, and sometimes I willfully disobey, but I must always repent because my sin has put me out of integrity with the Word, out of integrity with the Spirit, out of integrity with true fellowship, and out of integrity with my own conscience. Without repentance, sinful fruit abounds. Without repentance, shame and doubt rightly begin to set in and shipwreck my faith.

The Parable of the Sower
Matthew 13:13-23 says:

> This is why I speak to them in parables, because seeing they do not see, and hearing they do not hear, nor do they understand. Indeed, in their case the prophecy of Isaiah is fulfilled that says:

> "You will indeed hear but never understand,
> and you will indeed see but never perceive.
> For this people's heart has grown dull,
> and with their ears they can barely hear,
> and their eyes they have closed,
> lest they should see with their eyes
> and hear with their ears
> and understand with their heart
> and turn, and I would heal them."
> (From Isaiah 6:9-10)

> But blessed are your eyes, for they see, and your ears, for they hear. For truly, I say to you, many prophets and righteous people longed to see what you see, and did not see it, and to hear what you hear, and did not hear it.

> Hear the parable of the sower: When anyone hears the Word of the Kingdom and does not understand it, the evil one comes and snatches away what has been sown in his heart. This is what is sown along the path. As for what is sown on rocky ground, this is the one who hears the Word and immediately receives it with joy, yet he has no root in himself, but endures for a while, and when tribulation or persecution arises on account of the Word, immediately he falls away. As for what is sown among thorns, this is the one who hears the Word, but the cares of the world and the deceitfulness of riches choke the Word, and it proves unfruitful. As for what was sown in good soil, this is the one who

hears the Word and understands it. He indeed bears fruit and yields, in one case a hundredfold, in another sixty, and in another thirty. – ESV

What are the possibilities to explain the presence of longstanding, willful disobedience in a Christian?

1. One possibility is that I am not a real Christian after all. The Word does not resonate in me because my spirit is not really alive to God. I am a cultural or philosophical Christian, not one who is born again.

2. If I have become a Christian but do not understand, it is because I do not want to understand, not because I cannot understand. There is something willful about it, like not bothering to pursue the Lord to understand Him, or I want to preserve some privilege of sin I do not wish to give up.

3. Another possibility is that I have allowed myself to be persuaded to believe faith can't really change me because I still believe that what my flesh wants is what I want, and so become discouraged because I have regarded myself according to the flesh and not according to the spirit. (More regarding spirit and flesh is described in **Chapter 4 - My Nature Is My Spirit.**)

4. Or I may remain soulish in my thinking, like those in **1 Corinthians 3:1-3.** My mind is motivated to believe in times of great need, but when the need passes, I fall away. Or I obey when I'm in a mood that lifts me, and then disobey when I am no longer in that mood. (More of this is described in **Chapter 5 - Soul & Spirit.**)

5. There are times when I refuse to suffer for the sake of righteousness. I dread the pain of rejection by others when taking faith stands, or I resist the pain of withdrawal from behaviors that once gave me comfort, power or safety. I may resent the cost of discipleship, or I fear it. (These root sins of resentment and fear are described in **Chapters 9 & 10** respectively.)

6. Or I may just believe I can have it both ways. I want both God and my sin, so I exploit and abuse the Grace given by God to sin now and be sorry later. But this binge and purge behavior can diminish how sorry I actually am as time goes by, and it may eventually cause me to stop returning for forgiveness because of an increase in contempt for the Lord.

Contempt is blasphemy and can cause me to steer my ship into a reef to be destroyed. It is the inverse of the exhortation above in **1 Timothy 1:18-20**. Instead of holding faith in a good conscience, contempt is holding faith with a bad conscience. The fear of the Lord is the beginning of wisdom. If I lose it, I will be lost on the reef. **James 1:7** says, "the double-minded man is unstable in all his ways, and he can receive nothing from the Lord." This is often the case if I continually let the mindset of my flesh rule over the mindset of my spirit.

Do I know the answer for this corruption of conscience? **Yes.** Christ was tempted in every way as I am, but He did not sin. He not only suffered temptation, but also endured outrageous and unjust abuse! So then, who am I? I now have Christ's nature, so I can do as Christ did regarding temptation. My flesh is mine, but it is not me. I must persevere in faith. I must not be a fair-weather Christian who loves the free bread, miracles, insights, and being part of an exciting movement but then leaves Christ when the **cost** of discipleship is realized. That's what happens to seed that falls on stony soil, or seed that springs up quickly but then withers away because it has shallow soil that will only produce shallow roots, or seed that gets choked out by the cares of the world.

It has proved to be wonderful news that I can change the soil of my heart by believing I have the new nature revealed in the Word. I can access that truth and bring it into the everyday reality of my life by *acting as if* the Word of God is true, by making obedient choices in accordance with it. I am learning to obey Christ, my new Master, and to disobey Satan, my old master. I will always bear the fruit of the one I obey.

1 Samuel 15:22,23 says, regarding Saul's disobedience to God:
> Has the Lord as great delight in burnt offerings and sacrifices, as in obeying the Voice of the Lord? Behold, to obey is better than sacrifice, and to listen [*choose to pay attention and understand*] than the fat of rams. For rebellion is like the sin of divination and presumption is as the iniquity and idolatry. Because you have rejected the Word of the Lord, He has also rejected you from being king. – ESV (*Shank*)

Divination is an occult practice of summoning a spirit to serve the purposes of the witch or sorcerer. The diviner commands the spirits to perform tasks, execute curses, reveal hidden truths, et cetera. The evil spirit is to do the will of the diviner who *acts as if* he has divine authority. Rebellion against God, the Father of spirits, is putting my will above His will, like a conjurer. (More of this is described in **Chapter 15 – False Spirituality**.) Saul abused the authority God gave him by putting himself above the will of the Lord. This arrogance steadily worsened in Saul and arrogance becomes steadily worse in me if I do not repent. But God is no fool. He will not let that happen for long without doling out consequences. I must pay attention to those consequences when they come.

1 Timothy 4:1-2 says:
> Now the Spirit expressly says that in later times some will depart from the faith by devoting themselves to deceitful spirits and teachings of demons, through the insincerity of liars whose consciences have been seared, – ESV

Evil spirits will seem to give the witch, or even the disobedient believer, power to do what they want to do by granting them what their disobedience is seeking. This is because God will let me have what I want more than Him—if I persist in disobedience. At the same time, those spirits are corrupting faith and confidence of the disobedient, with false doctrine. The tendency of my flesh is to design my theology to conform to what I want to have permission to do. The tendency of my spirit, which is joined to Christ, is to want to *receive* my theological understanding from the Word of God and obey it, even when it hurts. When willful disobedience becomes a way of life, a moral inversion will eventually occur. Good becomes evil and evil becomes good.

In **2 Timothy 4:1-4**, Paul says to Timothy:

> I charge you in the presence of God and of Christ Jesus Who is to judge the living and the dead, and by His appearing and His kingdom: preach the Word; be ready in season and out of season; reprove, rebuke and exhort, with complete patience and teaching. For the time is coming when people will not endure sound teaching, but by having itching ears they will accumulate for themselves teachers to suit their own passions and will turn away from listening to the truth and wander off into myths. – ESV

The root of lawlessness draws on the desire of the flesh to disobey God. All believers have rebellious thoughts and urges. This comes from the enemy through the weakness of the flesh, as we have said. The flesh cannot be changed, but it will be destroyed. In Christ, we will receive a new body in the life to come which will never die and will not resist the will of God. In this life, I must persevere in living from the power of the Spirit of Christ in me, to overcome the world, the flesh and the devil, as Christ Himself did in His mortal body.

Unconditional Eternal Security & the Perseverance of Faith
1 Corinthians 6:9-11 says:

> Or do you not know that the unrighteous will not inherit the kingdom of God? Do not be deceived: neither the sexually immoral, nor idolaters, nor adulterers, nor men who practice homosexuality, nor thieves nor the greedy, nor drunkards, nor revilers, nor swindlers will inherit the kingdom of God. And such were some of you. But you were washed, you were sanctified, you were justified in the Name of the Lord Jesus Christ and by the Spirit of our God. – ESV (*Shank*)

The church in many parts of the world is ten miles wide but only a few inches deep. When the heat is turned up in tribulation, much of the church may evaporate, leaving clusters of puddles where only the deeper faith remains. One contributing factor is the moral passivity caused by the concept of *unconditional* eternal security for believers. It runs something like this:

> "I went forward in a meeting and gave my life to Christ. Or, I was baptized at birth. Now I'm free from the Judgment even if I don't go to church or change in any real way. Don't you dare raise any questions about the way I live to make me doubt my salvation. It's a done deal—I confessed Jesus as my Savior. We all sin, but I'll go to heaven in the end because I took the free gift. The evangelist said all I have to do is confess Jesus is Lord and my sins would be forgiven. I did that—now leave me alone."

Or the hollow comfort given the distraught mother at the funeral of her hell-raising son,

> "...but when he was a boy, he gave his life to Christ at Bible Camp, so he's in heaven now."

The truth is, we are not to say who is in heaven or not; God is the judge. It is our place as believers to warn and encourage faith and to work out our own salvation with fear and trembling. Please don't misunderstand me; I can have confidence that I am saved. There is an inner knowing that I belong to Christ when the Spirit bears witness to my spirit that I am His (**Galatians 4:6,7**). But eternal security is not unconditional. In addition to whatever the experience of a salvation moment may have been, there needs to be the clarity of **1 John 1:5-2:6** which says:

> This is the message we have heard from Him and proclaim to you, that God is light and in Him there is no darkness at all. *If* we say we have fellowship with Him while we walk in darkness, we lie and do not practice the truth. But *if* we walk in the light, as He is in the light, we have fellowship with one another, and the Blood of Jesus His Son cleanses us from all sin. *If* we say we have no sin we deceive ourselves, and the truth is not in us. *If* we confess our sins, He is faithful and just to forgive us our sins and to cleanse us from all unrighteousness. *If* we say we have not sinned, we make Him a liar, and His Word is not in us.

> My little children, I am writing these things to you that you may not sin. But *if* anyone does sin, we have an advocate with the Father, Jesus Christ the Righteous. He is the propitiation (*the Sacrifice that bears God's wrath and restores God's favor*) for our sins, and not ours only but also the sins of the whole world. And by this we know that we have come to know Him, if we keep His commandments. Whoever says "I know Him" but does not keep His commandments is a liar, and the truth is not in him, but whoever keeps His Word, in him truly the love of God is perfected. By this we may know that we are in Him: whoever says he abides in Him ought to walk in the same way in which He walked. - ESV (*Shank*)

So, *if* I maintain an internal honesty with regular confession of sin and repentance and strive to obey Him, I remain in fellowship with Him.

If I do not maintain an internal honesty, I am out of fellowship with Him and open to deception because I am walking in darkness.

If I refuse to maintain a life of obedience to Him, I am not in Him, even if I had an experience after praying the salvation prayer.

If as a believer, I refuse to repent and obey, I will begin to fall away.

If I walk more and more in darkness and disobedience, my faith will become meaningless.

The Greek Tenses
Some things can be lost or misunderstood in the reading of the English translation from New Testament Greek like the emphasis present in the original grammar or syntax. I will attempt to summarize a few points from the words of a 19th century theologian named **Daniel Steele, D. D.** from his book *Milestone Papers*. The chapter is called **The Tense Readings of the New Testament** and is available as a small booklet from

RevivalClassics.com, if you wish to explore his position in more detail.

Steele says there is an important tension between verses and phrases referring to the *once-and-for-all acts* of God and to *continuous and perpetual acts* of man. What God did and what we are to do—both must be properly understood. (This was first mentioned in **Chapter 3**, under the heading: **God's Part and My Part**.)

An example of the **aorist** tense—or a once-and-for-all act—is in **Romans 6:6-7**:

> We know that our old self was crucified [*once-and-for-all*] with Him in order that the body of sin might be brought to nothing [*destroyed*], so that we would no longer be slaves to sin. For he who has died [*once-and-for-all*] has been set free from sin. – ESV (Steele)

This verse teaches there has been an instantaneous death stroke to the old nature, *once-and-for-all*. If the Word of God does not lie, I must believe that it is true by faith that is *continuous and perpetual*. It is my responsibility to persevere in believing this truth and apply it to the self-interest inclination of my soul, and the weakness of my flesh (as explained in **Chapters 4 & 5**). **John 5:24** says, with two strong present tense examples:

> Truly, truly, I say to you, whoever hears [*continuously*] My Word and believes [*perpetually*] Him who sent Me has eternal life. – ESV (Steele)

There is an essential quality of perseverance to faith, not just a mental agreement that something is true. My part is not just doctrinal agreement. It's not just a one-time moment of faith with no follow-through. The acts of God are instantaneous. My acts as a believer are to be faithful by being continuous and persevering. One might say faith is a habit of believing, a habit or practice of righteousness. By the same token, the old habit of seeing myself as a slave to sin must now be rejected. God has given me grace to learn how to do this in Christ. The more I persevere in learning to live like this, the more fruit of the Spirit I will bear.

The overwhelming majority of verses referring to the *once-and-for-all* part God did and the *continuous and perpetual* part that I am to do, are clear. The only *once-and-for-all* part I can do is to choose to receive the Spirit of Christ into my spirit, making me a new creation, now possessing His new nature. That's because God Himself makes that choice a *once-and-for-all thing*! By the power of God, I am *once-and-for-all changed* into a person capable of righteous living. But I must persevere in believing this truth by making continuous and perpetual choices against temptation *as if* the Word of God does not lie!

Let us examine the profound mystery of **Hebrews 6:4-8**:

> For it is *impossible*, in the case of those who have *once been enlightened*, who have *tasted the heavenly gift*, and have shared in the Holy Spirit, and have *tasted the goodness of the Word of God* and the powers of the age to come, and *then* have fallen away, to restore them again to repentance, since they are *crucifying once again* the Son of God to their own harm and holding Him up to contempt. For land that has drunk the rain that often falls on it and produces a crop useful to those for whose sake it is cultivated, receives a blessing from God. But if it bears thorns and thistles, it is worthless and near to being *cursed*, and its *end is to be burned.*
> – ESV (*Shank*)

Yes, it is apparently possible to lose my salvation, but not because God is not faithful to keep me. If I am not faithful to believe and I allow myself to be deceived by persevering in disobedience, I may reach a point where I cannot be restored. Only God knows where this point is.

Even Paul says in **1 Corinthians 9:27**:

> But I discipline my body and keep it under control, lest after preaching to others I myself should be disqualified. [adokimos – *rejected*] – ESV (*Shank*)

Look at the force of **Hebrews 10:26-31**:

> For if we go on sinning deliberately *after receiving* the knowledge of the truth, there *no longer remains a sacrifice for sins*, but a fearful expectation of *judgment*, and a fury of fire that will consume *the adversaries.* Anyone

who sets aside the law of Moses dies without mercy on the evidence of two or three witnesses. How much worse punishment, do you think will be deserved by the one who has *spurned* the Son of God, and has *profaned* the Blood of the covenant by which He was sacrificed, and has *outraged* the Spirit of Grace?

For we know Him Who said, "Vengeance is Mine: I will repay." And again, "The Lord will judge His people." It is fearful thing to fall into the Hands of the Living God. – ESV (*Shank*)

I have heard so many say God was strict in the Old Testament, but because of Jesus, He is more compassionate. But this is not the line of reasoning in the New Testament book of Hebrews. If God was so severe a Judge when dealing with those of His people who rejected the laws of Moses, how much more severe will He be with His people in the church if they turn away from the grace of Christ!

Hebrews 10:32-39 goes on to say, regarding real Christians:

But recall the former days when, after you were enlightened, you endured a hard struggle with sufferings, sometimes being publicly exposed to reproach and affliction, and sometimes being partners with those who were so treated. For you had compassion on those in prison, and you joyfully accepted the plundering of your property, since you knew that you yourselves had a better possession and an abiding one. Therefore, do not throw away your confidence, which has a great reward. For you have need of endurance, so that when you have done the will of God you may receive what was promised. For, "Yet a little while, and the Coming One will come and without delay; but My righteous one will live by faith, and if he shrinks back [*falls away*], My Soul has no pleasure in him." (Habakuk 2:3-4) But we are not those who shrink back and destroyed [*utterly* apollumi], but those who have faith and preserve their souls. – ESV (Shank)

Can there be any doubt the plain reading of this text is directed toward Christians? How else do we explain the apostate church, the falling away, and the hearts that grow cold? In the **Book of Revelation Chapters 2-3**, the seven churches are warned that if they do not repent, there will be serious consequences. Those who remain faithful and overcome will receive rewards. In **Revelation 2:5**, Ephesus will suffer the *removal* of their lampstand from before the throne of God if they do not repent. Their whole church could be *rejected.*

In **Revelation 2:16**, the church in Pergamum is warned that the Lord will *come against* them with the Sword in His Mouth if they do not repent. Christ will *turn against* them. In **Revelation 2:20-23**, Thyatira is warned that those who still follow the Jezebel false prophetess will join in her afflictions and be *thrown* by Jesus into a great tribulation. In **Revelation 3:3**, Sardis is warned that if they will not wake up, Jesus Himself will suddenly *come against* them like a thief in the night. Those who remain faithful will not have their names *blotted out* of the Book of Life. Presumably then, those who do not repent *will be blotted out* of the Book of Life! In **Revelation 3:16**, Jesus says to Laodicea He will *spit them out* of His Mouth because they show their contempt for Him in being lukewarm.

Yikes! Am I in that place with my disobedience? Am I near to being cursed? Might I be thrown into the fire on the Last Day? *I am supposed to ask myself these questions!* This holy fear is in direct conflict with unconditional eternal security doctrine. The provocation of the fear of God is intended to drive away the contempt that allows me to stay in willful disobedience.

If I am tormented with this question, my faith is also provoked. If action in repentance is required, I am motivated to do something about it. But when I know I am persevering in my faith, I am fearless because I know I am in Him and He is in me.
Some may object to what I am saying, claiming this puts the Christian back under the Law. But we know salvation is impossible by keeping the Law. We can never earn our way to heaven. But the obedience of faith is meant to fulfill the moral Law as fruit, like Jesus did as the Pioneer and Perfector of our faith. By the inner witness of the Holy Spirit, the Lord has given us a clean conscience with a peaceful heart. When that

peace is troubled, we must seek Him and attend to what He shows us.

But you may ask, the New Testament says by faith *alone* we are saved. It says Abraham's faith was counted as righteousness before the Law was even given. You make it sound like faith + works = salvation. In reply I say, **yes** Abraham was saved by his faith alone, before the circumcision sign, but in **Genesis 26:4-5**, the Lord says to Isaac regarding the faith of his father Abraham:

> I will multiply your offspring as the stars of heaven and will give to your offspring all these lands. And in your offspring, all the nations of the earth shall be blessed, because Abraham obeyed My Voice and kept My *charge*, My *commandments*, My *statutes*, and My *laws*.
> – ESV (Shank)

My point is the same as the book of James. Salvation faith in Christ is to produce good works in Christ. We are new creations in Him. His faith is empowering ours. Do we all fall short of the glory of God? **Yes.** Do some do better than others? **Yes.** Will some receive greater rewards because of their fruit? **Yes.** Will others with less fruit still be saved? **Yes.** Is it possible for me to lose my salvation if I live a life of disobedience and contempt toward God? **Yes.** But it is not for you or me to say who will go to heaven and who will go to hell. Love must encourage and warn one another to be *continuous and perpetual* in our perseverance of faith, lest we be disqualified.

Do I have a problem with an expectation of needing to be perfect in order to be right with God? Then I have not understood the grace of God and need to be persevering with the Lord for the right understanding of the Gospel. God has given me grace to learn how to overcome in that area, too.

Do I have an inability to receive from God? Then there are still self-serving prideful conceits in my believing, and I have fallow ground that needs to be plowed. But in Christ, I have grace to learn how to overcome that as well.

The Root of Lawlessness must be cut off; it is more serious than the roots of bitterness, fear, and shame in the believer, because it draws from all three of them in its **conceits**. It is a direct rejection of the authority of God and the sacrifice of Christ, which produces a cold hard heart. It is very important to remember

Romans 10:6-11:

> But the righteousness based on faith says, "Do not say in your heart, 'Who will ascend into heaven?' (that is, to bring Christ down) or 'Who will descend into the abyss?' (that is to bring Christ up from the dead). But what does it say? "The word is near you, in your mouth and in your heart" (that is the Word of faith that we proclaim); because, if you confess with your mouth that Jesus is Lord and believe in your heart that God raised Him from the dead, you will be saved. For the Scripture says, "Everyone who believes *continuously and perpetually* in Him will not be put to shame." – ESV (*Shank}*

Romans 11:21 says:

> For if God *did not spare* the natural branches [Israel] *neither will He spare* you [Christian]. Note then the kindness and severity of God: severity towards those who have *fallen,* but kindness to you, provided you continue in His kindness. Otherwise you too [Christian] will be *cut off.* – ESV (*Shank*)

But you may say, what about verses like **2 Corinthians 1:22,** does it not say I am *sealed* in Christ? Are you saying God will take His Spirit away from a Christian?

> And it is God Who establishes us with you in Christ, and has anointed us, and Who has also put His *seal* on us and given us His Spirit in our hearts as a guarantee.
> – ESV (*Shank*)

And **Ephesians 1:13,14** that says:

> In Him you also, when you heard the Word of Truth, the gospel of your salvation, and believed in Him, were *sealed* with the promised Holy Spirit Who is the guarantee of our inheritance until we take possession of it, to the praise of His glory. – ESV (*Shank*)

Does this mean that after all we have been saying about my having a new nature in Christ and being in union with Him by the Holy Spirit thus creating a new man who loves righteousness—that God could take all that away from me? Am I not *sealed* in Him? Is not the Spirit in me a *guarantee*?

To that we can only say, look at **Romans 4:11,16**, regarding seals and guarantees in God's covenant with Abraham:

> He received the sign of circumcision as a *seal* of righteousness that he had by faith while he was still uncircumcised... That is why it depends on faith, in order that the promise may rest on grace and be guaranteed to all his offspring—not only to the adherent of the law but also to the one who shares the faith of Abraham, who is the father of us all. - ESV (*Shank*)

So, we can rightly conclude that the seals and the guarantees show God's good faith to us, but we must respond to that good faith toward Him with the righteous fruit of faith, or we break His seal. Did the circumcision seal of Israel save them when they turned away from God? **No.** If we in the church *spurn* the faith, *trample on* the Blood of Sacrifice, and *outrage* the Spirit of Grace, we will be *cut off.*

We must persevere in faith, not shrink back. Remember what we read in **Hebrews 10:26-31**. If Israel, without the indwelling Spirit was *cut off* for turning from the Law of Moses, *how much more* will the consequences be if we—who have been bought by the Blood of Christ and have been given the Holy Spirit—*turn away!* If those who were given little were cut off for *rejecting* what was given them, how much more will those who are given much be *cut off* if they *turn away* from the Lord? We must revere the whole Council of God; not just believe the verses we like and ignore the rest.

The fear of the Lord is the beginning of **wisdom**. The fear of the Lord is **clean**. Let us, like Paul, work out our salvation with fear and trembling, making integrity with God in our ways the highest priority. The joys of heaven await those who will believe by mixing faith with the Word and bearing righteous fruit.

But what about **John 10:27-30?**

> My sheep *hear* My Voice, and I know them, and they
> *follow* Me. I give them eternal life and they will never
> perish, and no one will snatch them out of My Hand.
> My Father Who has given them to Me, is greater than
> all, and no one is able to snatch them out of the Father's
> Hand. I and the Father are One. – ESV (*Shank*)

As Dr. Dale Yocum says, "Let us assert thankfully that this is a
beautiful passage about the security of the believer... we rejoice
in every Bible passage which proclaims (the believer's) assur-
ance and security; and there are many of them." but it is not
unconditional. It is for those who *hear* Christ's Voice and *follow* Him. It must be interpreted in the light of all the verses
referring to the subject. We can be assured that the Father's
Hand holds those of us who are believers, but our part is the
hearing and the *following*. Unbelievers are not His sheep, only
believers are His sheep. This passage does not include believers
who have chosen unbelief and unrepentant sin.
(See *CREEDS IN CONTRAST* by Dr. Dale Yocum pp. 144-146)

The foundation of the Reformation was to re-establish **Sola
Scriptorum**, Latin for the basis of all faith to be on the *scriptures alone*. Scripture must inform our theology. Our theology
must not force scripture to conform to what we want it to say.

Revelation 22:19 says:

> and if anyone takes away from the words of the book of
> this prophecy, God will *take away his share* in the Tree
> of Life and in the holy city that is described in this
> book. – ESV (Shank)

Only a believer has a share in the Tree of Life, and it can be
taken away from him. His share in eternal life is not unconditional.

John 15:6 says:

> If anyone does not abide in Me he is thrown away like a
> branch and withers, and the branches are gathered,
> thrown into the fire, and burned. – ESV (*Shank*)

To be a branch that is cut off, one must first have been part of the Vine.

But **Romans 8:38-39** says:

> For I am sure that neither death nor life, nor angels nor rulers, nor things presenter things to come, nor powers, nor height nor depth, nor anything else can separate us from the love of God in Christ Jesus our Lord. – ESV

God's love is not in question. But our abiding faithfulness to Him, is.

2 John 8-9 says:

> Watch yourselves so that you may not *lose* what we have worked for, but that you may win a full reward. Everyone who goes on ahead and *does not abide in* the teaching of Christ, does not have God. Whoever *abides* in the teaching has both the Father and the Son. – ESV (*Shank*)

We cannot *lose* what we never had. But we can lose Him if we don't abide in Him by keeping the teaching. But there is wonderful security that comes in following the teaching of God's Word. This is real security. God is love, He cannot deny His Own Nature. But His love has both kindness and severity.

Luke 12:10 Jesus says:

> And anyone who speaks a word against the Son of Man will be forgiven, but the one who blasphemes against the Holy Spirit will *not* be forgiven. – ESV (*Shank*)

Matthew 6:14,15 Jesus says:

> For if you forgive others their trespasses, your Heavenly Father will also forgive you, but if you do not forgive others their trespasses, *neither* will your Father your trespasses. – ESV (*Shank*)

Crisis

At this point you may say, "John, you are bringing me down, I hate what you are saying, this does not edify or build me up. In fact, you are attacking my confidence in my salvation in Christ. This is too severe, this is law." But as was quoted above, "be-

hold the kindness and severity of God." If our foundational assumptions are in the error that we can do whatever we want
and still be saved, we stay shallow, stop growing or even stop
listening to the conviction of the Holy Spirit—and trample on
the Blood of Jesus.

My lack of love for the Lord, my ingratitude that breeds grumbling contempt, my resistance to sacrifice all come from a refusal to see my own sin without understanding how Satan has
his way with me through my flesh.

Romans 7:13 says:
> Did that which is good, [the Law] bring death to me? By
> no means! It was sin, producing death in me through what
> is good, in order that sin might be shown to be sin, and
> through the commandment might become sinful beyond
> measure. – ESV

Notice when King Josiah heard the Law for the first time.
2 Chronicles 34:19,21 says:
> And when the king heard the words of the Law, he tore
> his clothes. ...Go, inquire of the Lord for me and for those
> who are left in Israel and Judah, concerning the words of
> the book that was found. For great is the wrath of the
> Lord that is poured out against us, because our fathers
> have not kept the words of the Lord, to do according to all
> that is written in this book. – ESV

My sin conviction is supposed to pierce my conscience made
dull by willful disobedience. My understanding of my sin's
gravity fills me with awe for the greater gravity of Christ's sacrifice, and inspires my heart to love Him all the more. I must
fear to insult Him again, and my soul must fear His wrath.
Those who have been forgiven much, love much, and we have
been forgiven more that we have begun to imagine. When we
"wrestle with the angel for blessing," we take our sonship with
Him seriously.

The "nothing to worry about" attitude of *unconditional* eternal
security is as harmful as the "bondage to performance" in perfectionism or legalism. Both are wrong and neither is the anti-

dote of the other. But holy fear of the Lord is the beginning of wisdom. The fear of the Lord is **clean**. Let us like Paul, work out our salvation with fear and trembling, making **integrity** with God in our ways, the highest priority. We are not saved by perfection, but by grace alone. But the joys of heaven await those who will believe by mixing faith with the Word and bearing righteous fruit, through obedience.

Remember what was said in **Romans 10:6,7**. To bring Christ down is to elevate myself above Him Who is my Judge. To raise Christ from the dead is only something God can do. It is not for me to say what will happen to others, that is not my job. My job is to fear the Lord, believe and obey Him, and warn my brothers and sisters to do the same—*lest we outrage* the Spirit of Grace and *be lost.*

My Lawlessness Inventory

1. List the ways I am resisting the will of God in my life.

2. List the excuses I make for that resistance.

3. What are the consequences for my disobedience?

4. What has God been unable to give me because of my resistance to Him?

5. What has God already given me to be able to obey?

6. Repent of each of them with *continuous and perpetual acts of faith* from **the power** of who I really am in Christ.

13

Male & Female Relationship Conceits

The inventories of the previous chapters have probably re-vealed some **conceits**—those self-serving assumptions, false securities, false dangers, unreal expectations, and ruthless enti-tlements that proceed from Satan through the mindset of the flesh, giving **license** to sin. These affect our thinking and be-havior from early childhood as our immature minds draw con-clusions to make sense of the circumstances of our family rela-tionships, traumas, unmet needs, et cetera. As we become adults with greater understanding and our powers of reason mature, we see that some of these assumptions are not true and often even harmful. But **conceits** left unchallenged will continue to act as invisible filters that distort what we per-ceive to be the truth.

As we have been saying, in a willful **conceit**, I make a deal to give myself permission to do something I should not, or to take advantage of someone in a wrongful way. To pacify my con-science, I will contrive a lofty reason to do a low thing. But, through a guilty conscience, these sinful choices begin to influ-ence who I believe I am. If I am reborn of the Spirit of Christ, my confidence in that reality can also be harmed by these **con-ceits** when they bear their inevitable fruit. How can I say I have the righteous nature of Christ when I just did *that*?

Who I believe I am also convinces me of who I believe I am not. Whichever master I obey gives evidence, true or false, as to whom I believe I belong. There will be fruit or consequences from those choices. **Conceits** become self-fulfilling prophecies in later life, as I follow what I misbelieve to be my way. The one with whom I identify defines what I believe I need, to be satisfied. My behavior is the expression of what I do to get what I need, to protect it, to use it, and to get more of it. Some behaviors express themselves as reflexive or automatic coping skills: hiding, lying, bullying, backstabbing, gossip, mockery, and the like. I believe it's very important to remember that I began with an identity that was shaped by the self-for-myself nature of Notgod, who still ruthlessly exploits my weaknesses in the flesh. He originally shaped my identity into a vehicle to express his sinful nature through me. By believing I have a new nature in Christ, I will learn to overcome if I practice making choices *as if* the Word of God is true. **Psalm 51:6** says:

> Behold, You delight in truth in the inward being, and You teach wisdom in the secret heart. – ESV

The basis for all intimacy is internal honesty. I cannot be in a relationship with God or anyone else without first being honest with myself. If I'm willfully naïve or unaware of what's going on within me, I will wrongly perceive what is happening around me with wrong perceptions or wrong assumptions. How can I possibly build anything real with others?

But we are afraid of real intimacy because we are afraid of the moral transparency of truth. We say we long for deep intimacy because we feel lonely. We want someone to meet our need. We want to be unconditionally loved, but our flesh does not want to pay the price of unconditional love in return. The flesh only wants to be cared for, but the Spirit of Christ wants to sacrificially care for others. The legitimate self-focus of the **soul** is to love and be loved—to understand and to be understood. But when the flesh resists the full engagement of our responsibility in fulfilling our part in this, we become weary, fearful, and dishonest about our motives.

The following examples of self-delusional patterns, or **conceits**, reveal a path to failure in the development of true intimacy or the capacity for a deep relationship.

When we're young, we don't plan to grow up to become someone who will be divorced, or who aborted a child, or whose body is ruined by STDs, or who lives with an abusive or cheating partner, or who will die alone without friends, or be an unmarried parent. But these kinds of things will happen to many of us if we don't strive to know and to act on the truth about ourselves and the truth about others, in the context of the truth about God. Since whom we will marry is the second most important decision we will make in life, we must guard our hearts and not "awaken love before its time" (**Song of**

Songs 3:5). The only decision more important than the one involving our marriage relationship is the one regarding our relationship with Jesus Christ.

I began with the flesh and a fallen nature, but I am called to put on Christ, to receive a new nature by the union of His Holy Spirit in my human spirit. With the power to put to death the deeds of the flesh, I am now a new creation in Christ.

1 Corinthians 15:42-49 says:

> So it is with the resurrection of the dead. What is sown is perishable; what is raised is imperishable. It is sown in dishonor; it is raised in glory. It is sown in weakness; it is raised in power. It is sown a natural body; it is raised a spiritual body. If there is a natural body, there is also a spiritual body. Thus it is written: "The first Adam became a living being;" the last Adam became a life-giving Spirit. But it is not the spiritual that is first but the natural, and then the spiritual. The first man was from the earth, a man of dust; the second Man is from heaven. As was the man of dust, so also are those who are of the dust, and as is the Man of heaven, so also are those who are in heaven. Just as we have borne the image of the man of dust, we shall also bear the image of the Man of heaven. – ESV

I am indebted to **Anne Wilson Schaef** and her book *Escape from Intimacy* for her collected observations. Although she does not address the Biblical spirituality of these issues, and seems to have no personal intimacy with Christ, her book has provided a wonderful opportunity for me to address God's Word with her data. In what follows, notice the recurring **conceits** and sinful payoffs that hinder or blindside the truth. These will continue to operate where they hide in my fallow ground—until I let the Holy Spirit plow my soul.

I must have my eyes wide open about myself as well as what may be true about the one to whom I am attracted. I must be prepared to see myself as either victim or perpetrator in the examples below. For what false payoffs am I selling out the truth? How have I made a skill out of lying, or how have I made a skill out of believing the lies of others? On pages **103 – 105** of *Escape from Intimacy,* Schaef lists a number of Pseudo-Relationship Skills I will label as **Schaef**. I have grouped similar false skills from her list.

Magical Thinking

My soul's desire without the influence of the spirit, causes me to see what it wants to see, not what is there. I seek to maintain the excitement of an emotional high at all costs because my welfare is tied to the object of my desire. The other person becomes either a tool for my agenda or an idol for my devotion. The following are examples of false intimacy skills with similar agenda attitudes and personal payoffs.

1. Schaef: "To be able to establish instant intimacy or quickly recognize a perfect mate, knowing nothing about the other person. This is 'love at first sight,' or desire without facts, creating a platform for seduction."

- I make a choice to believe what I want to be true without trying to find out what is actually true.
- The **conceit**: I can have an easy connection with you without breaking the spell of the moment.
- The *payoff:* You can be my ride for a while.

Psalm 36:1,2 says:

> Transgression speaks to the wicked deep in his heart. There is no fear of God before his eyes. For he flatters himself in his own eyes that his iniquity cannot be found out and hated. – ESV

2. Schaef: "To be able to pour out your life story and divulge intimate secrets without first establishing genuine trust. This is desire without boundaries, showing too much too soon in order to create a vehicle for an intimacy *con* to operate."

- One is deceived by the apparent openness of the other into revealing vulnerabilities that may later be exploited.
- The **conceit**: I can quickly form a sympathetic attachment with you to con you into dropping your guard.
- The *payoff:* I can help myself to what I want from you.

207

Psalm 119:29 says:

> Put false ways far from me and graciously teach me Your law! – ESV

3. Schaef: "To lunge ahead into a relationship based on a physical attraction or lust without giving reality a chance."

- This is desire without considering anything but *genital reasoning* and self-gratification, "hooking up," or "friends with benefits.
- The **conceit:** It's only sex, we're both adults with needs, we both get a little excitement and validation with no strings attached, and no one gets hurt.
- The *payoff:* I can get you to please my body without having to make a real commitment to you.

2 Timothy 3:13 says:

> ...evil people and impostors will go from bad to worse, deceiving and being deceived. – ESV

4. Schaef: "To be able, by intuition, to explain or understand the other person, not needing facts. Thinking we know what is hidden inside someone by convincing ourselves we have special powers."

- In fact, we just want to give our flesh permission to have what it wants. Women who stay involved with immature men must often resort to drawing upon their maternal instincts to stay in the relationship. Later they find themselves rejected because a man does not want to marry his mother, or he feels like he has become a project. On the other hand, men can push boundaries with immature women through exploiting flattery, or with an obsession mistaken for devotion. ˙
- The **conceit** for both: I know what you want—you have a desperate need for *me.*
- The *payoff:* I don't have to be *responsible* or consider the consequences to get what I want from you.

Psalm 36:3,4 says:

> the words of his mouth are trouble and deceit; he has ceased to act wisely and do good. He plots trouble on

his bed; he sets himself up in a way that is not good; he does not reject evil. – ESV

5. Schaef: "To be able to ignore other facets of life, in both parties, to keep the fantasy alive. Both parties make a deal to select only what supports their desire agenda. Does the other person have children? A mate? A demanding work obligation? Huge debt? Or a criminal record?"

- The **conceit**: I only have to see what I want to see. Everything will just work itself out because we love each other.
- The *payoff*: We don't have to spoil the magic of the moment by being responsible.

Luke 14:28-30 says:

For, which of you, desiring to build a tower, does not first sit down and count the cost, whether he has enough to complete it? Otherwise, when he has laid a foundation and is not able to finish, all who see it begin to mock him, saying, this man began to build and was not able to finish. – ESV

6. Schaef: "To be able to ignore faults and unshared values, hopes, and fears with a person you do not even trust or like."

- Some love to be flattered by seduction, to be desired. Others choose money or prestige. Some are just afraid of having to live alone.
- The **conceit**: I can overlook your faults so I can get the other things I want from you.
- The *payoff*: When I focus on all I can get from you, I don't have to deal with me.

1 Corinthians 12:11 says:

When I was a child, I spoke like a child, I thought like a child, I reasoned like a child. When I became a man, I gave up childish ways. – ESV

7. Schaef: "To be able to force the other person into your own romantic fantasies with special props, songs and symbols, which have no meaning outside the relationship."

- Desire driven by dream ideals and scripts with roles everyone else is supposed to play in my own show, starring me.
- The conceit: I can be the star of my own movie and you can be in the cast, in a supporting role.
- The *payoff:* I get to live my fantasy.

Proverbs 30:32 says:

> If you have been foolish, exalting yourself, or if you have been devising evil, put your hand to your mouth." – ESV

The Victim Mentality

Many of us have been victims of accidents or abuse. These are real injuries that have caused real pain and consequences. We are not minimizing those injuries. But a victim mentality uses the past or ongoing suffering as leverage for power over others through entitlement. I take the position of moral superiority over others in the sense that other people owe me, because of the bad things that have happened to me. By obligation, sympathy, or demand, I am entitled because of all the trials or even abuse I have suffered. A refusal to forgive empowers this conceit, as well the right of revenge. Another form of the victim mentality is self-sacrifice with conditions attached. This is a way of buying control. When the sacrifice is given and the expected reward is not forthcoming, it is construed as a personal insult or another betrayal. One becomes a martyr, but not to the righteousness of God, but the self-serving idols of self-esteem through exploited relationships.

1. **Schaef:** "To define everything in terms of how the relationship is doing."
   - If things are going well, I am fine. If the relationship isn't working, it's all my fault. This is not as charitable as it seems. I may say this in order to avoid the bad news about rejection, abuse, or other painful truth about the character of my partner. I insist it's up to me to save it. Pride is a coin with two sides: heads—I'm the best, tails—I'm the worst.
   - The conceit: I must work harder to fix this, because I'm worthless if this fails.

- The *payoff*: I am the *key* in this relationship. This is my project, my power and my reputation to manage.

1 John 5:21 says:

> Little children, keep yourselves from idols. – ESV

2. Schaef: "To be able to constantly lay aside personal needs for the sake of the relationship beyond healthy give and take. I can't say no to excessive demand or have boundaries to protect the honest and true things that are part of real love."

- There is always suppressed rage inside, but I never seem to need to take responsible action for healthy change."
- The **conceit**: I am a martyr for love, so you owe me.
- The *payoff*: Moral superiority is my *drug*.

Proverbs 11:2 says:

> When pride comes, then comes disgrace, but with the humble is wisdom. – ESV

3. Schaef: "To know how to compromise personal needs or to suffer endlessly, even at the expense of family, children and work. Similar to the martyr, this is personal obsession with low esteem that makes one become a resentful doormat."

- It is also the lifestyle of adultery for the offended spouse, while the obsessed adulterer is oblivious to the impact at home.
- The **conceit**: I am nothing without you; I'm worthless, so I have to take this.
- The *payoff*: I'll get you to say how precious I am some-day, for all my sacrifice.

Galatians 4:7 says:

> ...so you are no longer a slave, but a son, and if a son, then an heir through God. – ESV

4. Schaef: "To be able to lose boundaries and spiritual values in order to keep the relationship going, destroying the power of the truth."

- I'm a slave without power, so I must sell myself out—in order to be valued by you.

- The **conceit**: I will do anything for peace and security.
- The *payoff*: So I won't be rejected and have nothing.

Psalm 24:4-5 says:

> Who shall ascend to the hill of the Lord? And who shall stand in His Holy place? He who has clean hands and a pure heart, who does not lift up his soul to what is false and does not swear deceitfully, he will receive blessings from the Lord and righteousness from the God of his salvation. – ESV

5. Schaef: "To accept blame for everything."

- The most futile way of life is perfectionism, and this is negative perfectionism and is shame-based. It can be a way of deflecting personal rejection by others, by focusing on personal performance. It also carries the presumption that I am supposed to be a god, the buck stops with me. As if everything is up to me. I am the prime actor.
- The **conceit**: It's not me you reject; it's what I'm still doing wrong—but I can fix it for both of us.
- The *payoff*: I don't have to put the truth to the test, by staying in control.

Job 38:12,13 says:

> Have you commanded the morning since your days began, and the dawn to know its place, that it might take hold of the skirts of the earth, and the wicked be shaken out of it? – ESV

6. Schaef: "To be able to interpret intensity and jealousy as love. This is the battered-wife (or emasculated-husband) syndrome."

- Positive and negative emotional intensity is the drug. As the saying goes, "...those who will live in passion's house must be passion's slave."
- The **conceit**: You really love me—you don't mean to hurt me.
- The *payoff*: I don't have to stand up to you and risk losing you.

Romans 1:24-25 says:

> Therefore God gave them up in the lusts of their hearts
> to impurity, to dishonoring of their bodies among
> themselves, because they exchanged the truth about
> God for a lie and worshiped and served the creature ra-
> ther than the Creator, Who is blessed forever! Amen.

7. Schaef: "To be able to *shut off* feelings and awareness to
hang on to what I think I have."

- This is my rationalization for having no faith to deal
  with the evil in me or in you. It's avoiding pain to keep
  from losing the relationship.
- The **conceit**: I can just shut down.
- The *payoff*. Then I don't have to feel this pain.

Proverbs 31:6,7 *says in irony.*

> ...give strong drink to those who are perishing, and
> wine to those in bitter distress; let them drink and for-
> get their poverty and remember their misery no more.
> – ESV

8. Schaef: "To feel that the relationship has you, you don't have
it. Drama is everything. Failure to develop real intimacy skills,
intense battles, and sacrificial demonstrations defines the relationship."

- Sustained unforgiveness produces endless feuds.
- The **conceit**: I know I'm alive because I have a vital role
  in this drama.
- The *payoff*. I will stay in control—the problem is you,
  not me!

Titus 3:3 says:

> for we ourselves were once foolish, disobedient, led
> astray, slaves to various passions and pleasures, passing
> our days in malice and envy, hated by others and hating
> one another. – ESV

The Chameleon

The Chameleon is a lizard that can conceal itself from prey by
changing color to blend in with its environment. As a negative

intimacy skill, this is a form of narcissism that rejects personal values or preferences as a tactic, in order to blend with the life of another in a parasitical way.

1. Schaef: "To be able to be whatever the other person wants me to be. This is like the role-playing prostitute or predatory male. To become a perpetual child who takes the easy way of the dependent. Or conversely become the hunter in disguise, out to capture prey. My true agendas are concealed."

- The **conceit**: I can be whoever you need me to be in order to have you.
- The *payoff:* I don't have to risk an honest commitment to have you.

Proverbs 6:23-24 says:

> For the commandment is a lamp and the teaching a light, and the reproofs of wisdom are a way of life, to preserve you from the evil woman, from the smooth tongue of the adulteress. – ESV

2. Schaef: "To be able to completely enter the other person's world, taking on his/her feelings and issues, to use that person to escape my own life."

- This is common with a shame-based personality or one who has suffered abandonment. Relationships can become a cult.
- The **conceit**: If I can attach myself to you, I can have value by sharing in your value.
- The *payoff:* I don't have to deal with my past or do the hard work to overcome it.

Romans 16:18 says:

> ... such persons do not serve our Lord Christ, but rather their own appetites, and by smooth talk and flattery, they deceive the hearts of the naïve. – ESV

3. Schaef: "To have the skill of looking intimately involved while keeping safe behind a wall. This can be a predator biding time, the hidden agenda of the emotionally dishonest, or the desperately lonely trying to be accepted."

- The **conceit**: I can pretend I belong with you to see what I can get.
- The *payoff:* You will not reject me if you don't know the real me.

Psalm 55:20-21 says:

> His speech was smooth as butter, yet war was in his heart; his words were softer than oil, yet they were drawn swords. – ESV

4. P-RS: "To be able to attach to others who like me first, but who they are or what they are like, doesn't matter."

- This is the egocentric standard of a needy or bottomless person who is afraid to risk rejection by being a responsible adult or exercising real faith to trust God.
- The **conceit**: If you show you want me first, I'll know how to make the next safe move.
- The *payoff:* I don't have to risk rejection.

Proverbs 27:7 says:

> One who is full loathes honey, but to one who is hungry everything bitter is sweet. – ESV

The Knight and the Nurse

This is a **conceit** of grandiose narcissism. Knights and nurses are rescuers who appear to be merciful and eager to serve, but they are secretly acting out a strategy that will make them indispensably attached to and affirmed by their relationship target.

1. Schaef: "To believe that I have the skill to save you from the life you have made for yourself."

- I can change you even if you do not want to change.
- The **conceit**: I am your hero.
- The *payoff:* You are my trophy.

Proverbs 26:12 says:

> Do you see a man who is wise in his own eyes? There is more hope for a fool than for him.

2. Schaef: "To know how to fix the other person and quickly move in to meet needs, to make myself feel more important or better."

- I use the needs of others to prop myself up.

- The **conceit**: I am your healer.
- The *payoff*: You are to be forever grateful and belong to me.

Romans 8:12,13 says:

> So then brothers, we are debtors, not to the flesh, to live according to the flesh. For if you live according to the flesh you will die, but if by the Spirit you put to death the deeds of the body, you will live. – ESV

3. **Schaef**: "To know how to foster dependency and attach to another by being needed."

- This is control by obligation and mutual strokes.
- The **conceit**: I am vital—you need to stay close to me.
- The *payoff*: I can tie you to me.

Proverbs 23:3 says:

> Do not desire his delicacies, they are deceptive food.
> – ESV

4. **Schaef**: "To be the sole source of meaning in the other's life."

- This is possessiveness, enslavement, and false martyrdom.
- The **conceit**: You are mine; you can't live without me.
- The *payoff*: I will never have to be alone because I have you.

Galatians 4:8-9 says:

> Formerly, when you did not know God, you were enslaved to those that by nature are not gods. But now that you have come to know God, or rather to be known by God, how can you turn back again to the weak and worthless elementary principles of the world, whose slaves you want to be once more?" – ESV

The Predator

The hunter or the huntress—who is ruthless—is not seeking true relationship but use it as a pretense to gratify selfish desires. They are only capable of loving themselves. In a very insightful book called *Healing the Wounded Heart, The Heartache of Sexual Abuse and Hope of Transformation* by **Dan B. Allender**, the author describes the predator's process of "grooming" the innocent or naïve by "reading" their prey and appealing to unmet needs, making he or she feel special. A false bond of trust is established and then exploited with arousal. Then the child or adolescent suffers betrayal and harm through sexual conquest.

The victim is left with rage over the violation, and with shame and guilt in the pleasure of the arousal, causing a conflict with lasting consequences. The trauma is hidden by secrets and buried deep inside. Adult victims of sexual abuse are frequently plagued with an inability to emotionally and physically give themselves to their mates in what may well be an otherwise normal and loving marriage relationship.

Because genuine loving words and touch resemble the grooming tactics of the predator, those actions become triggers that cause the victim to emotionally relive the trauma of sexual abuse, provoking resistance and shutdowns that reject real and genuine intimacy. The same exploitation of needs and vulnerabilities are the strategies for seduction by a predator in dating situations as well—when their target mistakes the grooming process for love.

1. Schaef: "To be able to form a connection, but not know how to be a friend."

- I'm out to get but not to give, I'm a user of people. I have no reciprocal response to your needs.
- The **conceit**: I can use you, but you can't use me.
- The *payoff*: I can get what I want and then move on.

Isaiah 13:11 says:

> I will punish the world for its evil, and the wicked for their iniquity; and lay low the pompous pride of the ruthless. – ESV

2. Schaef: "To be able to hook another person with manipulation and management of their impression of me, with an acceptable image."

- These are narcissistic seduction techniques of image projection.

- The **conceit**: I can control you by playing to your vanity.
- The *payoff*: I can have whatever I want from you, but you can't have the real me.

Proverbs 26:24-26 says:

> Whoever hates disguises himself with his lips and harbors deceit in his heart; when he speaks graciously, believe him not, for there are seven abominations in his heart; though his hatred be covered by deception, his wickedness will be exposed in the assembly. – ESV

3. **Schaef:** "To be able to use honesty as a con."

- I can fake intimacy—flattering you by sharing secrets—to create an impression of special intimacy.
- The **conceit**: What a woman wants is sincerity. Once you have that faked, you have it made. Or, what a man wants is to have his ego stroked. Once you have him flattered, you have it made.
- The *payoff*: Having it made.

Proverbs 26:28 says:

A lying tongue hates its victims, and a flattering mouth works ruin. – ESV

4. **Schaef:** "To be able to turn the tables when caught, induce sympathy, or escape responsibility for bad behavior. Cunning and slippery, they can successfully read the weaknesses of others while concealing their own. By being liars, they stay sick or addicted."

- The **conceit**: I'll always make you pay.
- The *payoff*: You can't make me take responsibility for myself.

Genesis31:41-42 says after Jacob speaking to Laban, his father-in-law:

> I served you fourteen years for your two daughters, and six years for your flock, and you have changed my wages ten times. If the God of my father, the God of Abraham and the fear of Isaac had not been on my side, surely now you would have sent me away empty handed.

God saw my affliction and the labor of my hands and rebuked you last night. – ESV

5. Schaef: "To develop skills in communication to form attachments while withholding true agendas."
- Bait and switch.
- The **conceit**: I can make you surrender to me by telling you what you want to hear.
- The *payoff*: Then I can ride you to where I want to go.

In **Genesis 30:30-36** After Jacob came to an agreement that he would take all the speckled and striped goats and sheep, leaving Laban all the pure and desirable sheep and goats:

> Laban said, "Good! Let it be as you have said." But that day Laban removed the male goats that were striped and spotted, and all the female goats that were spotted, every one that had white on it, and every lamb that was black, and put them in charge of his sons. And he set a distance of three days' journey between himself and Jacob, and Jacob pastured the rest of Laban's flock.
> – ESV

6. Schaef: "To never take **no** for an answer."
- This is about what I want, not what you want. Hardball control matters more than you do. To possess, not share.
- The **conceit**: I always get what I want.
- The *payoff*: I can have you, whether you want me or not.

1 Kings 21:1-16 says:

> When Naboth refused to sell his vineyard to Ahab, King of Israel. Queen Jezebel had false charges brought against Naboth so he would be stoned to death. Then she told her husband to take the vineyard, and he did. (summarized by Shank)

7. Schaef: "To be willing to make the other person a tool to get high, not a soul to be cherished. People are prey."
- The **conceit**: I matter, you don't.
- The *payoff*: I'll use you until I get tired of you.

2 Samuel 13:1-22 says:

> Tamar was raped by Amnon, then she was despised and cast off by him. (summarized by Shank)

It's important to be aware of false intimacy ploys. I have seen my behavior and assumptions in many of these examples. I've fallen for a lot of these tricks, too. I've even been manipulative in some of these ways. I deeply regret them. I'm grateful beyond measure for my forgiveness in Christ and the forgiveness by others. It makes it easier to forgive others when I see I have been no better in my ways than those who took advantage of me—because it is a holy thing to confront one's own unholiness—God heals and changes me.

Chapter 13 Study Questions

1. What is a pseudo-relationship skill or a false intimacy skill?

2. What is magical thinking in a relationship?

3. What is the manipulative power of the victim mentality?

4. What are the techniques of the chameleon?

5. What is self-serving about the knight and the nurse?

6. What is the ruthlessness of the predator?

7. What have I seen in myself and in others from these false intimacy skills?

14

Chapter 13 comprises "vertical bars" of **conceits** and *payoffs*. What follows is a set of "horizontal parallel bars" intersecting these **conceits** and *payoffs* bars, creating complex systems of life controlling behaviors and addictions. Together they form the grid of an iron prison door.

Narcissism & Relationship Addictions

Narcissists have either lost touch with or have rejected their true selves. They construct a false image of themselves to present to the world, *misbelieving* the false image is more useful in achieving personal needs and agendas. Maintaining this false image takes a lot of energy, but time will eventually reveal the real person beneath the image the narcissist tries to project.

From the examples in the previous chapter on true and false intimacy, we saw many **conceits** used to manipulate other people as tools to achieve sinful *payoffs*, often with ruthless tactics. We also saw conceits that enable ourselves to buy into the tactics of predators, by seeing only what we want to see. There are whole **systems of conceits** involved in maintaining this artificial identity projection. An artificial projection involves habits of self-manipulation that force the truth aside in favor of short-term gains, at the expense of considerable damage to the conscience. Many of us who are now believers come from narcissistic belief systems learned from our old master and refined to perfection in our old nature. As a new creation in Christ, we now have the grace to learn how to break these systems and patterns of unbelief and restore our conscience to integrity with the Truth.

Otto Kernberg, a prominent psychoanalyst, says, "narcissists present various combinations of intense ambition, grandiose fantasies, feelings of inferiority and over dependence on external admiration and acclaim ... with chronic dissatisfaction about themselves... with conscious and unconscious exploitiveness and ruthlessness toward others." - from *Narcissism, Denial of the True Self* by **Alexander Lowen, MD**.

Romans 1:28-32 says:

> And since they did not see fit to acknowledge God, God gave them up to a debased mind to do what ought not to be done. They were filled with all manner of unrighteousness, evil, covetousness, malice. They are full of envy, murder, strife, deceit, maliciousness. They are gossips, slanderers, haters of God, insolent, haughty, boastful, inventors of evil, disobedient to parents, foolish, faithless, heartless, ruthless. Though they know God's decree that those who practice such things deserve to die, they not only do them but give approval to those who practice them. – ESV

While these traits are common among those who have rejected God, those of us who say we believe must let the Spirit of God have His way in plowing our fallow ground, so that we can root out old conceits and begin to bear His fruit more effectively; otherwise, we will continue to bare Satan's fruit in willful blindness. Narcissism is a major component in both chemical and behavioral addictions. What follows are examples of behavioral addictions, which draw heavily upon the **conceits** of narcissism.

Sexual Addiction

Both men and women can be sexual addicts. Patrick Carnes says In OUT OF THE SHADOWS, "The addict substitutes a sick relationship for a healthy one with others. The addict's relationship with a mood-altering experience becomes central to life."

> **Level 1** – Addicts use pornography, strip shows, prostitutes, and commit frequent infidelity. Usually both parties are addicts.

> **Level 2** – Addicts are involved with voyeurism, exhibitionism, stalking, fetishes, and high-risk acting out. These behaviors can result in civil and legal consequences.

> **Level 3** – Addicts are involved with rape, incest, and other violent crimes against the innocent.

Strong legal consequences result from these offenses.
– adapted from *Out of The Shadows* by **Patrick Carnes**

Just as God has a self-for-others nature, real love is about the other person. Real love is based on real intimacy and giving to the other. Sexuality is good, not evil. It is God's wedding present. In Genesis, sexual relations were designed by God and were called good along with everything else God made. Sin and the Fall came later. The New Testament compares the love between a husband and wife to that of the love between Christ and the Church, His bride.

Promiscuity ruins females with broken hearts, bitterness, unwanted pregnancy, abortion, or loss of fertility from STDs. For men, nothing retards the full development of a young male into becoming a real man like promiscuity. If a boy can easily have what only a responsible husband should have, why should he grow up? If a young female gives herself to an immature male for a pitcher of beer and a pizza at a party, why should she be surprised if he moves on to another the next weekend, just because he can? Why should she be surprised that the object of his involvement is sex, not who she is as a person?

Women who eventually marry after experiences of manipulation and abandonment often take it out on their husbands by venting their rage against the sins of *all men* they have known, while often ignoring their own part in it. They also resent the fact that they had to compete with other promiscuous females to hold the men they eventually lost. Husbands who have been promiscuous have a tendency to return to pornography or even affairs, finding it difficult to stay interested in one woman, especially if she has real needs of her own, or has lost interest in him sexually. Only a fantasy woman will wait quietly in a drawer until she is needed.

For these reasons, the Bible *forbids* sex before or outside marriage, but *commands* it after marriage, except by mutual agreement for a season. Though commanded, this is not to be about guilt and manipulation. It should have the frequency of communion, for love, honor, and affirmation. "Do this often in remembrance of Me."

223

1 Corinthians 7:5 says:

> Do not deprive one another [*of conjugal rights*], except perhaps by agreement for a limited time, that you may devote yourselves to prayer; but then come together again, so that Satan may not tempt you because of your lack of self-control. – ESV (*Shank*)

Does another person make me sin? **No**, it is my choice to sin. Can I be the agent of temptation for another? **Yes**, but I must not be.

Romance Addiction

Schaef also says in **Chapter 2** of, *Escape from Intimacy*, "Both men and women can be romance addicts. Romance isn't evil, but its misuse is. When romance becomes an end in itself, the other person doesn't matter. The other person is soon rejected for another romantic involvement. Like sex addicts, romance addicts take from the most sacred and vulnerable aspects of human interaction to feed their addictions. Their partners are just props in the fantasy to keep it alive. Childish idealism drops the lover they have come to know for a new one who is unknown and mysterious. Manipulative control of the romance, is key. Players come and go."

> "**Level 1** – Addicts are preoccupied with romantic fantasy, which often involves ideal or unavailable lovers. They are obsessed with romance books, movies, soaps, and the like, but are not yet acting out. Family and friends suffer because the addict is devoted to escape from responsibility.
>
> **Level 2** – Addicts have affairs, liaisons, and multiple marriages. Lovers, children, and finances suffer. Continuing to cherish a victim status, they continue to be victims. They seek out the perfect mate to prove to themselves they are perfect.
>
> **Level 3** – Addicts need a more intense fix by seducing partners and trying to force them into preconceived romantic ideals. Increasing the thrill to dangerous and

bizarre situations, even acting out with strangers. Some even try to precipitate violence and jealousy to get the thrill of being desired above all else. But the romance addict is self-absorbed and has no concern for what happens to the contenders! Their narcissism keeps them unaware of the needs or pains of others. They steadfastly refuse to take responsibility for their actions. Their perfectionism prevents them from learning how to create real intimacy with a real person, by honestly facing their own flaws as well as the flaws of others." – adapted from *Escape from Intimacy* by Ann Wilson Schaef pages **51-52**

"The female romance addict finds it necessary to play the innocent damsel in distress, staying naive to escape moral accountability. The male counterpart attempts to own the woman he gallantly rescues as a trophy and is intent on keeping her dependent upon him. This keeps them both from growing up and being responsible. Marriage is often an intense drama. The romance addict uses increasingly ruthless control to force the partner into preconceived relationship scripts. They are constantly amazed and offended at their partner's failure to conform to their very special needs. If he really loved me, he would magically know how to treat me. Or, if she really loved me, she would gratefully adore and please me. The endless disappointment of unfulfilled fantasy expectations feed a victim mentality. Real life demands, with practical needs and responsibilities, suffer. Familiar routines are boring—mystery and adventure must be found elsewhere." (Summary from Schaef's chapter on Romance Addiction)

Relationship Addiction

Schaef's summary from **Chapter 3** of her book: "Relationship addicts don't have relationships—they have hostages. Prolonged emotional dishonesty dulls the senses and deepens compulsivity. Needing a partner, they are unable to be alone. The relationship may not even be sexual or romantic, but they have intense jealousy over the *supply* of their stash—if my best friend has another friend, there won't be enough for me. Experts in the techniques of relationship, they often have an openness con, doing all the right things to protect their exclu-sive access to their target. Appearing to be interested and at-tentive, they are really looking for hooks. They share feelings, but not the ones that would scare away their prey. They even cling to destructive people in desperation.

> **Level 1** – Addicts are externally referenced—needing another to have value, meaning and purpose. They re-place their former frustrated friends quickly without grieving or taking stock of what just happened. They must always be in some kind of intense relationship. Either positive or negative intensity is craved.

> **Level 2** – Addicts are driven to have a particular rela-tionship with a particular person, while lying to them-selves about what is really going on. They are jealous and intolerant of the other person's past history, re-sponsibilities or needs, because they were not part of it. They are suffering martyrs, but never go for something better. Old relationships are easily reignited, despite the fact that all this was done before and proved fruit-less! They are often bottomless in their need for the ex-clusive attention of their prey."

"Sex addicts come on... romance addicts move on... and rela-tionship addicts hang on." – adapted from *Escape from Intimacy* by Anne Wilson Schaef page 101

The Addiction Cycle
It's vital to understand that these three forms of addictive be-havior all have a cycle of thought and emotion associated with acting out those behaviors, driven by a system of corrupting conceits. If there is no intersection of spiritual power and truth with my conceits, I am left with trying to fix my thoughts and feelings by altering my mood. Emotional pain is pain in my soul.

Start at the top and proceed clockwise.

The Soul & the Addiction Cycle

I've adapted this chart from a free graphic download on addiction cycles. Most diagrams like this refer to chemical addictions. But we are discussing behavior or processes addictions—that is, how one reasons or rationalizes one's situation in compulsive behavior cycles.

> 1. The cycle begins at the top of the chart with EMOTIONAL PAIN. There is real pain here from my wounds, anger over offenses, fears about what could happen again, and shame about my behavior in response to the pain of my wounds.

> 2. Moving clockwise, emotional pain leads to a CRAVING FOR RELIEF. Who doesn't want the pain to stop? The question is, will I turn to God or Notgod, Christ or Satan? Do I want to fix my problems, or do I just want to fix my pain?

> 3. The desire for relief becomes PREOCCUPATION WITH ACTING OUT BEHAVIOR, which grows stronger and stronger as a temptation. Because of longstanding habits learned from my old master, my flesh is eager for the old solution, even though I now have a new nature in Christ. I must learn new habits of believing and response.

4. I make a choice to ACT OUT COMPULSIVE BEHAVIOR, choosing to believe I cannot suffer withdrawal with endurance, I will succumb to acting out in the old ways.

5. Acting out creates a SHORT-TERM HIGH, RELIEF OR NUMBNESS. The pain is momentarily relieved with pleasure or satisfaction, revenge or comfort. But I have only temporarily jumped into unreality without solving any of my problems. My conscience has now been dulled. My focus is distracted. I am emotionally insensitive. I have become unaware of the matters at hand that need my attention.

6. The temporary numbness is followed by NEGATIVE BEHAVIOR CONSEQUENCES. My insensitivity causes blunders in judgment, alienation of friends and family, poor job performance, and it is a huge waste of time.

7. The consequences produce DEPRESSION, GUILT AND SHAME. When reality inevitably returns, I am painfully aware of some of what I have done. I have no excuses for the damage I have caused, though I try to justify myself. I blame God for how He made me, or I blame you. I insult you by minimizing my offenses with excuses. I insult God by minimizing my confession. Or, ashamed of myself, I try to hide from both.

8. The depression, guilt, and shame lead me once again to LOW ESTEEM, SELF LOATHING and PROMISES TO CHANGE. Because my guilt and shame are stabbing me with the sharp point of consequences, I feel remorse. But my remorse is more about myself, so I hate myself. I feel hopeless, but I hate feeling hopeless, so my remorse becomes shallow and does not last. I promise to change. But I cannot fully change my ways without changing my operator. If my operator is now Christ, I must learn how to draw on His power in me to be transformed into His likeness, to be able to suffer change.

Healing and Brain Training

By the time compulsive behavior becomes a full-blown addiction, acting out has caused my brain to normalize the intensified levels of its own chemical stimulation or sedation. This causes an altered adjustment of my brain's normalcy bias. Since I am not a scientist, I can't specifically explain how behavior affects brain chemistry or how, in turn, brain chemistry affects behavior. However, I do know that my brain has the capacity to learn habits in order to streamline the response processing to daily circumstances. Similar events trigger similar responses. Repetition of habits allows the brain to respond to the same triggers without having to rethink the process again. I know the addicted brain's normalcy bias does not think things are normal unless it has regular large charges of the stimulating brain chemicals that are created by intense mood alteration activity. I also know destructive habits were learned by my body and my soul from my old operator. This is my flesh contending with my spirit, demanding satisfaction.

My new operator is Jesus Christ, and I am a new creation in Him. He is teaching me new habits of believing that are exposing and destroying my former **conceits** while strengthening my perseverance in faith. I have learned that withdrawal from the old habits is survivable. Giving in to sin is not inevitable. My brain is learning a new normal. My healing began with His Blood, which sanctifies me, and with receiving His Holy Spirit, Who empowers me. My healing is increased by learning what this all means, by acting *as if* what the Word says is true in my choices. I'm learning more and more how to bear His fruit because He is making me a willing slave of righteousness.

Romans 6:17-18 says:

> But thanks be to God, that you who were once slaves of sin have become obedient from the heart to the standard of teaching to which you were committed, and, having been set free from sin, have become slaves of righteousness leading to sanctification. – ESV

What God has done is *instantaneous* and *eternal.* What I am to do is to be *perpetual* and *persevering.* In the life to come, those who have believed will be instantaneously and eternally completed in the righteousness of Christ. Those who have not believed will be instantaneously and eternally condemned in their unrighteousness. If I love God and also love the lost, I must strive to be the best and most effective example of the expression of Christ I can be, so I can help as many of them as I can to see Christ in me, the hope of glory for them also.

Real Relationship Skills

As Schaef asserts, "real intimacy takes **Time + Truth + Trust**." It takes time to know each other in truth and to learn if we can trust each other. There is a balancing that must occur between our one-ness and our two-ness, in marriage. Real love must make accommodations, and real love *wants* to. But dishonesty and selfishness will exploit the good will of the other if we are unequally yoked. The more areas we agree on, the less tension. But no two people are identical in needs, drives, or temperament. Two people who are spiritually healthy can make loving accommodations in all non-moral, preferential conflicts. But if they are not spiritually equal, the weaker one will constantly pull the other down to a lower level of fruitfulness and energy. Opposites attract to increase capacity in one-ness. But we must not be opposite in spirit.

What follows is a list of Healthy Relationship Skills taken from pages **140-141** of Schaef's book, as well as some skills I have added myself.

Schaef: "To be able to wait in faith, for intimacy to grow."
The **Song of Solomon 8:4** says:
> I adjure you, O daughters of Jerusalem that you not stir up or awaken love until it pleases. – ESV

Schaef: "To be honest about my own needs and to honor them without selfishness."
- By knowing myself and knowing you, I'm better equipped to know if you and I are compatible.

2 Corinthians 6: 14 says:

> Do not be unequally yoked with unbelievers. For what partnership has righteousness with lawlessness? Or what fellowship has light with darkness? – ESV

The unhappiest marriages I've witnessed are the ones where the wife said, "I knew he wasn't a Christian, but I thought he was a good man." Or the husband who said, "I desired her beauty so much, I thought I could live with her spiritual and emotional problems."

Schaef: "To care for, but not enable another."
- My charity does not compromise my spiritual and moral values for you.

Proverbs 22:24-25 says:

> Make no friendship with a man given to anger, nor go with a wrathful man, lest you learn his ways and entangle yourself with a snare. – ESV

Schaef: "To not be emotionally dependent on another."
- I don't need you to make me okay. The best relationships are not two halves making a whole, but rather two whole people sharing with each other, making each other better. I must pay no attention to such things as the Jungian theory that my *soul/animia* has an invisible opposite that must be fulfilled by a partner who is completed by my *animia*. This is pagan thinking, because in Christ, I am in fact whole and complete and lacking nothing in Him.

James 1:4 says:

> And let steadfastness have its full effect, that you may be perfect and complete, lacking nothing. – ESV

Schaef: "To be unwilling to turn your life over to anyone but God."

- If I keep God's ways first, He will keep me. I will then be able to let an unhealthy relationship go. I have only one Master, Christ!

Matthew 6:33 says:

But seek first the kingdom of God and His righteousness, and all these things [*you need*] will be added to you. – ESV (Shank)

Schaef: "To see my own faults as clearly as I see those of others."

Matthew 7:3-5 says:

Why do you see the speck that is in your brother's eye, but not notice the log that is in your own eye? Or how can you say to your brother, "Let me take the speck out of your eye," when there is a log in your own eye? You hypocrite, first take the log out of your own eye, and then you will see clearly to take the speck out of your brother's eye. – ESV

Schaef: "To be willing to take the risk of being real with another for the sake of integrity."

- We must be willing to let any darkness from our past be known by the one we want to marry before getting married.

Proverbs 28:13 says:

Whoever conceals his transgressions will not prosper, but he who confesses and forsakes them will receive mercy. – ESV

Schaef: "To have the good sense to not be intimate with one you do not yet trust."

- If I have the Spirit of Christ, I have His discernment informing my conscience. I must believe and pay attention to what the Lord is showing. I must not sell out to sin and become blinded.

Proverbs 11:13 says:

> Whoever goes about slandering reveals secrets, but he who is trustworthy in spirit keeps a thing covered.
> – ESV

To have a humble and teachable spirit. I've written a song called Powers That Be, with this chorus: *A wise man will learn from his foolishness and a wise man will learn from the wise. A wise man will change his ways and let the Spirit open his eyes.*
Proverbs 29:1 says:

> He who is often reproved, yet stiffens his neck, will suddenly be broken beyond healing. – ESV

Schaef: "To be willing to risk anger or rejection for the cause of good."

- I must speak with prophetic courage that is *without* self-righteousness.

Proverbs 27:5-6 says:

> Better is open rebuke than hidden love. Faithful are the wounds of a friend; profuse are the kisses of an enemy.
> – ESV

Schaef: "To know that love cannot be created or manipulated—it is a gift from God."

- God is love! He loves because He cannot deny His Own Nature, not because I could ever earn it. The rock of His love is the Rock on which I stand. Christ's faith is upholding my faith. In Him I live and breathe and have my meaning. I have no nature of my own to express. But let me not misrepresent Him.

True Love

1 Corinthians 13:4-8a says:

> Love is patient, it is kind, it does not envy, it does not boast; it is not proud, it is not rude, not self-seeking, or easily angered. Love keeps no record of wrongs, does not delight in evil, but rejoices in the good, rejoices in the truth. It always protects and always trusts, it always hopes and perseveres. Love never fails—and my

God is love, my God is love, my Lord is love. – from *Lord of Love* / **Shank** / Peniel Music

When I am honest with myself, I know I fail at expressing love like this. Resentment, fears, wounds, shame, and guilt warp my perceptions and responses to others, and even to God. But God is good and wants to give me a clean heart. Jesus took the condemnation in my place so God can give me a new heart. If I humble myself and agree with God, He will strengthen me with His Spirit and lead me out of the old ways of my former master. The following is a warning about blinding **conceits** that can corrupt intimacy. It also shows how we can protect ourselves.

Why Wait?

Many have heard that God wants us to be virtuous and respectful of the power to bring new life into the world. We are also aware that God will bless us if we obey. We have all been warned about the risk of unwanted pregnancy, as well as the ravages of sexually transmitted diseases. Many around us believe the answer is safe sex or some kind of serial monogamy. Discussions on this level are heard every day. You may be tired of hearing all of this being rehashed over and over. Or maybe you think your relationship with someone is an exceptional case, and you will be able to avoid the consequences that have come to others.

Consider the lessons learned from those who've lived out the painful consequences of these deceptions. Sexual intimacy is the highest level of intimacy possible between a man and a woman. And it's from this wonderful gift of loving intimacy that God meant new life to come forth within the safe bonding of marriage. It's the deepest expression of our affection, acceptance, nurturing, and honor. This kind of intimacy must be enclosed in the highest level of trust between two people. That trustworthiness takes *time* to discover and to develop, and it is meant to culminate in a marriage covenant with God, loving and keeping each other in that sacred trust.

Attraction is the earliest stage of romantic love. When attraction is mutual, it then leads to the excitement of *infatuation*. This is all normal, but it is important to realize that the root of the word for infatuation is *fatuous*, which means foolish. You might say a state of infatuation is a state of *infoolishment.*

At this time, everything about the other person is so very good. All that he/she does seems wonderful or even perfect. It feels like true love. But it's not true love yet—it's a bargain. You're happy because you are getting a good deal, a perfect person, and you are made to feel wonderful just by being with that person. The relationship seems to maintain itself without much effort. This is the point of greatest susceptibility to self-deception and foolishness.

Many of us have moved from infatuation straight into sexual union. Our judgment is impaired by the euphoria of infatuation. Then a kind of blindness caused by the ecstasy of emotional bonding—which naturally occurs with sexual intimacy—steamrolls us into commitments deeper than we are ready or able to maintain. When the underlying infatuation eventually runs its course, the whole thing usually breaks down with disillusionment, painful breakups, or even worse, a marriage filled with agony and bitter disappointment.

Real love is not possible until there is real intimacy, and real intimacy is not possible without a *mutual exchange of faults.* Part of what comes with sexual union is a tremendous bonding of our souls. This soul-tying is designed to help us overcome all outside threats and distractions to our unity with one another. This is essential in a marriage, because a safe and secure nest must be provided for the children to grow in later. But when entered into outside of marriage, this soul-tying can block our ability to see one another objectively, and the result is a temporary form of blindness.

When we give a relationship a chance to get past infatuation and are not yet blinded by the ecstasy of sexual union, we give one another the opportunity to let our weaknesses, shortcomings, and even our darker secrets be known. This is a risk. Many relationships end here, and many of them should. We must be careful to take on only what we truly believe we can handle. God means for us to understand what we're doing with the choices we make. He wants our love for each other to be a free and informed choice, just as it is in all our covenants with Him. And after our commitment to Christ, marriage is one of the most important covenants we will ever make.

God's love is overflowing to others. I believe this is why He made us: to be in fellowship with us as He is in fellowship within the Godhead. God is in relationship with Himself. The Spirit glorifies the Son and the Son glorifies the Father. Being made in His image, we can know that real love is not about ourselves, but it is about blessing the other person. We have desire for the other person, but we're not ruled by it. When we are willing to lay down our own life for someone else, then we have God's real **agape** love.

When we see the fault the other person has and still want to be all we can be for them in spite of those faults, we have real love. This must be a freewill choice with our eyes wide open. If we are putting God first in all this process, He will surely bless us and even add much more. Putting God first is doing it His way. If we can't set the temptation to selfishness aside, to be all we can be for someone else, we will be overwhelmed by children who, by their very dependence will demand everything we have to give in raising them.

In worldly thinking, people are drawn together by infatuation because it's in their own selfish interest to be with someone who is a good deal or bargain and who satisfies desires. When infatuation eventually diminishes and the faults eventually show, it is no longer a deal. One says to the other, "I am no longer happy. The relationship is over because it is no longer in my selfish interest for us to be together."

What a tragedy if children are on the way before this is recognized. Or we have ruined ourselves for anyone else with something like HIV. We must be humble and respectful of the weakness of our flesh in the face of strong temptation. We must also be wise in choosing with whom we will spend our lives, because all of us have baggage that will require the grace of our partner to endure. Does the person you say you love build you up in faith and encourage your best, or do they appeal to your weaknesses and encourage sin? We must not let ourselves be ruled by the flattery of being desired.

Even in Christ, we all have selfish temptations that are all too easily rationalized. We must put God first. If we believe God is good, we can trust Him. If we cannot trust Him, we do not really believe He is good. But God is not motivated by anything other than His Goodness. When He says "You shall not do this..." He says it from out of His Goodness. When He says, "You shall do that..." it's out of His Goodness also. HE HAS NO OTHER MOTIVATION IN HIS ACTIONS, IN HIS PLANS, OR IN HIS COMMANDMENTS!

But the narcissism of sin gives great power to the ruthless to exploit and oppress the weak. Justified by self-delusional **conceits** men oppress women and children, and women manipulate men. When women without virtue give themselves to men without honor—they kill their own children or bring them up without fathers. Where there is no answerability to God, merciless selfishness will breed violence, especially with defenseless children. A self-entitling victim mentality denies that the death of a human life has occurred in an abortion, or that the abandonment of one's family does not matter. When we disobey the Lord, men, women, and children are all betrayed. Hear what He has to say to you; He means to give you a blessing that will last the rest of your natural life and that will even impact the next life, because a godly partner will help you bear more spiritual fruit for the Kingdom now, and you will receive greater reward in the Kingdom to come.

Chapter 14 Study Questions

1. What is narcissism?

2. What is the differences between sexual, romance and relationship addicts?

3. How does the addiction cycle work?

4. What is a normalcy bias?

5. What false intimacy skills do I need to change in myself?

6. What is true love?

7. How does abstinence protect me from marrying the wrong person?

III: The Passionate Worship of True Spirituality

15

Magic, Mysticism & Curses

> *To know wisdom, is to know God.*
> *To know God is to understand deception.*
> *To understand deception, is to see how*
> *the serpent had his way with me.*

... be wise as serpents but innocent as doves. – Matthew 10:16 ESV

There are some basic assumptions in conflict between the true spirituality of the Bible and false spirituality of paganism. It is important to be clear about these differences in order to prevent a syncretistic framework from compromising true faith with the distortions of magic and idolatry. Syncretism seeks to blend two or more opposing belief systems which are incompatible, into a forced or compromised view of reality by disregarding the foundational logic of each. Only the willfully ignorant or naïve will say all religions are the same. But with God, there is no fellowship between darkness and light.

> "In both magic and pagan religion, the operation of spirits, who are both personal and conscious, is assumed. Prayer and sacrifice through a priest or priestess seeks the favor of the spirits. On the other hand, the witch or sorcerer makes demands of them (spirits). Both act as mediums. But the laws of magic are a complete misconception of both the laws of science and the Laws of God. Magic is a wrong understanding of cause and effect that makes it a false science and a false understanding of the order and uniformity of nature."
> – Frazer

Sympathetic Magic
In his excellent book, *The Golden Bough*, **Sir James George Frazer** says there are two false supporting assumptions for Sympathetic Magic, which I now summarize below from pages 11-13 of his book:

"First, that like affects like, or, an effect resembles the cause. This is said to be in accordance with the **Laws of Similarity**. For example, the use of charms that are made to resemble a person are said to have the power to affect that person, like a voodoo doll. If the image suffers a wound, so will the man. If an effigy is burned, the man's soul is said to be damned. If the puppet is buried, the man will die. If an image of a god is worshiped, the god in heaven is adored through it. Charms based on these Laws of Similarity may also be called **Homeopathic** or **Imitative Magic**."

This is why the magical mindset of the Philistines in **1 Samuel 6:4** was to humbly return the Ark of the Covenant to Israel on a new wagon, drawn by two milk cows that had never worn a yoke. Included was a guilt offering of *five golden tumors* and *five golden mice*, so the God of Israel would lift the *resembling* plagues of tumors and mice that had been laid on the *five cities* of the *five humbled lords* of the Philistines, because they had captured the Ark of the Covenant and mocked the God of Israel.

But **Exodus 20:4-5a** says:

You shall not make for yourself a carved image, or any likeness of *anything* that is in heaven above, or in the earth beneath, or in the water under the earth. You shall not bow down to them or serve them..." – ESV (*Shank*)

The reasoning is that a manmade image is not to be used as a sacred thing to worship false gods, or even to worship the True God. Idolatry of this kind is **Sympathetic Magic**. God alone is Holy! Faith is not about what we see with our eyes or touch with our hands. Jesus Christ is our only Mediator with God and His Spirit is joined to us if we are born-again Christians. As I said earlier, we are the **naos** of God; we are where God is in our lives because we are joined to Him, and we are a new creation in Him. When we assemble with two or more fellow believers, the Word says He is in the midst of us. The born again are also seated at the Right Hand of God in the heaven. God's Word does not lie. Just because this may be difficult to grasp conceptually, doesn't mean we can't act on that truth of

Scripture by faith. Idolatry is misplaced trust, however sincere or well-intended an idolater may be. We do not kiss the feet of Christ if we kiss the feet of a statue of Him. Idolatry of this kind is the practice of **Sympathetic Magic**.

The Laws of Contagion or Contact

Frazer says, "The second false assumption of magic is that things that once were in contact with each other maintain some connection even when far away from each other."

For example, if I have your hair or fingernail clippings, I am said to have power over you to affect you with a spell through what was once part of you. A medium holding something personal that belonged to a missing person claims to have a vision of where that person is, even if deceased. If the medium's prediction happens to be true, it's because the demon through him or her is sweetening the deception with accurate details in order to misdirect people away from the true God.

In **Acts 16:16-18**, a slave girl who was a medium accurately stated that the apostles were "servants of the Most High God, who proclaim to you the way of salvation." The Greek says she had a spirit of a **python**, which means she had powers like the **Pythia**, the priestesses whom the pagans sought for prophetic counsel at such places as the Oracle of Delphi. (*It would not surprise me if the origin of the term in English, a pithy saying, came from the name of these alleged wise women.*) Paul cast out the spirit in her because the demon was hoping to give credibility to the slave girl, so to later undermine the new church being established in Philippi with a false prophetess, after the apostles moved on.

Acting through mediums, demons are well known to lie, wholly or in part. A place where a tragedy or outrage has occurred is falsely said to become accursed or haunted. These assumptions are also based in the reasoning of **Laws of Contact** or **Contagion**. If a place or an object could actually be spiritually contagious, how could you sleep in a hotel bed where fornication, rape or incest may have occurred? How could you buy anything at a second-hand store? It might be fun to have an autograph or a possession once owned by a famous person, but nothing of their spirit is transferred to me if I now own it, good or evil.

Real curses come from unrepentant sin. *No* spiritual curse is passed to another by mere physical contact or proximity. I believe the advice in **1 Timothy 5:22** not to be quick to lay hands on someone, has less to do with contracting a demon from them than it does in giving the person a false sense of being right with God, and identified as being one with us when they may have no real intention of repentance. Sin contaminates the unrepentant and may cause consequences for the innocent, but one is not corrupted by evil-spirit influences unless one willingly participates in sin.

Proverbs 26:2 says:

> Like a fluttering sparrow or a darting swallow, an undeserved curse does not come to rest. – NIV

Some may argue that the verses in **Leviticus 13:51** and following, that refer to a house being unclean, are an example of spiritual contamination of a piece of property. Nonsense! Those verses are about hygiene, not demonic realms. There are demonic strongholds in the world, but that is because of people in those regions who have given themselves to disobedience. *Unrepentant sin opens one to demonic control.* Sinners and the demons they obey, occupy lands and places through the rebellious unbelief of the local population. Christians are to boldly go into those places to bring the light of the Gospel. When Paul was directed by the Spirit not to enter some cities, it was because he was to go where he was commanded. Those forbidden cities may not have been ready for the Gospel yet, distracting him from God's purpose at that time. Are not all powers and principalities under my feet in Christ Jesus at the Right Hand of the Father? If Christ is for me, who can prevail against me? Even if I die, I overcome in Him.

So, as a personal choice, do I decline to go into a mosque because I am afraid of the spirit there? **No**. When Moses first encountered the Lord at the burning bush, God told him to remove his shoes because he was on holy ground. That was because the Lord was revealing Himself there. Therefore, I will not give the mistaken impression that I think the mosque is holy ground by removing my shoes to enter. This is my policy. A missionary to Islam may not believe he is restricted in the same way by the Holy Spirit because of ongoing dialogue regarding the Truth. But followers of Mohammed are not won for the Lord by aspects of faith we may have in common with them, but rather by realizing what they have believed is a lie and are thereby convicted to repent of their sin.

This is an issue of counterfeit spirituality not spiritual unity. What fellowship has darkness with light? Some may say this is a disputable matter like eating food offered to idols. "An idol is nothing," (**1 Corinthians 8:4**) and we are to eat food offered to us by a host without condemnation, and not enquire if it is unclean. But if it is revealed that the food was offered to an idol, we are to refrain, so not to give the impression the god they worship is equal or equivalent to the Lord Jesus Christ. Jehovah is the God of Abraham, Isaac and Jacob, in the lineage of Christ. Allah is the old moon god of pagan Arabia. That's why the crescent is still his symbol. Mohammed falsely claims blessing from God comes down through Abraham in Ishmael and Esau. He was a false prophet! I find nothing wrong with visiting places that have been historically pagan for the sake of history or art, but I will not enter if I must first show reverence.

God Created Fixed Laws for Creation
The magical worldview sees a universe that is not governed by fixed physical laws. Magic does not care about the observation of facts or phenomena gained by the repeatable experiments of science. Instead, magic sees the universe as *elastic and variable*, subject to the whims of capricious gods or spirits who can be influenced by a medium to gain advantage. The magician never questions what is going on. If the spell does not work, perhaps a stronger magician is prevailing in opposition. But magic only has power over people who believe in it. Evil spirits deceive the superstitious because sin is blinding and it holds the unrepentant in bondage. Frazer observes that some wizards "are naïve and puzzled by poor results, but the best of them *know* they are charlatans, using tricks and lies to manipulate their followers." Christians must not fall under the bondage of su-

perstition, mixing false spirituality with the truth. This is what syncretism is. Again, in Christ we are seated above all the other spirits by God the Father. We must be holy (*separate*).

Frazer makes interesting comparisons between the mindsets of pagan religion, magic and science, which I will summarize and interpret below. **Sympathetic Magic** creates false sciences. Instead of astronomy, magic produces astrology. Instead of chemistry, magic gives us alchemy. Instead of a medical doctor, magic creates a witch doctor.

He notes that in pagan religion:
> "the priest or priestess is a supplicant who comes before the deity to worship, offer sacrifice, and to pray. The attitude is one of humility and a desire to please, that the favor of the gods may be granted. Ritual and ceremony are significant with sacred procedure and sacred objects. The priest or priestess acts as a medium through whom both the people and the gods, speak. They believe the miraculous is possible at any time because the capricious gods can grant favors for those who adore them on a whim, or so they may get revenge over the interests of rival deities."

However, with magic, "the wizard or the witch threatens the spirits with insults and curses if they do not perform the spells demanded. Their attitude is haughty and arrogant. A spirit [*demon*] is summoned. Exchanges are made. Ritual and ceremony are also significant with magical procedure, along with charms and fetishes. Drugs are often part of the process. An induced experience enhances deception by creating a highly suggestible, mediumistic state of mind that opens one up to demonic influence. The miraculous is expected because there are no fixed physical laws to prevent it, as well as the belief that reality can be massaged into whatever the witch wants it to be ..."

The scientist "chooses not to invoke spiritual involvement with the process of discovery or achieving his goals. Since he knows the laws of nature are fixed, he

tries to find a way to solve problems by practical experimentation, building on what has been proven as physically possible, to discover new applications. His attitude should be detached, to let the facts take him
where they will. The miraculous is not a considered
factor."

To these comparisons, I would like to add a definition of Biblical Christianity absent from Frazer's analysis.

The Biblical Christian sees the observable world as designed by God with repeatable and provable laws govern-
ing all physical processes. God's logical design of nature
with repeatable fixed laws of function, make scientific observation possible. The most backward cultures in the
world see spirits in nature who must be placated—
scientific experimentation is sacrilege to them.

A Christian also sees there are spiritual forces opposed to
God and to man. Sin is as undermining to the moral and
spiritual world as entropy and decay are to the physical
world. Both lead to death. Our mediator is Christ for this
life and the next. We must be humble, teachable, and obedient to His commands. When we pray, we seek His will
in what we ask, knowing He loves us. He is not an imper-
sonal force, nor a tyrant subject to whims, but a personal
God Who has given us His Spirit that we may know Him
and grow to be more like Him. We take authority over
powers and principalities because of the Blood of Jesus,
not by power in ourselves or other spirits. God gives us favor in Christ. When the miraculous does happen, it is an
extraordinary occurrence by the Sovereignty of God, to reveal Himself and show His ministers as credible.

Personal example

Once a good friend of mine and I had conversations with a
young man who professed to be a Satanist. He had suffered un-
speakable abuse as a boy, having been repeatedly raped. In his
late teens, he was about to commit suicide when he heard a
voice telling him not to do it. He said that voice was Lucifer
and he had a wonderful plan for his life. So, he became a fol-

lower of Satan, believing a convoluted and false doctrine. Interestingly, he had high moral standards and spoke with contempt for members of his coven who were carrying on with what he regarded as stereotypical fornication, drug use, and curses.

This led to lengthy exchanges between us, and he seemed to be carefully reexamining what he believed to be true, when the Christ of the Bible was explained to him on intimate terms. Finally, he asked me to pray to God to ask Him if He had anything to say to this young man. So, I prayed and the Lord gave loving and compassionate words to him about what he had suffered, but also a serious warning to repent, because he was close to being completely swallowed by the serpent of deception, and soon would be unable to see the Light at all.

I wrote down all that I heard from the Lord and met with him again. After I read him the message, he sniffed with condescending contempt. Then he said:

> "You almost had me. If you were really hearing from God, you would have said certain words I was waiting to hear, that an All-Knowing God would have spoken to *prove* what you say is true. But I didn't hear *those words!*"

He was putting God to *the test*. He wanted God to jump through his hoop! He didn't care about God's moral truth or the peril he faced. Like the wizard above, who commands the spirits they conjure to do his will, he was demanding God to perform. He was not interested in receiving the truth and righteousness of the Word. He was not ready to submit to God even if he heard the words he was waiting for, because the next time he wanted to hear from God, he would set another of his own preconditions before he would obey. God is gracious, but He does not jump through hoops like a trained animal. Or, as C. S. Lewis says in The Chronicles of Narnia, "Aslan is not a tame lion." That young man was not ready for Jesus to be his LORD. He turned away and did not repent. May the Holy Spirit continue to pursue him and lead him to salvation.

Ceremony & Ritual

Ceremony and ritual that is more than a dignified procession has more in common with idolatry than with true spirituality. Ceremony as an element of respect or remembrance is good, but corrupted when it involves sacred objects and sacred procedures. Magicians have magic words and ways of saying them. Pagans have special ritual prayers. Christians should not. Certainly, traditions have their place in helping us see we are part of history. Israel was commanded to remember the feast days and celebrate them because they commemorate what God did for them in the past.

Jesus said of communion that we should receive it often in remembrance of Him. It's *not* a magic ceremony, but rather a time to examine ourselves and repent of the sins that can rob us of faith and dishonor His sacrifice for us. Memorizing and quoting Scripture is good to build understanding in the Word and to stand in faith. Proscribed prayers and chants that emphasize procedural technique, are opposed to real faith in the power and goodness of God. Appealing to the flesh, they can become more like spells than the simple faith exercised in Christ by any believer who believes he is at the Right Hand of God by grace. The only Priestly Mediator required is Christ. In fact, the Greek word for priest (**hiereus**) is not listed at all among the offices of the church where apostles and prophets, evangelists, pastors and teachers are listed.

The flesh can make an idol out of anything, even in the worship of God. Sometimes the Holy Spirit will manifest His Presence in a dramatic or even miraculous way to encourage our faith. At other times, He may appear to be silent to see if we will believe without seeing. Sometimes He is displeased with something going on in the congregation and is waiting for us to repent. Instead of humbly asking Him to show us if there is a hindrance, some churches decide to praise until "God shows up."

This can be a demand that God *prove* Himself to be there, when He has already said He is in the midst of two or three of us, whether we feel Him or not. This is not faith but could even be a provocative insult. God will not be conjured. This kind of sin allows evil spirits to give false prophecy and deceive the congregation into following false doctrines of demons. I have known of several false revivals with bizarre manifestations that sensual leaders permitted to go unchecked because the people flocked to their churches to experience thrilling wonders. Real revivals come from real repentance. More will be said in **Chapters 17** and **18** regarding **True Gifts of the Spirit.**

Mysticism

Related to magic and pagan religion is mysticism practiced for its own sake. This is not the same as a revelation of our union with Christ based on the work of Christ and the transforming indwelling of the Holy Spirit, as described in preceding chapters. The Holy Spirit makes that union with Christ real to us. There is no human contrivance involved.

Speaking of contrivance, let me illustrate by my own experience. As a young man, I left my nominal Christian faith to search for something that was more experientially powerful. I studied most of the world's major religions and even the occult. Gradually, I fell into the use of psychedelic drugs and allowed myself to fall under the influence of Indian philosophy as well. One night, after taking some powerful LSD, the Lord intervened. I was alone and peaking—at the top of my high.

When I saw my profound vulnerability, I cried out to God in terror. He spoke to me very clearly. He said He knew I was looking for Him and that I wanted to experience what it might be like to stand in His Presence, but I was opening myself to evil. He said, "If you want to experience Me, you need to deal with Me on My terms, *not yours.* I Am the Lord!" He told me I was allowing myself to be deceived by inducing an experience of what it might be like to be in His Presence. What I was actually doing was spiritual masturbation.

It shocked me to hear my mystical pursuits referred to in this way. One may argue that God would never say a phrase like spiritual masturbation. But a bride and a bridegroom have real intimacy with each other, like Christ and His church. I quit my drug use immediately. If you are offended by this language, see how He graphically described the spiritual prostitution of Israel and Judah in **Ezekiel 23**.

At that time, I had no real relationship with Him that would constitute a real experience of Him. He also said, "You know how it is when you're reading something difficult to understand—then you understand it? You experience a flash in your mind that reinforces your comprehension. The flash underscores the meaning of what you read. But when you use these drugs, that same flash goes off over and over, but without comprehending anything real. You think you're grasping profound truths, but your hands are empty. In fact, you're allowing yourself to be deceived by believing lies Satan is telling you, because you have turned away from Me. You must deal with Me on My terms, not yours. I Am the Lord!"

So, I was the first among my friends to quit drugs in 1968. I knew Who was speaking to me. It was Jesus. But I had a strong prejudice against the church. I said I thought it was too bourgeois, because I had only heard anecdotal sermons in nominal churches, without any deep spiritual content.

A few weeks later I was in my Yoga class. I loved my guru, who was a real Brahman priest from India. I thought I could worship Jesus through yoga and so refrained from chanting the names of Krishna or Shiva. I had done all the preliminary physical exercises and poses to gratify my muscles so they wouldn't distract me. I had done all the breathing exercises to give my brain a big hit of oxygen. As we began to meditate, the Lord spoke to me again. "You are still trying to induce an experience of being with Me without being in a relationship with Me on My terms, not yours. I Am the Lord!"

I quit yoga, but it took three more years before I was born again. I told myself and others that I believed in Jesus but hated the hypocritical church. While church members have problems that can be rightly criticized, the deeper reason for the delay in becoming part of a church family was because I still didn't want to give up opportunities for sexual encounters when they came along. My delay was really due to my hypocrisy, not the church.

Our union with Christ is real because it is God's doing, *not* a human technique. Visions came to the prophets because God wanted to show them something real, not because they were ascetics inducing trance states through drugs, sensory deprivation, fasts, or conjuring. Induced mystical experiences reinforce lies by opening us up to counterfeit experiences with demons. The Word shows all that is not of God is of *Notgod*, the *Unmaker*. God will not be summoned because of our selfish will. Madmen or drug users often claim to see or even to be God. But for some reason, while I was in the midst of hallucinatory satanic activity, He heard my fearful cry and broke into my delusion and took me out of it – *twice!* Then He patiently waited for me to come to Him later with all of my heart.

Chapter 15 Study Questions

1. What is the Law of Similarity in sympathetic magic?

2. What is the Law of Contagion in sympathetic magic?

3. What causes someone to fall under the power a curse?

4. What are the effects of believing in either fixed or elastic laws in creation?

5. Why are objects and places not inhabited or haunted by spirits?

6. What is wrong with an induced spiritual state?

16

True Worship & Prayer

God is Spirit, and they that worship Him must do so in Spirit and in Truth. – ESV

Revelation 4:1-11 says:

> After this I looked, and behold, a door standing open in heaven! And the first voice, which I heard speaking to me like a trumpet, said, 'come up here, and I will show you what must take place after this.' At once I was in the Spirit, and behold, a throne stood in heaven, with One seated on the throne. And He Who sat there had the appearance of jasper and carnelian, and around the throne was a rainbow that had the appearance of an emerald. Around the throne were twenty-four thrones, and seated on the thrones were twenty-four elders, clothed in white garments, with golden crowns on their heads. From the throne came flashes of lightening, and rumblings and peals of thunders, and before the throne were burning seven torches of fire, which are the seven spirits of God, and before the throne there was as it were a sea of glass, like crystal.
>
> And around the throne, on either side of the throne, are four living creatures, full of eyes in front and behind: the first living creature like a lion, the second living creature like an ox, the third living creature with the face of a man, and the forth living creature like an eagle in flight. And the four living creatures, each of them with six wings, are full of eyes all around and within, and day and night they never cease to say,
>
> "Holy, Holy, Holy, Is the Lord God Almighty,
> Who Was and Is and Is to Come!"
>
> And whenever the living creatures give glory and honor and thanks to Him Who is seated on the throne, Who lives forever and ever, the twenty-four elders fall down before Him Who is seated on the throne and worship

Him Who lives forever and ever. They cast their crowns before the throne, saying,

"Worthy are You, our Lord and God,
to receive glory and honor and power,
for You created all things, and by Your will they existed
and were created." – ESV

Notice the creatures with eyes all over them, inside and out, showing they see everything, outer deeds and inner motives. We must not be foolish and try to gloss over what we have done or still doing with contempt for the Holiness of the Lord. True worship, beginning with confession and repentance, pleases God.

The Holy Approach
In the Old Testament, there are many instructions given about how to approach The God Who Is Holy. The attitude of our approach is to show no presumption. One of several ways of viewing the Old Testament with New Testament eyes is seeing what are called *types* and *symbols*. A type is a spiritual illustration or a picture of a spiritual truth. It can be like the way the life of Joseph portrays the life of Christ in being rejected by his brothers, falsely accused, later exalted to the right hand of a king, then revealing himself to his brothers and forgiving them. All types fall short at some point because no human can compare to Christ. But a person like Joseph or David, or the temple high priest, illustrate aspects of the life and purpose of Christ in picture form, even though all of them fall far short of the true righteousness of Christ, Whom they may unwittingly prefigure.

In **Leviticus 8**, we read about the consecration of Aaron and his sons as priests. Notice that they were first washed with water, removing the contamination of the world, then made sacrifice for their own sin before they could approach God on behalf of others. Much of the teaching of the clean and the unclean were illustrations given to teach a sense of how sin defiles us in the sight of God and must be removed *before* approaching Him.

The Bronze Sea was a giant washbasin filled with water for washing the priests *before* they served, and to clean the edible parts of the animals used in sacrifice. The beauty of holiness is to be cleansed from sin. In ancient times, when Israel wandered forty years in the wilderness, God first instructed the people about His Law and how He was to be worshiped. They used the spoil from Egypt—their "back paid wages" to make the articles of the temple of gold, silver and precious stones. The women of Israel gave their mirrors of polished bronze to be melted down to make the Bronze Sea for the cleansing of the priests. Beauty is an Old Testament type for holiness. Washing is a type of righteousness.

After being washed, Aaron was given new clothes. Pure white robes with sashes, gave him the righteous dignity he needed to stand for the people, set apart for holiness before God. He also put on the ephod, a golden breastplate adorned with jewels, representing each of the tribes of Israel. These jewels were over his heart so he would remember the people for whom he was to intercede. Inside a pocket in the ephod the Urim and Thummim were kept, two stones used in consulting the will of God for the people, with yes and no answers, for this or that decisions. A white turban was placed on his head, showing he was under God's authority. And on that turban, was a golden crown with a plate inscribed with the words, "Holy to the Lord." He was anointed with oil—a symbol of the Holy Spirit and His equipment of power, wisdom, authority, and the uncreated Life of God, which was now upon him in his office.

He brought in the blood of innocent animals whose sacrifice pointed to Jesus, the Innocent Lamb of God without blemish, Who was sacrificed for us. The blood on the right ear of the high priest purified his ability to hear from God. The blood on his right thumb sanctified the work of his hands. The blood on his right big toe showed God's favor wherever he went. The fire that burned up the sacrifice was the acknowledgement of the damnation we deserve, which is taken away by the sacrificial substitution of Christ. Man is made higher than the animals, but an innocent animal was better than a sinful man, because animals aren't devious. Now that Christ the Perfect has come, no more animal sacrifices are needed.

The intercession of the Son, Who is both High Priest and Sacrifice, is greatest of all! The book of **Hebrews** profoundly explains how Jesus completely fulfills the Righteous demands of God and renders the shadow copies of the earthly temple and sacrifices, obsolete. But God Is Holy! Even though the born again can now sit at His Right Hand in Christ Jesus, we must not show *contempt* for the Lord in our boldness before Him, by forgetting to examine ourselves before we serve or ask something of Him. God Is Holy! We must fear and honor Him with truth in our inward being.

Kinds of Prayer – Praise & Adoration

The glory of the Lord is overwhelming when we glimpse it. Praising God for Who He Is has moved me to fall on my face and want to try to cover my head with floor tiles. On my face like that, I know I am only approaching reality. I want to hide and cry out "Holy, Holy, Holy is the Lord!" The Rock broken open for me to hide in, is Christ! Like Moses, I see only a limited part of the Glory of the Lord. There must be no casual contempt in my conversing with Him. I want to wash His Feet with my hair and tears for His forgiveness. I despise my sin when I look on Him Whom I have pierced!

Isaiah 6:1-7 says:

> In the year that King Uzziah died I saw the Lord sitting upon a throne, high and lifted up; and the train of His robe filled the temple. Above Him stood the seraphim. Each had six wings: with two he covered his face, and with two he covered his feet, and with two he flew. And one called to another and said: "Holy, Holy, Holy is the Lord of hosts; the whole earth is full of His Glory!

> And the foundations of the thresholds shook at the voice of him who called, and the house was filled with smoke. And I said: "Woe is me! For I am lost; for I am a man with unclean lips, and I dwell in the midst of a people of unclean lips; for my eyes have seen the King, the Lord of hosts!

Then one of the seraphim flew to me, having in his hand a burning coal that he had taken with tongs from the altar. And he touched my mouth and said: 'Behold, this has touched your lips; your guilt is taken away, and your sin atoned for. – ESV

After the fantastic visions of the Glory of the Lord in the calling of Ezekiel in **Ezekiel 1:1-3:15**, "...he sat down overwhelmed for seven days." Though most of us have never had experiences like these, our spirits know the Holiness of God from His Word if we are alive to Him.

In the forgiveness of Christ, we also see the beauty of His Holiness. We spontaneously want to keep **Matthew 22:37**:

You shall love the Lord Your God with all your heart, with all your soul and with all your mind. – ESV

When our guilt and condemnation are taken away, we rejoice with all our hearts! In **Luke 19:40**, when the Pharisees told Jesus to restrain the zeal of His disciples, He answered:

I tell you, if these were silent, the very stones would cry out. – ESV

Psalm 150

Praise the Lord!
Praise God in His sanctuary;
　　　praise Him in His mighty heavens!
Praise Him for His mighty deeds;
　　　praise Him according to His excellent greatness!
Praise Him with trumpet sound;
　　　praise Him with lute and harp!
Praise Him with tambourine and dance;
　　　praise Him with strings and pipe!
Praise Him with sounding cymbals;
　　　praise him with loud clashing cymbals!
Let everything that has breath praise the Lord!
Praise the Lord!" – ESV

It's very important that I express vigorous joyful worship of the Lord in both private and public settings. I may not feel like it sometimes, but this is something I should do in the spirit—

in the obedience of faith. Praising God when I don't feel like it is the sacrifice of praise David speaks of. I praise God even when my soul feelings may not want to. My flesh is weak and my soul has its moods and subjective self-interested focus. (*See* **Chapter 5 Soul & Spirit**.) But I am spiritual, transformed by the presence of the Holy Spirit in my spirit.

My attitude shows me what spiritual view I am taking, Christ's or Satan's. Changing that view is changing my attitude. The corrected view must now direct the mood of my soul, to do what is right. I am to bring my flesh into subjection so that faith will prevail. I'm no longer living from mood faith like a child. If I let my flesh rule, I deny the power of God to transform me deeds of the flesh overcome me. If I cannot overcome the weakness of the flesh in myself, why should the demons obey me when I stand against them, on behalf of myself or others?

As a young missionary in Amsterdam around 1975, I was praying as I knelt over a sofa. My spirit was calling out for more of God, but my flesh was experiencing a growing dread as I sensed the Lord was drawing near me. At that time, I still only saw myself as distant from God; His Presence was only known to me as transcendent—high and far away. I had received His Spirit but didn't yet realize the deeper reality of God's *immanence*—His *union* with my spirit. I can remember thinking that if the Glory of the Lord enters this room, I'm going to turn into a puddle of hot grease on the floor. Then the Lord spoke to me and said, "Get into the Rock!"

I opened my eyes and saw that I had been trying to burrow under the cushions of the sofa to hide. Then I remembered the story of Moses when he asked to see the Glory of the Lord. The Lord told him to get into a rock that was broken open, to hide lest he look on the Lord's face and die. When Moses got into the rock, the Lord covered the crack with His Hand as He passed by and Moses was permitted to see only His Back, and live. At that time, I did not correctly understand what it meant to be in Christ Who is my Rock. That revelation did not fully reach me until years later. But after this experience I wrote this song after **Exodus 33:17-23**.

The Cleft in the Rock
Come unto Me all ye who fear Me
Come unto Me all ye who tremble before Me
Come unto Me all ye who feel so unworthy
I have a place wherein I will hide thee
I have a place wherein I will hide thee

A Rock broken open to hold and protect thee
With My own Hand I will clean and heal thee
This is the place wherein I will seal thee
Deep in the Rock you can stand before Me
Safe in the Rock you can stand before Me
From *Yeshua* / Peniel Music 2005 / johnbyronshank.com

As I have already stressed, we should never try to induce a spiritual revelation experience, but sometimes they come when we are immersed in ministry or serious intercession. If we just do the minimum in service and don't stretch our faith, why should we expect God to show us something we don't think we need? But we should not be hasty to see visions! If they are from God, more will be expected of us because of what we now know. To whom much is given, much is expected. But a vision that is not from God will bring deception.

Thanksgiving
We must gratefully acknowledge God as the source of all the blessings around us. It is just as important to thank Him for each thing He is doing in our lives one-by-one. Like praise, this is a spiritual attitude, not just a mood. Not being grateful creates bitterness, and bitterness breeds contempt, and contempt justifies sin in our lives and a falling away from God. Soon everything God is doing makes no sense because our foolish hearts are hardened and our minds are darkened. Gratitude is an attitude. Love is also an attitude, not just an emotion. How else can we be commanded to love the Lord our God with all our heart, with all our soul, and our mind? How else can we be commanded to give thanks? If God is enthroned on the praises of His people, it is not because He needs our praise, but because we need to be rightly aligned in our believing to find favor and blessing in what we do. Being rightly aligned is not

just getting our compass to point in the right direction, it is in walking and leaping and praising God with all our might! In Him alone is truth, power and light.

1 Thessalonians 5:16-18 says:
> Rejoice always, pray without ceasing, giving thanks in all circumstances; for it is the will of God in Christ Jesus for you. – ESV

Psalm 118:1-4 I've personalized this psalm in a song:
Your Love Endures forever
I will give thanks to You, You are so very, very good;
Your love endures forever...
Your love endures forever...
Your love endures forever, Amen.

You answered me and You set me free,
You live in me, I will not be afraid.
O what can a man do to me?
For You are always with me,
My help and my triumph over my enemies.

I take my refuge in You, O Lord,
No trust in the ways of a man.
I take my refuge in You O Lord above,
No trust in the princes of the land.

Though my enemies surround me,
In Your Name, I cut them off!
They surround me on every side,
In Your Name, I cut them off!
They swarmed over me like angry bees
But they burned up just like dry thorns,
In Your Name I cut them off, I cut them off!

Your Right Hand, Jesus, has done mighty deeds,
I will not die, but I will live!
Your Right hand, Jesus, has lifted me on high,
I will proclaim what you have done!
Your Right Hand, Jesus, has done mighty deeds!
You have purified me with fire,
But You have not given me over to death.

You have opened up for me the gates of righteousness!

I will give thanks to You, You are so very, very good;
Your love endures forever...
Your love endures forever...
Your love endures forever, Amen.

From *Yeshua*/Peniel Music 2005 / johnbyronshank.com

Confession

There is symmetry in positive and negative confession. We
know we believe in the love and goodness of God when we
confess what is true about Him. We know we believe in the
love and goodness of God when we honestly confess our sins.
Positive confession is to say aloud what is true about what
God has done and is doing, in my life. Negative confession is to
admit whatever wrong I have done, to bring me back into
alignment with the truth.

John 4:24 says:

God is a spirit and they that worship him must worship him in spirit and truth. – ESV

Psalm 51:6 says:

Behold, You desire truth in the inmost being. – ESV

Revelation 19:10 says:

The testimony of Jesus Christ is the spirit of prophecy.
– ESV

Confession keeps me honest and keeps me from betraying my
Lord by undermining the truth of the gospel with hypocrisy.
The truth restores soundness of mind and releases the power
of God to work mightily in me as well as in others. Truth is
also the cure for double mindedness that fosters **conceits**
which give permission for me to have compartments inside
myself where sin can continue to flourish, even though I am a
child of God.

I am completely known by God, I should let myself be fully
known by a few trustworthy accountability partners of the
same sex. I should be transparent with my wife, being quick to

confess and repent my offenses and to forgive hers as well. She should to the same. See **Chapter 8** for more on partners under **Accountability & Discipleship.**

Romans 10:8-10 says:
> But what does it say? 'The Word is near you, in your mouth and in your heart' (that is, the Word of faith that we proclaim); because if you confess with your mouth that Jesus is Lord and believe in your heart that God raised Him from the dead, you will be saved. For with the heart one believes and is justified, and with the mouth one confesses and is saved. – ESV

Psalm 32:1-7 says:
> Blessed is the man whose transgression is forgiven,
> whose sin is covered.
> Blessed is the man against whom the Lord counts no
> iniquity,
> And in whose spirit, there is no deceit.
>
> For when I kept silent, my bones wasted away
> Through my groaning all day long.
> For day and night Your Hand was heavy upon me:
> My strength was dried up as by the heat of summer.
>
> I acknowledged my sin to You,
> And did not cover my iniquity;
> I said, "I will confess my transgressions to the Lord,"
> And You forgave the iniquity of my sin.
>
> Therefore, let everyone who is godly
> Offer prayer to You at a time when You may be found;
> Surely in the rush of great waters,
> They shall not reach him.
> You are a hiding place for me;
> You preserve me from trouble;
> You surround me with shouts of deliverance." – ESV

Petition
These are requests for the needs of others as well as for myself, addressing a wide diversity of situations, and for guidance in how to deal with them. Because the prayers of the righteous

avail much, confession of who I am in Christ gives confident boldness of faith, so long as internal honesty about my own sin is maintained. He is in me and I am in Him.

Hebrews 5:7 says:

> In the days of his flesh, Jesus offered up prayers and supplications, with loud cries and tears to Him Who was able to save Him from death, and He was heard because of His reverence. – ESV

Mark 11:12-14, 20-26 says:

> On the following day, when they came from Bethany, He was hungry. And seeing in the distance a fig tree in leaf, He went to see if there was anything on it. When He came to it, He found nothing but leaves, for it was not the season for figs. And He said to it, "May no one ever eat fruit from you again." And His disciples heard it.

> (*The next day*) ...As they passed in the morning, they saw the fig tree withered away to its roots. And Peter remembered and said to Him, Rabbi, look! The fig tree You cursed has withered. And Jesus answered them, "Have faith in God. Truly, I say to you, whoever says to this mountain, 'Be taken up and thrown into the sea,'" and does not doubt in his heart, but believes that what he says will come to pass, it will be done for him. Therefore I tell you, whatever you ask in prayer, believe that you have received it, and it will be yours. And whenever you stand praying, forgive, if you have anything against anyone, so that your Father also, Who is in Heaven may forgive you your trespasses. – ESV

There's that call to righteousness again. Do I believe I am a righteous new creation in Christ, and am I also manifesting evidence of that confession with holy fruit? But this time that issue is set in a puzzle. Why did Jesus curse the fig tree for not having fruit when it was not even the season for it to bear fruit? When the disciples saw the withered tree, Jesus said, "Have faith in God," then went on to talk about faith to be able to throw a mountain into the sea. The lesson is this: Jesus did an *arbitrary* thing in cursing the fig tree. If God in heaven will grant an *arbitrary* request spoken in faith with righteous integrity, how much more will He grant a request for something that has *merit* if I have faith? Do I believe I have favor with God because I am in Christ and He is in me?

James 5:13-16 says:

> Is any among you suffering? Let him pray. Is anyone cheerful? Let him sing praise. Is anyone among you sick? Let him call for the elders of the church, and let them pray over him, anointing him with oil in the Name of the Lord. And the prayer of faith will save (**sosei** – *heal*) the one who is sick, and the Lord will raise him up. And if he has committed sins, he will be forgiven. Therefore, confess your sins one to another that you may be healed. The prayer of a righteous person has great power as it is working. (**energi**) – ESV (Shank)

Intercession

Intercession is to stand in the gap between God and another, who either cannot or will not stand for himself. I believe an intercessor must have a practical understanding of the following:

Christ being both God and man has empathy. He can identify with the suffering and temptation of mankind, knowing what it's like to be one of us.

Hebrews 4:14-16 says:

> Since then we have a Great High Priest Who has passed through the heavens, Jesus the Son of God, let us hold fast our confession. For we do not have a High Priest Who is unable to sympathize with our weaknesses, but One Who in every respect has been tempted as we are, yet without sin. Let us then with confidence draw near to the Throne of Grace, that we may receive mercy and find grace to help in time of need.
> – ESV

As the Son of God, seated at the Right Hand, He has the influence and power with the Father to act mightily on our behalf, because God has put all powers and principalities under His feet.

Ephesians 1:19-22 says:

> ... and what is the immeasurable greatness of His power
> towards us who believe, according to the working of
> His great might that He worked in Christ when He
> raised Him from the dead and seated Him at His Right
> Hand in the heavenly places, far above all rule and au-
> thority and power and dominion, and above every name
> that is named, not only in this age but also in the one to
> come. And He put all things under His feet and gave
> Him as Head over all things to the church, which is His
> body, the fullness of Him Who fills all in all. – ESV

As an intercessor, I must embrace by faith my *position* in
Christ, that I am a new creation in Christ, with a nature that is
now like His, because His Holy Spirit is joined to me, even
though I am still weak in my flesh. My flesh is mine, but it is
not **me**. Therefore, I must not presume to approach the Lord,
knowingly harboring unconfessed sin. But by believing who
Christ has made me to be, I will boldly approach my Father in
faith and stand in the sin-gap between God and another who
cannot or will not stand in faith for himself!

Hebrews 10:19-22 says:

> Therefore, since **I** have confidence to enter the holy
> places by the Blood of Jesus, by the new and living way
> that He opened for **me** through the curtain, that is,
> through His flesh, and since I have a Great Priest over
> the house of God, **I** can draw near with a true heart in
> full assurance of faith, with **my** heart sprinkled clean
> from an evil conscience and **my** body washed with wa-
> ter. I will hold fast the confession of **my** hope without
> wavering, for He Who promised is faithful.
> – ESV (Shank)

My weakness helps me to identify with the weakness of others, and my position at the Right Hand helps me to identify
with Christ as His child, with all powers and principalities
under my feet, in Him. I am not there by any merit of my own. I
cannot imagine the true significance of this, but I can make a
choice to *believe* it is true about me, and *act* on it with a
choice, because the Word of God does not lie! This is a choice

by my spirit, not the mood or opinion of my soul or the presumption of my flesh.

Ephesians 2:4-10 says:
> But God, rich in mercy because of the great love with
> which He loved **me**, even when **I** was dead in **my** tres-
> passes, made **me** alive together with Christ—by grace **I**
> have been saved—and raised **me** up with Him and
> seated **me** with Him in the heavenly places in Christ Je-
> sus. In grace, **I** have been saved through faith. And this
> is not **my** own doing; it is a gift of God, not as a result
> of **my** works, so that **I** may not be able to boast. For **I**
> am His workmanship, created in Christ Jesus for good
> works, which God prepared beforehand, that
> I should walk in them. – ESV (Shank)

The Word of God that does not lie also says in **Matthew 18:18**:
> Truly, I say to you, whatever you bind on earth will be
> bound in heaven and what you loose on earth will be
> loosed in heaven. – ESV

Putting all these truths together, we have promises from the
Lord that can revolutionize faith and reveal audacious strategies in the Holy Spirit. In interceding for my beloved son, I
learned that I must first take a stand against his sin by telling
him it was putting his soul in jeopardy. *Right and wrong were
clearly delineated.* Having done that, I tried to find every other
way possible to encourage him. We talked often of things we
both enjoyed. When he suffered hurts, I mourned with him.
When he had successes, I rejoiced with him. I often encouraged him to faith as far as he would let me. I shared with him
my own struggles with sin. I shared my own triumphs and
failures. Sometimes he threatened to cut me off when I said
something he didn't like hearing, but I remained patient because I loved him and I knew he loved me.

I also tried to educate myself in the powers of the besetting
sins that held him so tightly. There were lies at the bottom of
his assumptions about himself. There were also deceptive rein-
forcements that were the consequence of disobedience. There
were soul ties to fellow sinners. There was shame and con-

demnation. Of course, I made many mistakes, but I did as much as I could to understand what it must be like to be in his shoes. Because Jesus knows what it is like to be in my shoes, I never judged him for his temptations. I most certainly have plenty of my own.

Clearly, my son was suffering spiritual blindness because of his own sin. Blindness, deafness, and a hard heart are the consequences we all have when we refuse to repent. However, because my son was able to use *my sins* as an excuse to dismiss my calls to return to the Lord, the Spirit led me to make amends for many sins I had committed against him as his father. Whenever I saw one, I confessed it to the Lord and to my son and asked for forgiveness. Sin had ruined my integrity as a messenger. Love motivated me to restore that integrity for my son's sake. It also drove me to repent of how I had misrepresented the Lord. I began to open up more of my process in dealing with my temptations, from a Biblical point of view. My son knew about my successes and failures. I acknowledged many of my fears and weaknesses as well. Sometimes he used these confessions against me, but so what! This is my son; I would die for him, if necessary.

About a year before my son repented, the Lord told me to stop exhorting him to go to church. He told me my son would go just to get me off his back, not because his heart was ready. He must not go until the Lord had prepared the way for him. So, I told my son what the Lord said to me and my son was relieved. All my cards were on the table for him to see. God's love was there to see, too.

Christ is both man and God. He knows what it's like to be both. The Word became flesh and dwelt among us. My role as an intercessor requires identification with both the righteousness of Christ and the weakness of sinful man. In identifying with Christ, I must see myself as a new creation in Him, as being like Him in spirit. I must also confess any active sin and plead the Blood for myself first, that I may approach God in the Righteousness of Christ. Then I claimed verses like **Ephesians 2:4-10**, which declare that I am seated at the Right Hand, above all powers and principalities, which are under Christ's

Feet. Because I am in Him, these powers are also under **my feet**. This is God's doing, not **mine**. Then, in the favor Christ has from His Father, I stand in the place of **my** son Jonathan, for whom I am interceding and say:

> Lord I plead the Blood for him also. I stand in his place as You stood in mine and took the punishment I deserved, pleading mercy for me. Your grace enabled my eyes to be opened, my ears to hear and my heart to understand, that I might repent. I pray for mercy that You will not give him the punishment his sins deserve, either. I pray that his eyes will be opened, that his ears will be able to hear and his heart will be able to understand, and that You will grant him the gift of repentance. Because You said what we bind on earth is bound in heaven, I bind the power of Satan and restrict his interference. I bind Jonathan to the will and love of God. Because You said that what we loose on earth will be loosed in heaven, I loose the bonds of deception that blind him. I pray Lord that You will loose Your love, favor and mercy on Jonathan as I lift him up to You. I commit him to You in Jesus' Wonderful Name, amen!

Then I needed to stand on what I was trusting for, as I waited patiently for the answer, being willing at all times to speak when the Spirit told me to, or be silent, to do as the Spirit told me to do, or to get out of the way. It's important to see intercession as action as well as words. Over the course of my stand, I must be prepared to fast, exhort, encourage, and rebuke when necessary. Sometimes when I'm asking God to say such and such to the one I'm praying for, He will say, "Go and say those words to him yourself—you are My instrument!"

Be willing to experience rejection, condemnation, discouragement, and false starts. I found it necessary to turn him over to the Lord for whatever consequences necessary to bring about repentance. But remember, the one for whom you are praying has a free will and must come to a willing surrender. Only God knows what it will take and when it will happen. The Lord has proven repeatedly that He is a rewarder of those who seek

Him. Now it is my joy to be in wonderful fellowship with my son, whom the Lord has delivered and restored to faith!

Fasting

To humble one's self with fasting is also part of prayer. Fasting may be going without food for a period of time or it may be giving up a favorite food or activity for a season. It may be skipping a meal to spend time in prayer. It may be abstinence from meat or solid food for a while. But remember that fasting is a *work* and one must do it in *secret*, away from the regard and reward from men. Fasting does not hire God to do something we want like a magician deals with an evil spirit. Stay away from making a vow as an incentive for your request to be granted. This is not to be a *deal* with God. Do not be ensnared with condemnation by making a vow. Be righteous for righteousness sake because of who you are in Christ. Do not fast without drinking water. Agree with God beforehand how severe it will be and for how long. Sometimes Satan will come along and pretend to be the Holy Spirit saying, "If you really love me, go for another week."

If you have agreed with God what you are giving up, and for how long, stick to it. The Lord loves a cheerful giver and a heart that freely wants to please Him, and He will help us keep our commitment. In fact, you will find in fasts that go longer than two days, a sense of being lifted by the Holy Spirit sets in. We fast in His strength, not our own. A kiss that is spontaneously given is worth a hundred that are granted when requested. A voluntary sacrifice for the sake of love is most pleasing to God. If you are not yet spiritually mature, be humble and ask a more experienced Christian, and take his advice. If you are unhealthy or diabetic, ask for medical advice. Be honest, humble and teachable, for all else is vanity. Don't compare yourself to others who may be stronger or weaker than you are.

Isaiah 58:6-12 says:

> Is this not the fast that I choose:
>> To loose the bonds of wickedness,
>> To undo the straps of the yoke,
>> To let the oppressed go free,
>> To break every yoke?

Is it not to share your bread with the hungry?
> And bring the homeless poor into your house;
> When you see the naked, to cover him,
> And not hide yourself from your own flesh?
> [*family needs*]

Then shall your light break forth like the dawn,
> And your healing shall spring up speedily;
> Your righteousness shall go before you;
> The glory of the Lord shall be your rear guard.

Then you shall call, and the Lord will answer;
> You shall cry, and He will say, 'Here I Am.'
> If you take away the yoke from your midst,
> The pointing finger, and speaking wickedness,
> If you pour yourself out for the hungry
> And satisfy the desire of the afflicted,

Then shall your light rise in the darkness
> And your gloom be as noonday.
> And the Lord will guide you continually
> And satisfy your desire in scorched places
> And make your bones strong;
> And you shall be like a watered garden,
> Like a spring of water,
> Whose waters do not fail.

And your ancient ruins shall be rebuilt;
You shall raise up the foundations of many generations;
You shall be called the repairer of the breach,
The restorer of streets to dwell in. – ESV

Matthew 6:16-18 says:
> And when you fast, do not look gloomy like the hypo-
> crites, for they disfigure their faces that their fasting
> may be seen by others. Truly, I say to you, they have re-
> ceived their reward. But when you fast, anoint your
> head and wash your face, that your fasting may not be
> seen by others, but by your Father Who is in secret.
> And your Father Who sees in secret will reward you.
> – ESV

Imprecation

This is a lesser-known way to pray. These are prayers of warfare that invoke the wrath of God on our enemies. **Psalms 35, 58, 69, 83,** and **109** are Old Testament examples.

But Jesus says in **Matthew 5:44**

> ...love your enemies and pray for those who persecute you. – ESV

Romans 12:20 says:

> If your enemy is hungry, feed him... – ESV

Ephesians 6:12 says:

> For we do not wrestle with flesh and blood, but against the rulers, against the authorities, against the elemental powers over this present darkness, against the spiritual forces of evil in the heavenly places. – ESV

Since this is true, I believe prayers of imprecation should rarely be used against people but be more directed against the *spirits* that are driving them. But the gospel tells us that those who do not repent will suffer the same fate as the evil spirit whom they follow, when God judges the earth. Consequences are the great motivator for the sinner to repent. They certainly have been for my repentance. But prayers for consequences should never become a **conceit** to "sanctify" bitterness or to withhold forgiveness. I can have enemies through no fault of my own, but if I am at fault, I must strive to be reconciled so far as I am able. I must forgive all, including those who will not forgive me, humbly accepting my consequences in peace for what I may have done. And trusting God to help me bear up when I am innocent. The wrath of the Lord is righteous!

Psalm 35:1-10 says:

> Contend, O Lord, with those who contend with me;
> Fight against those who fight against me!
> Take hold of shield and buckler and rise to my help!
> Draw the spear and the javelin against my pursuers!
> Say to my soul, "I am your salvation!"
>
> Let them be put to shame and dishonor who seek my life!

Let them be turned back and disappointed
Who devise evil against me!
Let them be like chaff in the wind,
With the angel of the Lord driving them away!
Let their way be dark and slippery,
The angel of the Lord pursuing them!

For without cause, they hid their net for me;
Without cause, they dug a pit for my life.
Let destruction come upon him when he does not
    know it!
And let the net he hid ensnare him;
Let him fall into it – to his destruction! – ESV

Psalm 58:1-11 says:

Do you indeed decree what is right, you gods?
Do you judge the children of man uprightly?
No, in your hearts you devise wrongs;
Your hands deal out violence on earth.

The wicked are estranged from the womb;
They go astray from birth, speaking lies.
They have venom like the venom of a serpent,
Like the deaf adder that stops the ear,
So that it does not hear the voice of the charmers
Or of the cunning enchanter.

O God, break the teeth in their mouths;
Tear out the fangs of the young lions, O Lord!
Let them vanish like water that runs away;
When he aims his arrows, let them be blunted.
Let them be like the snail that dissolves into slime,
Like a stillborn child that never sees the sun.
Sooner than your pots can feel the heat of the thorns,
Whether green or ablaze, may He sweep them away!

The righteous will rejoice when he sees the vengeance;
He will bathe his feet in the blood of the wicked.
Mankind will say, "Surely there is a reward for the
    righteous;
Surely there is a God Who judges the earth. – ESV

Excommunication

In 1 Corinthians 5:1-5, Paul sends an unrepentant sinner out of the congregation. Verses **4-5** say:

> When you are assembled in the Name of the Lord Jesus and my spirit is present, with the power of our Lord Jesus, you are to deliver this man to Satan for the destruction of his flesh, so that his spirit may be saved in the Day of the Lord. – ESV

This prayer seems to have achieved its desired effect in the repentance of the sinful man in **2 Corinthians 2:5-11**:

> Now if anyone has caused pain, he has caused it not to me, but in some measure—not to put it too severely—to all of you. For such a one, this punishment by the majority is enough, so you should rather turn to forgive and comfort him, or he may be overwhelmed by excessive sorrow. So, I beg you to reaffirm your love for him. This is why I wrote, that I might test you and know whether you are obedient in everything. Anyone whom you forgive, I also forgive. Indeed, what I have forgiven, if I have forgiven anything, has been for your sake in the presence of Christ, so that we would not be outwitted by Satan; for we are not ignorant of his designs. – ESV

So, a prayer-stand of **imprecation/excommunication** by the whole congregation at Corinth results in repentance. This is not something we do alone, but with the agreement of the church. Then the congregation is to forgive and reinstate the man who repented, so that excessive sorrow or morbid shame does not cause the man to fall away in condemnation or the church to be corrupted by a prideful judgmental spirit. Forgive the one who repents. Continued shunning will foster *morbid shame* and *hopelessness,* defeating the power of grace to heal.

Chapter 16 Study Questions

1. What does it mean that God is Holy?

2. What is the difference between prayers of praise and prayers of thanksgiving?

3. What are positive and negative confessions?

4. What is the difference between petition and intercession?

5. Christ is both God and man. Why must an intercessor identify with Christ, and how do we identify with the one for whom we are praying?

6. What are some things we must remember to do when we fast, and what things should we remember not to do?

7. What situations warrant prayers of imprecation?

17

Personal Gifts of the Spirit

In Genesis, we read that God created the heavens and the earth. He created man in His image and gave him dominion over it. We were to rule the earth in God's Name and under His direction. The angels are able to visit the earth on God's errands, but the only beings allowed to dwell here legally are those who enter by the doorway of birth.

John 10:1-5 says:

> Truly, truly, I say to you, he that does not enter the sheepfold by the door but climbs in by another way, that man is a thief and a robber. But He Who enters by the door is the Shepherd of the sheep. To Him, the gatekeeper opens. The sheep hear His Voice, and He calls His own sheep by name and leads them out. When He has brought out all His own, He goes before them, and the sheep follow Him, for they know His Voice. A stranger they will not follow, but they will flee from him, for they do not know the voice of strangers.
> – ESV

Evil spirits do not come into the world by the lawful door of birth the way Christ did. They are thieves and robbers, coming to corrupt and undermine the Kingdom of God and the dominion over the earth God gave to Adam and his descendants. Because of the Fall and the deception of Sin, we are susceptible to thieving malevolence.

The Father, the Son, and the Holy Spirit are co-equal. The Father leads for the sake of order. A husband and wife are equal in value, but the husband is to lead for the sake of order. Jesus never contended with the Father for more control, but in His incarnation, Jesus emptied Himself of His own intrinsic power, when in beautiful submission, He legally entered the earth through conception by the Holy Spirit, in the virgin birth.

Philippians 2:5-7 says:

> Have this mind among yourselves, which is yours in Christ Jesus, Who, though He was in the form of God,

did not count equality with God a thing to be grasped, but made Himself nothing, taking the form of a servant, being born in the likeness of men. And being found in human form, He humbled Himself by becoming obedient to the point of death, even death on a cross. Therefore, God has highly exalted Him and bestowed on Him the Name that is above every name, so that at the Name of Jesus every knee should bow, in heaven and on earth and under the earth, and every tongue confess that Jesus Christ is Lord, to the glory of God the Father. – ESV

Having given up His own glory and powers, which He had in heaven, He did not begin His public ministry until He was baptized by John and received the power of the Holy Spirit. By the Spirit, He outwitted the enemy, endured abuse, saw into the hearts of men and perform miracles. Jesus was submissive to His Father's will. So are we to be.

But Satan saw God's power and authority as something he wanted to grasp. In **Isaiah 14:13-15**, The Lord said to him:
You said in your heart, "I will ascend to heaven; above the stars of God. I will set my throne on high; I will sit on the mount of assembly in the far reaches of the North; I will ascend above the heights of the clouds; I will make myself like the Most High." But you are brought down to Sheol, to the far reaches of the pit.
– ESV

For this offense, he was thrown down from heaven, not because God was selfish, but because Satan was grossly incompetent to be in the driver's seat and would have wrecked the whole universe, which only Christ in His mighty power can direct and hold together! And Satan's self-centered nature would have made paradise a hell.

When I was about four years old, I used to stand up on the back seat of our 1948 Plymouth and watch my father drive the car. There were no seat belts in those days. I looked over his shoulder and watched him put in the keys and push the starter button to make the engine go. I thought that I could do that too. One summer day I invited my three-year-old brother to go for a ride with me in Daddy's car. The car door must have been open; I don't remember how we got in, but I remember seeing my little brother sucking his thumb and giggling with excitement in his corner of the back seat. I was standing in the front seat on the driver's side, so I could see through the windshield.

I didn't have the keys, but I pushed the starter button. The motor didn't start, but the lurch of the starter-motor caused the car to roll about twenty or thirty feet, because we were on a small hillside. We hit a tree that stopped us from rolling into doctor Schroeder's yard or into his house. Naturally, my father was appalled at such an unthinkable thing happening to his small children, and he ran to see if we were injured. I was like Satan in the way I presumed, in the ignorance of my youth, that I could do what only my father could do. But Satan is *no child* and has *great malice* in his heart. His intentions are evil!

Luke 3:21-22 says:

> Now when all the people were baptized, and when Jesus also had been baptized and was praying, the heavens were opened, and the Holy Spirit descended on Him in bodily form, like a dove; and a Voice came from heaven, "You are My Beloved Son; with You I am well pleased." – ESV

Many say that Jesus could do all His miracles because He is the Son of God, but we can't because we're only human. But by seeing Jesus' example, the same power given to Him by His baptism in the Spirit, is to be ours because He is not only our Lord and Savior, He is also the Pioneer and Perfector of our faith! Avoid this **conceit** someone has said, "I don't want the gifts, I just want Jesus and *nothing more.*" Better to say, "I want Jesus and *nothing less.*" For the believer in Christ, the exercise of the power of the spiritual gifts is not presumption, but faith.

Hebrews 12:1-2 says:

> Therefore, since we are surrounded by so great a cloud of witnesses, let us also lay aside every weight, and sin which clings so closely, and let us run the race that is set before us, looking to Jesus, the founder and perfector of our faith, who for the joy that was set before Him

endured the cross, despising the shame, and is seated at the Right Hand of the throne of God. - ESV (*Shank*)

The Greek word for founder (*from* **arche**) is sometimes translated pioneer. It's also the root from which the branch springs, like the Vine image of Christ that produces fruitful branches in those who are grafted into Him.

Remember **Galatians 2:20b** where it says:
... And the life I now live in the flesh I live by the faith **of** [tou] the Son of God, Who loved me, and gave Himself for me. - RSV (Shank)

The word for perfector (*from* **teleo**) can also be translated finisher, to bring to an end, or completion. So Christ, the "**alpha and omega**" is the founder of my faith and also the perfector of it in me. His faith upholds mine and sets the example for me by demonstrating what the Holy Spirit can accomplish in believers. Jesus limited Himself to being born in the flesh, but He exercised miraculous power by the same Spirit Who indwells me, *not using* the power that He temporarily set aside, which He had in heaven. What He started in Himself by the Spirit, He completes in me, by the same Spirit.

John 14:12-14 says:
Truly, truly, I say to you, whoever believes in Me will also do the works I do; because I am going to the Father. Whatsoever you ask in My Name, this I will do, that the Father may be glorified in the Son. If you ask Me anything in My Name, I will do it. - ESV

Some say Jesus was only speaking to His disciples, not to us. Others say the works we will do were evangelizing the world, not signs and wonders. But the verse says "whoever believes in Me will do the works that I do." There is no specificity as to what those greater things are, or limits as to what they can be.

Gifts of Grace (Charismata)
1 Corinthians 12:4-13 says:
> Now there are varieties of gifts, but the same Spirit; and there are varieties of service and the same Lord; and there are varieties of activities, but the same God Who

empowers them all in everyone. To each is given the manifestation of the Spirit for the common good. For to one is given through the Spirit the word of wisdom, and to another the word of knowledge according to the same Spirit, to another faith by the same Spirit, to another gifts of healing by the one Spirit, to another the working of miracles, to another prophecy, to another the ability to distinguish between spirits, to another various kinds of tongues, to another the interpretation of tongues. All these are empowered by One and the same Spirit, Who apportions to each one individually as He wills. – ESV (*Shank*)

Many churches are wary of the Gifts of the Spirit because of the disorder that they have heard of or seen in charismatic meetings. But those fears block the Power of God among them as much as neglected order does where the Gifts are in fact encouraged. Note also that the use of utterance in the ESV is the Greek **logos**, which literally means Word, as in the Book of John, which says, "... in the beginning was the Word and the Word was with God, and the Word was God ...." I take this to mean something more forceful and authoritative than just an utterance. The text should say a **word** of wisdom, and a **word** of knowledge.

Proverbs 14:4 says:
> Where there are no oxen, the manger is clean, but abundant crops come by the strength of the ox. – ESV

A man could plant little without an ox in Jesus' day. But an ox requires maintenance and cleanup in the manger. Little is accomplished by human effort and knowledge. It takes the power of the Holy Spirit for breakthrough in both heaven and on earth, just like the power of an ox breaks the ground for a farmer by pulling a plow.

All intimacy is messy; vulnerability and strong emotions are part of it. When we are in love, sometimes we gush. A congregation that is shouting in the joy of the Lord is not doing something wrong, but the leaders of the church need to keep order as well as check intruding spirits that may try to bring deception into an emotionally vulnerable assembly, through errant doctrine, or to undermine the testimony of Christ through a loss of self-control.

1 Corinthians 13:8-13 says:

> Love never ends. As for prophecies, they will pass away; as for tongues, they will cease; as for knowledge, it will pass away. For we know in part and we prophesy in part, but when the perfect comes, the partial will pass away. When I was a child, I spoke like a child, I thought like a child, I reasoned like a child. When I became a man, I gave up childish ways. For now, we see in a mirror dimly, but then face to face. Now I know in part; then I shall know fully, even as I have been fully known. So now faith, hope and love abide, these three; but the greatest of these is love. – ESV

Some argue from this verse that what is referred to as the *perfect* which is to come means the *canon* of the scriptures, so the time of prophesy and tongues were only for the apostolic age when the writers of the New Testament were alive. But if this is true, why do we still need to acquire knowledge? Knowledge has not ceased, so neither have prophecies and tongues. But knowledge increases more and more in these days; including the knowledge of God in those very scriptures. The perfect that is coming refers to the return of Christ to the earth!

These verses also speak of maturity and the growth of our understanding and self-control. In this life, we see even the wisdom of scripture in part, or even dimly, at times. But when we see Christ face-to-Face, what more is there to learn? Then we will know even as we are fully known by Him.

1 Corinthians 14:39 says:

> So my brothers, earnestly desire to prophesy, and do not forbid the speaking in tongues. But all things should be done decently and in order." – ESV

If the time of prophecy and tongues is over, why does Scripture give instructions as to their proper use? As has been said by others, clear light can be broken by a prism into a spectrum of many colors from the same beam. So, the ministries to which we are called, given by the same Spirit, reveal varieties of gifts and services. The gifts are *tools*, not badges of honor. Believers tend to express different combinations of the gifts appropriate to their respective callings in service. If you are not in ministry of some kind, you probably do not know how God has equipped you supernaturally. Whoever is keen or sharp in spirit to know, will come to know. Whoever is dull in spirit will never know. I agree with those who find it helpful to group the gifts in following three categories. First, we will define the gifts in a brief summary form. Later we will go into more detail.

Gifts of Revelation

<u>Word of Wisdom</u> (**logos sophia**) —This is special insight into God's purposes and intentions. When carried by prophecy, it can foretell the future in the sense of what God is about to do. It does not have to be spoken aloud to be in operation but can also be a strategic guide in how to deal with an important situation.

<u>Word of Knowledge</u> (**logos gnosis**) —The revealing of hidden facts. Sometimes hidden sins or deep desires are revealed to convict a sinner or encourage a believer. This gift can also be prophetically spoken aloud or held in discretion as the Spirit directs. The one who receives it may use it for prayer focus, counseling or for taking specific action.

<u>Distinguishing Spirits</u> (**diakrisis pneumata**)—For the identification of the sources of spiritual influences, good or evil. This diagnostic gift is especially helpful in deliverance, intercessory prayer, or for the overseers of worship and testimony in the assembly, to determine if a word given is from God, or not. Counterfeit experiences and messages are exposed with this gift.

Gifts of Power

<u>Faith</u> (**pistos**) —This is greater than the basic faith required for salvation, even though it is the same Greek word. The emphasis is "to another is given faith," an *exceptional* thing not faith common to all believers. It is the power to trust, to wait for the Lord to do something promised or needed that only He

can do. It can be a spoken word of faith to proclaim confidently what is believed for, that it will be received, as in **Mark 11:24-26**. Or be a stand that encourages others to join in faith to glorify God for what He is about to do. It can also be a silent long-suffering perseverance in prayer despite evil hindrance, even when all others have given up, as in intercession.

Miracles —The working (**energeia**) of powers (**dunamis**) is a miraculous, temporary intervention to change or modify the laws of nature at the direction of the Spirit, for the purpose of stimulating faith and upholding a messenger as being from God.

Healing—Gifts of healing (**iaomai**) is the miraculous intervention of healing into the natural course of disease or injury. Notice the plural—gifts. Some have observed specialization in healing certain kinds of diseases. Others say the plural means various and diverse occasions of healing. These gifts do not mean one should not seek medical help when sickness occurs, as they are miraculous exceptions to the natural order of things. There will be further discussion on this subject in **Chapter 18**.

Gifts of Edification
Prophecy (**propheteia**) This is a supernatural utterance in a known language. It is a speaking forth of encouragement to build up the body of Christ. The simple exercise of this gift does not necessarily mean one has received the *office* of a prophet (see **Chapter 19**) as listed in **1 Corinthians 12:28**. That office is a recognition one should not seek for himself but should be recognized by the church after long-term evidence of reliability and wisdom.

Kinds of Tongues (**glossai**)—The gift of tongues is a supernatural utterance in a language unknown by the speaker. Some may despise this gift as foolish. But to the humble, it's wonderful to be able to pray beyond one's personal understanding, in the will of God, by the Spirit. Be careful what you despise or find of little value in the Kingdom of God! As the Apostle Paul says in **1 Corinthians 14:18**:

> I thank God that I speak in tongues more than all of you. – ESV

Interpretation of Tongues (**hermeneuo glossai**) —This is the ability to reveal the meaning of an unknown tongue. In a public use of tongues, an interpreter needs to be present so the whole congregation may benefit from the meaning. Privately, God can also reveal things to us as we worship in tongues, by the gift of interpretation, especially if we ask God to give us this gift, as Paul urges us to do in **1 Corinthians 14:13**.

> Therefore, one who speaks in a tongue should pray for the power to interpret. – ESV

How do I know the Voice of God?

If I see myself in the eyes of my flesh, I will always doubt. If I am in willful disobedience, I am already deceived and act in presumption. But if I am eager to be led by the Lord, I will obey His Voice. He says that if I love Him, I will keep His commandments. The more I say yes to His commands, the clearer His Voice becomes. He speaks clearly in His Word. He will never tell me to do anything that contradicts His Word. He cannot deny Himself. Obedience to His Word shapes my conscience and gives understanding to the mindset of my spirit. The more clarity I have about soul and spirit, (*see* **Chapter 5**) and the more I have plowed my fallow ground (**Chapters 8-14**), the better I am at discerning **conceits** that justify disobedience. Pulls that come through my flesh to disobey, are not coming from me anymore. I must believe I am a new creation in Christ. My old nature has been crucified in Him. His Word says I now have a new nature in Him, and I must believe it. My flesh is mine, but it is not me.

As I mature, I must learn to stop letting my mood or circumstances define me, or to determine what I really want to do, because I am in Christ and He is in me. His will is to do the will of His Father, and because I am in Him, I must choose to believe that His will is shaping my will also. I exercise faith by mixing it with the Word, taking *action* with righteous choices and deeds in *obedience*. His Word is a lamp to my feet and a guide to my choices. His rod of discipline and His staff of protection comfort me because He disciplines me. He loves and protects me from my enemy. I can receive correction because pride no longer prevents me from having the humility to learn from others. I have grace to learn from my consequences. I take responsibility for my choices. I forgive others so there is no snare to cause Satan to provoke God's justice against me.

Therefore, I will be bold in exercising authority at the Right Hand of God, where His Word says He has placed me in Christ. No power or piety or works of my own put me there. I believe God has equipped me also with spiritual gifts to be used as important tools for the ministry to which He has called me. Those He has called He has also equipped. He gives me grace to learn to live more and more like this.

The Gifts in More Detail
The Word of Wisdom
The word of wisdom is not the unusual insight of scholars or mystics, it is not the ability to organize or manage, not prudence or discretion, and is not sanctified common sense. The infinite inventory of facts in the Mind of God is His Knowledge. His plan and purpose of His predestined will, is His Wisdom. It is sometimes predicting of the future in prayer times and can be carried in prophecy, though it is at the discretion of the receiver whether it is spoken aloud to others. The spirit of the prophets is subject to the prophets. Sometimes it is meant only for guidance in prayer or counseling. A personal example comes to mind.

In the late seventies, we had returned from Amsterdam where we had been missionaries. The news media told a story about some Mullikan terrorists from a former Dutch colony. They had taken some young school children as hostages. Like many others back in Holland, I was seriously praying for the children to be released. Then, an image came to my mind of the children all getting sick. They were throwing up everywhere in the classrooms where they were held. The rooms smelled of a putrid odor and the children were all crying. Then I saw their captors becoming alarmed and disgusted with the situation, deciding to let the children go. So, I prayed that this would happen to break the standoff. The following afternoon, news came over the radio where I was working. I can't remember all the details, but the announcer said that the children being held hostage were released because they all got sick. Amazed, I shouted out to my colleagues, "That's exactly what I prayed would happen!" Those around me were startled and must have thought I was crazy.

Let me be clear about this. I was not the one who set the children free; it was the Lord, and God may have given the same vision to others to pray as well. But I am a witness; this was a word of wisdom showing what God was going to do, and He did it! Here are some Scripture examples of the word of wisdom:

1 Thessalonians 4:15-18 says:

> For this we declare to you by the Word of the Lord, that we who are alive, who are left until the coming of the Lord, will not precede those who have fallen asleep. For the Lord Himself will descend from heaven with a cry of command, with the voice of an archangel, and with the sound of the trumpet of God. And the dead in Christ will rise first. Then we who are alive, who are left, will be caught up together with them in the clouds to meet the Lord in the air, and so we will always be with the Lord. Therefore encourage one another with these words. - ESV

Without the Lord revealing His hidden plan of the rapture, we could not know about it and be encouraged.

Acts 27:21-26 says:

> Since they had been without food for a long time, Paul stood up among them and said, "Men, you should have listened to me and not set sail from Crete and incurred this injury and loss. Yet now I urge you to take heart, for there will be no loss of life among you, but only the ship. For this very night there stood before me an angel of the God to Whom I belong and Whom I worship, and He said, 'Do not be afraid, Paul; you must stand before Caesar. And behold, God has granted you all those who sail with you.' So take heart men, for I have faith in God that it will be exactly as I have been told. But we must run aground on some island." - ESV

Events happened just as Paul said they would in the verses that follow in the rest of the chapter.

1 Kings 21:17-19 says:

> Then the Word of the Lord came to Elijah the Tishbite, saying "Arise, go down to meet Ahab king of Israel, who is in Samaria; behold, he is in the vineyard of Na-both, where he has gone to take possession. And you shall say to him, 'Thus says the Lord, in the place where dogs licked up the blood of Naboth shall dogs lick your own blood.'" – ESV

God was about to punish Ahab and his wife Jezebel for their treachery in the murder of Naboth, as well as all they had done to lead Israel into sin. No matter what Ahab did to try to avert it, the purposes of God revealed in this word of wisdom came true exactly as foretold in **1 Kings 22:37-38**.

<u>Word of Knowledge</u>

This is not amplified human knowledge gained by study or experience; it is a revelation of facts hidden from man but known by God, and it is a mighty aid to counselors and intercessors. When it comes, it is not always spoken in public, but may also be used with discretion in counseling or in witnessing situations. Natural knowledge comes whether we walk with God or not, by observation, conversation, reading, and reflection. Knowledge that comes from knowing God for a long time is wonderful but is not specifically a word of knowledge. The first three chapters of the Book of Revelation reveal what God alone knew about the spiritual realities of the seven churches. He says to each in turn, "I know your works ... but this I have against you ... Return to Me and I will give you ... To those who overcome, I will give ..." So it is among individual believers as well.

As a new Christian in 1971, I was visiting a church where the power of the Spirit was in strong manifestation. I had invited some friends to come with me. After an outdoor public meeting had ended, we moved into a large three-stall garage to get into the shade to escape the August heat. Members of that church were coming to the two elders who were ministering. The people came to receive guidance and correction from the

Holy Spirit. There was a great brokenness among them. All were encouraged, but some received correction first. Then the elders turned to those of us who were guests, saying that the Lord also wanted to speak to some of us.

I was electric with both excitement and fear. I wanted the Lord to speak to me, but as a new Christian, I was afraid of what He might expose in me. The two elders came toward us, and the crowd made way for them. I felt myself gently pushed out of the way as they approached my two friends. They called the wife by name, even though they had never met. They also warned her to repent before some serious personal and spiritual consequences would befall her, regarding adultery. Despite the clear sign to her of being called by name and the strong message of warning, she refused to repent. In the years that followed, great harm came from her unfaithfulness, just as the elders had warned.

In **1 Samuel 9:15-20** we see both the word of wisdom in God revealing His plan for Saul, and a word of knowledge regarding the unknown status of his father's lost donkeys.

> Now the day before Saul came, the Lord had revealed to Samuel: "Tomorrow about this time I will send you a man from the tribe of Benjamin, and you shall anoint him to be prince over My people Israel. He shall save My people from the hand of the Philistines. For I have seen the affliction of My people, because their cry has come up to Me." When Samuel saw Saul, the Lord told him, "Here is the man of whom I spoke to you! He it is who shall restrain My people." Then Saul approached Samuel in the gate and said, "Tell me, where is the house of the seer?" Samuel answered, "I am the seer. Go up before me to the high place, for today you shall eat with me, and in the morning, I will let you go and will tell you all that is in your mind. As for your donkeys that were lost three days ago, do not set your mind on them, for they have been found. And for whom is all that is desirable in Israel? Is it not you and your father's house?" – ESV

Notice that the word of wisdom reveals that the following day God would send the man He had chosen to be king. The revelation—that the lost animals were found and that the Spirit would reveal all that was on Saul's mind—was a word of knowledge.

2 Kings 6:15-17 says:

> When the servant of the man of God rose early in the morning and went out, behold, an army with horses and chariots was all around the city. And the servant said, "Alas my master! What shall we do?" He said, "Do not be afraid, for those who are with us are more than those who are with them." Then Elisha prayed and said, "O Lord, please open his eyes that he may see." So, the Lord opened the eyes of the young man, and he saw, and behold, the mountain was full of horses and chariots of fire all around Elisha. - ESV

Acts 9:11 says:

> And the Lord said to him, 'Rise and go to the street called Straight, and at the house of Judas look for a man of Tarsus named Saul, for behold, he is praying, and he has seen in a vision of a man named Ananias come in and lay his hands on him so that he might regain his sight. – ESV

John 2:24-25 says:

> But Jesus on His part did not entrust Himself to them, because He knew all people and needed no one to bear witness about man, for He Himself knew what was in man. – ESV

John 4:17-18 says:

> The woman answered Him, "I have no husband." Jesus said to her, "You are right in saying, I have no husband; for you have had five husbands and the one that you now have is not your husband." – ESV

<u>Faith</u>
There is a progression that may be observed in degrees of faith. Norman Grubb says that in order to sit down in a chair, one must believe the chair will hold the one who will sit in it.

Romans 1:16-17 says:

> For I am not ashamed of the gospel of Christ: for it is the power of God unto salvation to everyone that believeth; to the Jew first, and also to the Greek. For therein the righteousness of God is revealed from faith to faith, – RSV (Shank)

As others have said:

Natural faith is the ability to accept the existence of Jesus based on historical records.

Saving faith (**Acts 16:31**) is the ability to believe God has removed the judgment that separated me from Him in Christ, making me a new creation.

Fruitful faith (**Galatians 5:22**) is the ability to obey God daily, resulting in a transformation of my character and to be a blessing of others.

Miracle faith, or as some define it, *a word* of faith (**1 Corinthians 12:9**), is the ability to believe God will honor my words as they come by His Spirit, for a miracle comes to pass. As a spoken word of faith that comes to pass is a Gift of Powers, Miracle Faith is the power to wait unwaveringly for God to do what He has promised, or to stand for what we have believed and trusted Him for.

In **Daniel 3:16-18**, the story of Shadrach, Meshach and Abednego, the men defied the command of the king to bow down to his idol, even if it meant being thrown alive into the fire:

> O Nebuchadnezzar, we have no need to answer you in this matter. If this be so, our God Whom we serve is able to deliver us from the burning fiery furnace, and He will deliver us out of your hand, O king. But if not, be it known to you, O king, that we will not serve your gods or worship the golden image you have set up.
> – ESV

Their faith was rewarded in their deliverance by an angel of the Lord, who was standing with them in the midst of the same fire that had killed some of the guards who had thrown them into it. The flames had no power over their bodies, their hair was not singed, their cloaks were not harmed, and there was not even the smell of soot on them. The ropes were burned off, but they stood again before the astounded Nebuchadnezzar, and he blessed their God! Their extraordinary word of faith was upheld.

In **Daniel 6**, Daniel has to either stop worshiping God or be thrown to the lions. He faithfully submitted to his circumstances and trusted God with the outcome. And God delivered him! Like Satan, who tries to work the justice of the Word of God against the children of God—the satraps conspired to hold king Darius to his own unbreakable law, to destroy Daniel. One can see how this gift will be one of the most important during the coming tribulation when one cannot buy or sell without worshiping the Beast.

In **Romans 4:20-22** says regarding Abraham:
> No distrust made him waver concerning the promise of God, but he grew strong in his faith as he gave glory to God, fully convinced that God was able to do what He had promised. This is why his faith was counted to him as righteousness. – ESV (*Shank*)

Abraham trusted God to fulfill His promises and through his Descendant Jesus, salvation came to all of us!

In **2 Kings 4:1-7** says:
> Now the wife of one of the sons of the prophets cried to Elisha, "Your servant my husband is dead, and you know your servant feared the Lord, but a creditor has come to take my two children to be his slaves." And Elisha said to her, "What shall I do for you? Tell me what you have in the house?" And she said, "Your servant has nothing in the house except a jar of oil." Then he said, "Go outside, borrow vessels from all your neighbors, empty vessels and not a few. Then go in and shut the door behind yourself and your sons and pour into all these vessels. And when one is full, set it aside. So, she went from him and shut the door behind herself and her sons. And as she poured they brought the ves-

sels to her. When the vessels were full, she said to her son, "Bring me another vessel." And he said to her, "There is not another." Then the oil stopped flowing. She came and told the man of God, and he said, "Go sell the oil and pay your debts, and you and your sons can live off the rest." – ESV

The wife of one of the sons of the prophets, gathered empty vessels at Elisha's direction, and they waited in faith as the vessels were all miraculously filled with oil to sell for provision in a time of famine. God provided for them because they waited in faith for His deliverance.

In **Genesis 49:1-27**, Jacob speaks a word of faith over all his descendants. All his words came to pass in the tribes that grew from each of his sons.

In **Exodus 12**, the people waited in their homes and ate their Passover meal, with blood over their doors, as Moses directed them. God brings forth their release from slavery in a single night with His judgment on Egypt. They waited in obedience by faith.

Chapter 17 Study Questions

1. What is the role of the gifts of the Spirit today?

2. How can I be confident that I am hearing from God and not another spirit?

3. What are the differences between a word of wisdom and a word of knowledge?

4. How does the word of faith differ from other kinds of faith?

18

The Only Autonomous Being

Who is like unto Thee?
There is no one in all the earth,
The stars and under the sea,
There is nobody, there is nobody,
There is no one like Thee!

O Lord and Master, pouring forth grace Adonai,
Nourisher, Satisfier, O El Shaddai,
Elohim God Almighty, El Elyon Most High,
Eternal El Olam is hidden from our eye!

Jehovah-Ro'i, the Lord is my Shepherd,
Jehovah-Nissi, the Lord is my Banner,
Jehovah-Tsidkenu, the Lord is my Righteousness,
Jehovah-Rapha, the Lord is my Healer.

Jehovah-Jireh, the Lord my Provider,
Jehovah- Shalom, the Lord is my Peace,
Jehovah-Shammah, the Lord is among us,
Jesus, the fullness of God dwells in Thee!
Jesus, Your Spirit of God dwells in me!
Who is like God?/ *Yeshua*/johnbyronshank.com/iTunes

As we have been saying, there is only One Autonomous Person in the universe: God. All other living beings and nonliving things derive their existence from Him. All of the hosts of heaven were made by Him, all spirits and all men, all the stars and planets in their courses, beasts in their ways, seasons in their times. Only He has the power to call into being that which is not. He called creation into being. He spoke and there was light. He said "let there be" ... and it was so!

Operations of Powers (Dunamis)

A miracle has been described as a supernatural intervention into the course of natural events or a temporary suspension of natural processes by an act of Divine Power. There are two prominent words for power in the New Testament.

Dunamis is the ability of God to call into existence that which is not, *absolute power.* Operations of powers (energeo dunamis) is given to us in the gifts of the Spirit. As His children, with His Spirit joined to our spirits, power and righteousness are given. The second significant word for power is **exousia**. This is the power and privilege of *delegated authority* as an office or calling from God. A master, a prince, or anyone set into authority has **exousia** power to exercise influence as an agent of God, even if they abuse it. Those who misuse what God has given will answer for it. The believer who recognizes his position at the Right Hand in Christ, acts in His Name. Before Pentecost, the disciples were given exousia authority to cast out demons and heal the sick. (**Matthew 10:1**) After Pentecost, they were given **energeo dunamis** by the Holy Spirit. (**Luke 24:49 and Acts 1:8**)

It's important to recognize that Satan's power is almost never stated as **dunamis**, but rather **exousia** power. Contrary to popular fiction and horror movies, he is not able to call into being that which is not. Though heavenly rulers and powers are referred to as **dunamis**, one must assume these were gifts and callings given before the Fall. Rebelling angels left their posts and now misuse their gifts and callings, apparently as demons. **Romans 11:29** says, "...for the gifts and callings of God are irrevocable."

The predestined *plan* of God has already anticipated all the evil generated by the sins of high powers and low men. He Himself does no evil but the Lord is bending all things to His wonderful purposes in Christ. They are under His Feet. Though Satan gives his dunamis of irrevocable gifts and callings to the beast in **Revelation 13:1-2**, he still has only temporary authority to manipulate and to deceive what is created by God:

> And I saw a beast rising out of the sea, with ten horns and seven heads, with ten diadems on its horns and blasphemous names on its heads. And the beast that I saw was like a leopard: its feet were like a bear's, and its mouth was like a lion's mouth. And to it the dragon gave his power [**dunamis**] and his throne and great authority [**exousia**]. – ESV (Shank)

Satan is manifesting himself through the beast. God permits the strong delusion they create, which deceives those who refuse to repent. So, the Lord calls a house into being from nothing. Satan can only break windows, leave the water running, wreck the furniture and so on, but he cannot do what only God can do, to call the house into being, from out of nothing.

God gave miraculous power to Moses to bring down the plagues (**Exodus 7:14-12:32**) and open the Red Sea (**Exodus 14:16**) so Israel could pass through on dry ground, as well as providing water from a rock in the wilderness (**Exodus 17:5-7**). Elijah was given power to call down fire on a wet altar in a test between Baal & Jehovah (**1 Kings 18:38**). Jesus raised the dead, multiplied food, walked on water, turned water into wine (all four **Gospels**). Paul strikes Elymas the magician with blindness for opposing the gospel. The proconsul saw this and believed in the power of God (**Acts 13:9-12**).

The Bible has many examples of miracles, great ones like those above and small ones like withering the fig tree with a curse. One of the sons of the prophets who followed Elijah was Elisha. Elisha had a determination to receive a great blessing from the Lord, as did his father Jacob before him, who wrestled with the angel of the Lord for His blessing of favor. Elijah was about to be taken up to heaven. Elisha was determined to be there when it happened. When Elijah told the prophets, who traveled with him to stay back, Elisha refused to obey out of his zeal. Elijah kept saying to Elisha that he should come no further with him at Gilgal, at Bethel, at Jericho, and at the Jordan River, but Elisha would not heed. Then Elijah rolled up his cloak and struck the river. The waters parted for him and he crossed. Elisha followed him over. When Elijah asked Elisha what he wanted from him, Elisha said he wanted a double portion of the Spirit that was on Elijah. He was not rebuked for his request.

Instead, Elijah said in **2 Kings 2:10-14**:
> "You have asked a hard thing; yet, if you see me as I am taken from you, it shall be so for you, but if you do not see me, it shall not be so." As they went on and talked,

> behold, chariots of fire and horses of fire separated the
> two of them, and Elijah went up in a whirlwind into
> heaven. And Elisha saw it and cried, "My father, my fa-
> ther! The chariots of Israel and its horsemen!" And he
> saw him no more.
>
> Then he took hold of his own clothes and tore them in-
> to two pieces. And he took up the cloak of Elijah that
> had fallen from him and went back and stood on the
> bank of the Jordan. Then he took the cloak of Elijah
> that had fallen from him and struck the water, saying,
> "Where is the Lord, the God of Elijah?" And when he
> had struck the water, the water was parted to one side
> and to the other, and Elisha went over. – ESV

Notice the persevering faith of Elisha, and pay close attention
to his faith, *putting on* Elijah's cloak. He *put off* his own
clothes and tore them in half. This is like my rejection of my
old identity, my old man. He then *puts on* his master's cloak.
This is like the command in Scripture for me to *put on* Christ,
my new identity, my new man! The old man has no power to
overcome, but the new man has supernatural power to overcome in Christ. And by extension, the new man also has access
to the supernatural power of the gifts of the Holy Spirit.

Was Elisha rebuked for his spiritual ambition? **No.** Was Jacob
rebuked for wrestling for blessing? **No.** Was Peter rebuked for
wanting to be able to walk on water like Christ? **No.** Is my desiring the spiritual gifts vain? **No.**

1 Corinthians 14:1 says:
> Pursue love, and earnestly desire the spiritual gifts, es-
> pecially that you may prophesy. – ESV

Why am I encouraged to desire and pursue these gifts and
their power? It's because they are to bring glory to God and
blessings to others. In pursuing the Lord, I must express faith
by being diligent with myself about my weaknesses and sins. I
must humble myself. I must be responsible with what is entrusted to me. If I am faithful with little, He will set me over
much. I must pursue integrity by *putting on* Christ and *put-*

ting off my old ways. But it's not my righteousness God will honor, but the righteousness of His Son in me. To believe that God can use "even me" is essential, because I am believing that I am at the Right Hand of God in Christ Jesus. Believing is *acting as if* what the Word says is true, in my whole walk. An occasional high spike of faith from God, beyond my normal level of living may happen sometimes because God is merciful. But I am called to a consistent obedience of faith in all circumstances, period. God is no fool. He knows if I mean what I confess. He knows the true desires of my heart.

<u>Gifts of Healings</u>
While the skills the medical profession are God-given, and the human body has God-given capacity to fight disease and heal wounds, the gifts of healings in this verse refers to supernatural cures (**iaomai**) for bodily infirmities above and beyond the natural means God has already provided. Sometimes the gift is used for spiritual and soul healing as well. The healing miracles of Jesus were not only acts of mercy to those who were sufferng, but also gave evidence that Jesus is Who He said He is.

In similar fashion, healings performed through His church show the favor of God on His ministers. The Power of Christ to triumph over death in the resurrection is also made more credible by healings. People are drawn to the gospel, moved to repentance, and glorify God because of them, especially in countries where the gospel has not been known. Healings are merciful evidence that the Word of God is true. As the Blood atones for our sins, the Stripes are for the healing of the body in this life as well as the next.

It is reported by missionaries in countries like India and other parts of the East, where the gospel has not been known, that they have more frequently observed miraculous healings. In the West, where hearts have grown cold and the love of God's righteousness is in decline, miracles of this kind happen less often. When Jesus was in Nazareth, He was not able to perform as many signs in His hometown, because the people had a skeptical contempt from knowing Him as just another kid from the neighborhood.

Matthew 13:57 says:

> And they took offense at Him. But Jesus said to them, "A prophet is not without honor except in his hometown and in his own household." – ESV

The West is becoming more and more like Nazareth. Familiarity breeds contempt in the West where diluted Christianity has become dull and is considered socially irrelevant. Seminaries ordain shepherds who are not even born again! They have merely fulfilled academic criteria for ordination and are more concerned with reshaping the gospel to suit the politics of the times. The blind, lead the blind in the name of Christianity, in many churches. But true repentance and revival can change all that.

Isaiah 53:5 says:

> But He was wounded for our transgressions;
> He was crushed for our iniquities;
> Upon Him was the chastisement that brought peace,
> And with his stripes we were healed. – ESV

Matthew 10:7-8 Jesus speaking to the twelve, said:

> And proclaim as you go saying, "The kingdom of heaven is at hand." Heal the sick, raise the dead, cleanse lepers, cast out demons. You received without paying; give without pay. – ESV

1 Corinthians 12:9 refers to gifts of healing. Recall from **Chapter 17**, some have observed that healing in certain categories of specialization is given to different people. Some have grace for success with blindness, others for hearing, and some for the lame. Some have grace for heart ailments, psychological problems or deliverance. I don't think the verse necessarily means specialization just because gifts are described in the plural. As I said earlier, it could as easily mean there are opportunities for many healings for those with this gift. But the Spirit distributes the gifts severally as He wills.

I have no preferential opinion about either way of seeing it. Healing is granted in response to faith in a variety of circumstances. In **Mark 2:1-4**, the substitutionary faith of friends is honored for the sick person who was lowered down through the roof. In **Matthew 9:20-22**, acting alone, the faith of a woman who suffered a blood discharge for twelve years, is granted healing. In **Matthew 9:25**, the faith of the father for his young daughter is honored in what was a raising from death. As in **Mark 9:28**, the most common situation, the faith of both the minister and the sufferer are honored.

James 5:14-15 says:

> Is anyone among you sick? Let him call for the elders of the church, and let them pray over him, anointing him with oil in the Name of the Lord. And the prayer of faith will save the one who is sick, and the Lord will raise Him up. And if he has committed sins, he will be forgiven. – ESV

This verse has a promise we can stand on because of the authority Christ has given to the office of the elder: the prayer of faith will save the one who is sick—the Lord will raise him up.

Why are people not healed?

I believe this gift is in operation today. Sometimes the prayer for healing manifests right away and sometimes it comes later. Sometimes long intercessions seem to be fruitless, but faith must persist against unbelief. I'm still standing in faith for healing in some persistent infirmities in friends which have not yet come to pass. But I continue to stand for them. Here are some Biblical reasons healing prayers do no produce results.

In **Matthew 17:19-20**, lack of faith is rebuked:

> Then the disciples came to Jesus privately and said, "Why could we not cast it out?" He said to them, "Because of your little faith. For truly I say to you, if you have faith like the grain of a mustard seed, you will say to this mountain, 'move from here to there,' and it will move, and nothing will be impossible for you." – ESV

Galatians 4:13-14 says:

> You know it was because of a bodily ailment that I preached the gospel to you at first, and though my condition was a trial to you, you did not scorn or despise me, but received me as an angel of God, as Christ Jesus. – ESV

Redemptive suffering—where God has a purpose in sickness to humble, or to draw someone to seek Him, or for identification with the sufferings of others in prayer, or to develop perseverance in faith, or to demonstrate the sufficiency of grace for all circumstances. Concerning Paul's thorn in his flesh, its remaining in him was not lack of faith in healing; he was an instrument of healing in many. He sought the Lord for relief three times, then accepted God's answer.

2 Corinthians 12:7 says:

> So, to keep me from becoming conceited because of the surpassing greatness of the revelations, a thorn was given me in the flesh, a messenger of Satan to harass me, to keep me from becoming conceited. Three times I pleaded with the Lord about this, that it should leave me. But He said to me, "My grace is sufficient for you, for My power is made perfect in weakness." Therefore, I will boast all the more gladly of my weaknesses, so that the power of Christ may rest upon me. For the sake of Christ then, I am content with weaknesses, insults, hardships, persecutions, calamities. For when I am weak, then I am strong. - ESV

The Gospels and Acts have many examples of healings for the purpose of revealing the Son of God to unbelievers, as gifts of grace. But unconfessed sins need repentance before healing can occur with believers when receiving communion, especially criticism, resentment, bitterness or an unforgiving nature.

1 Corinthians 11:27-32 says:

> Whoever, therefore, eats the bread or drinks the cup in an unworthy manner will be guilty concerning the body and blood of the Lord. Let a person examine himself, then, and so eat of the bread and drink of the cup. For anyone who eats and drinks without discerning the body eats and drinks judgment on himself. That is why many of you are weak and ill, and some have died. But if we judged ourselves truly, we would not be judged. But when we are judged by the Lord, we are disciplined so that we may not be condemned along with the world.
> - ESV

Sometimes another person is to be the instrument.

1 Corinthians 12:30 says:

> Do all have gifts of healing? Do all speak in tongues? Do all interpret? – ESV

A refusal to see medicine, diet, exercise, and personal behavior as factors contributing to the disease and allowing sickness to flourish, is another. The body is the temple of the Holy Spirit, requiring care and responsible maintenance.

Timing is a factor. Some healings occur immediately, but some are delayed until obstacles are removed, or until attitudes change. Some healings occur in stages through a process of healing involving growth.

Some root causes of sickness are physica*l*, like infections, broken bones, cancers—these are diseases and afflictions in the body.

Some diseases originate in the soul—psychosomatic, originating in mental or emotional stresses that arise from fears, traumas, anxieties, bitterness, angers, and condemnation.

Some are demonic in origin—disease in the spirit. Demonic possession, demonic harassment, curses and life controlling sin habits allowed to flourish because of long standing unbelief, disobedience, or unforgiveness.

Wise advice I have heard

If persons are convinced that their sickness is from God, don't try to talk them out of it. You may be persuasive verbally, but they may not be convinced on a deeper level. Their doubt will bring condemnation—like, I just can't seem to receive from God. Better to wait until they are ready inside. Similarly, we must also be careful not to obligate someone to believe because of our zeal. While God does honor the faith of the minister alone in some cases, one must be sensitive about possibly leading someone to discredit faith itself if they are not ready to go further.

There may be obstacles like those listed above, hindering favor for healing, but God is Sovereign and He will do as He pleases, out of His Goodness. He knows the highest good in each situation. Pray for those who willingly seek prayer, accept them as they are, be gentle and truthful with them. Don't urge someone go forward for healing who is not ready to believe.

Ministry of Healing
- I have learned some helpful advice from people who have more experience in this gift.
- First, listen to what the sufferer says is wrong and listen to what God says to do.
- Be free *not* to pray if your guidance is not yet clear or you perceive the sufferer does *not yet* have the faith to believe for healing.
- Do not give in to pressure to perform.
- Be honest about what you see or do not see.
- Be free to pray for those who come forward in faith and also for those for whom you feel a compassionate burden.
- Listen for root causes.

The laying on of hands and anointing with oil affirms identification with the sick and the favor of the Holy Spirit, as in James 5:13-16:

> Is anyone among you suffering? Let him pray. Is anyone cheerful? Let him sing praise. Is anyone among you sick? Let him call for the elders of the church, and let them pray over him, anointing him with oil in the Name of the Lord. –ESV

Be sensitive to the sufferer's needs, but know that healing comes from God by faith, not necessarily by bodily contact. Seek the guidance of God while praising Him. Whether there is a perceived manifest Presence or not—is not the point. Is not the Spirit of the Lord indwelling you at all times? If two or more of us are praying together, is He not in our midst? Leave manifestations of the Holy Spirit to the Holy Spirit. He decides when they are given. We believe we are joined to Him and Him to us, making us a new creation. I find phrases like "God showing up" in a prayer time to be insulting to Him. He is not conjured by our worship. He does not have to prove He is with us. More likely, He is waiting to see if we will prove ourselves faithful by trusting in Him, not by sight or with our feelings.

Pray specifically and in detail as guidance from the Lord comes to you, and encourage the sufferers to repeat after you, so they can speak forth their own faith. Emphasize the hope of health and positive results from the perspective of being seated at the Right Hand.

Pray with an aggressive confidence, believing what you say, as Jesus says in **Mark 11:22-26**:

> And Jesus said to them, "Have faith in God. Truly, I say to you, whoever says to this mountain, 'Be taken up and thrown into the sea,' and does not doubt in his heart, but believes that what he says will come to pass, it will be done for him. Therefore I tell you, whatever you ask in prayer, believe that you have received it, and it will be yours. And whenever you stand praying, forgive, if you have anything against anyone, so that your Father also, Who is in heaven may forgive you your trespasses." – ESV

If I am asking for God's grace in healing after many times offending Him, I must also be giving grace to those who have offended me. If I have Christ's nature in me, shall I not treat others with the same mercy and grace that He has given me? If I do not, how will I be able to pray without doubt that His power will move through me? A guilty conscience will always steal my confidence. It is not enough that I believe God heals if I do not walk in faith with some consistency in other areas of my life. If I have faith, I will have learned to make some progress in resisting sin and walking in victory in more areas of my life as well. I will not be perfect in my walk, but unforgiveness is a serious disobedience that offends God, poisoning my confidence before Him. I must not be like the wicked servant who was forgiven a huge debt by his master, then turned around to demand full satisfaction for a small debt that was owed to him by another.

When we pray for healing, only say "if it be your will" if you are uncertain of it—not because we doubt the goodness and power of God to heal.

Mark 9:21-24 says:

> And Jesus asked his father, "How long has this been happening to him?" And he said, "From childhood. And it has often cast him into the fire and into water, to destroy him. But if You can do anything, have compassion on us and help us." And Jesus said to him, "If You can!" All things are possible for one who believes." Immediately the father of the child cried out and said, "I believe; help my unbelief!" – ESV

Pray with Thanksgiving because God always answers prayer, even if it is not in a way we expect. Pray in the Spirit.

Romans 8:24-27 says:

> For in this hope we were saved. Now hope that is seen is not hope. For who hopes for what he sees? But if we hope for what we do not see, we wait for it with patience.
>
> Likewise, the Spirit helps us in our weakness. For we do not know what to pray for as we ought, but the Spirit Himself intercedes for us with groanings too deep for words. And He Who searches hearts knows what the mind of the Spirit is, because the Spirit intercedes for the saints according to the will of God. – ESV

Discerning of Spirits

This is not the gift of discernment, as some call it, but discerning spirits. This gift is not spiritual mindreading. It is not psychological insight or character assessment. It is not the power to discover faults in others.

Sometimes the Holy Spirit gives us a prophetic word as a gift of discerning of spirits, which exposes hidden motivations by spirits that are not from God, though they may have the appearance of being so. Counterfeit spirituality is rampant. If we do not know God's Word, or do not have the gift of discerning spirits mentioned above in **1 Corinthians 12:10**, we must wait to see what fruit a hidden agenda bears. Alas, this means we must often wait until painful consequences and appalling foolishness occur, that discredit the church of Christ. Better to be able to wield the two-edged sword of the Word—and have the gift of discerning spirits.

Ephesians 6:12 says:
> For we do not wrestle against flesh and blood, but against the rulers, against the authorities, against the cosmic powers over this present darkness, against spiritual forces of evil in the heavenly places. – ESV

Jeremiah 28 shows the testing of a true and a false prophet. In verses 13-17, the Lord reveals the truth:
> Go, tell Hananiah, "Thus says the Lord: You have broken wooden bars, but you have made in their place bars of iron. For thus says the Lord of hosts, the God of Israel: I have put upon the neck of all these nations an iron yoke to serve Nebuchadnezzar king of Babylon, and they shall serve him, for I have given him even the beasts of the field." And Jeremiah the prophet said to Hananiah, "Listen Hananiah, the Lord has not sent you, and you have made this people believe in a lie. Therefore, thus says the Lord: Behold, I will remove you from the face of the earth. This year you shall die, because you have uttered rebellion against the Lord." In that same year, in the seventh month, the prophet Hananiah died. – ESV

In the revealing that the Lord had not sent Hananiah we see discerning spirits. In the revealing God's plan for Hananiah we see a prophetic word of wisdom, which came true in two months. The vocal gifts like prophecy can often carry several gifts at the same time, as the Holy Spirit chooses. In prayer, don't we often speak praise and thanksgiving at the same time? Do we not often pray both petitions and intercession together?

Some diseases and infirmities are caused by spirits.

Luke 13:10-17 says:

> Now He was teaching in the synagogues on the Sabbath. And there was a woman who had a disabling spirit for eighteen years. She was bent over and could not fully straighten herself. When Jesus saw her, He called her over and said to her, "Woman, you are freed from your disability." And He laid His Hands on her, and immediately she was made straight, and she glorified God. But the ruler of the synagogue, indignant because Jesus had healed on the Sabbath, said to the people, "There are six days in which work ought to be done. Come on those days and be healed, and not on the Sabbath day." Then the Lord answered him. "You hypocrites! Does not each of you on the Sabbath untie his ox or his donkey from the manger and lead it away to water it? And ought not this woman, a daughter of Abraham whom Satan bound for eighteen years, be loosed from this bond on the Sabbath day?" As He said these things, all His adversaries were put to shame, and all the people rejoiced at the glorious things that were done by Him. – ESV

Sometimes deafness, dumbness and blindness have spiritual causes. **Matthew 12:22-28** says:

> Then a demon-oppressed man who was blind and mute was brought to Him, and He healed him, so that the man spoke and saw. And all the people were amazed, and said, "Can this be the Son of David?" But when the Pharisees heard it, they said, "It is only by Beelzebul, the prince of demons, that This Man casts out demons." Knowing their thoughts, He said to them, "Every kingdom that is divided against itself is laid waste, and no city or house divided against itself will stand. And if Satan casts out Satan, he is divided against himself. How will his kingdom stand? And if I cast out demons by Beelzebul, by whom do your sons cast them out? Therefore, they will be your judges. But if it is by the Spirit of God that I cast out demons, then the kingdom of God has come upon you." – ESV

Obviously, some afflictions have emotional or psychosomatic origins, and some can have physical causes. The gift of discerning spirits can show if an infirmity is organic or spiritual in nature. Notice that He says He casts out demons by the Spirit of God. As the Pioneer and Perfector of our faith, Jesus is showing us that the same Holy Spirit Who filled Him at His baptism—after He had emptied Himself of the Power He had in His own right as the Son of God before His incarnation—*is in us now.* The Holy Spirit was the Power by which He performed His miracles on earth. We must believe we now have both the nature and favor of God by the Holy Spirit's indwelling. If we truly believe the old nature we had before is dead and have *put on* Christ, the kingdom of God is now within us with power. Therefore, we are to show we have believed by being more like Christ in His ways, saying **no** to evil, with more and more success.

As we said in **Chapter 15** of this book, the slave girl spoke the truth in saying the apostles were proclaiming the way of salvation. She was not rebuked until the Holy Spirit showed Paul she had a demon. A thing is not necessarily from God just because it is spiritual or supernatural, or even a true statement. The spiritual root agenda was exposed by the gift of discerning spirits.

1 Timothy 4:1 says:

> Now the Spirit expressly says that in later times some will depart from the faith by devoting themselves to deceitful spirits and doctrines of demons ..." – ESV

For this very reason, the church is to be equipped with this gift of discerning spirits.

2 Thessalonians 2:8-12 says:

> And then the lawless one will be revealed, whom the Lord Jesus will kill with the breath of His Mouth and bring to nothing by the appearance of His coming. The coming of the lawless one is by the activity of Satan with all power and false signs and wonders, and with all wicked deception for those who are perishing because they refused to love the truth and so be saved.

Therefore, God sends them a strong delusion, so that they may believe what is false, in order that they may be condemned who did not believe the truth but had pleasure in unrighteousness. – ESV

This is one of the few verses where Satan's power is **dunamis**. The Holy Spirit stands aside and lets the fullness of the devil's own nature and energy be manifest without God's restraint for a short time before the Judgment Day. But his dunamis is false signs and wonders!

Thoughts on Demons and Spirits

I don't refer to a sin as a spirit because it blurs the areas of personal responsibility to be righteous. For example, fornication and drunkenness are sins and should not be personified as spirits to be exorcised, even though Satan's hold in these areas may need to be rebuked.

I think calling someone's attitude a spirit can also be confusing. For example, saying someone has a bitter spirit does not mean possession when it is only a figure of speech. A demonic presence can express bitterness, but discerning spirits must clarify what is specifically happening.

I also avoid calling various atmospheres spirits. To say a church has a "cold spirit" or a "different spirit" may be an accurate assessment of its spiritual health, but it could also be a slanderous insinuation or outright condemnation of another part of the body of Christ. If a church needs changing, pray for it or talk to the leaders about specific problems. Be careful with judgments.

Personal Experience

This gift has been valuable to me in counseling, evangelism, and in intercession, where getting to the root of things is critical. It has occasionally been expressed when I was not expecting it. Once I was sitting in the audience at a Christian conference, listening to a speaker on the subject of worship. He was making much of what we can receive from the heavenly regions while praising the Lord. As I listened, I became increasingly aware that something was wrong, even though I did not necessarily hear doctrinal error. There was something in the man that God was angry about.

That night, I sought the Lord about what was troubling me, and He said I was to say that because God is Holy, He is offended if we approach Him without dealing with our own sin first. The next morning, I approached him respectfully and gave him the word I received about his teaching on worship, that the Lord wants us to be clean before we go before the people in His Name, especially if we are leading others in worship. The Lord wants us to be pure in heart, confessing and repenting of known sin.

He was very subdued in the morning lecture after being quite flamboyant the night before. When he finished speaking, he packed up all the merchandise he had for sale and left. I was criticized by some of the pastors and elders for unsettling a guest speaker before he was about to teach. A month later, that same speaker announced that he was stepping down from ministry because of a longstanding adulterous affair with one of his worship team singers. God did not reveal the nature of the man's sin to me but wanted me to warn him. He was guilty of presumption in making worship a show, instead of a sincere expression of truth in the inward heart.

Prophecy
Prophetic insight and proclamation is a manifestation of the Spirit in a known language that reveals something of God's Mind that does not originate in the mind of the speaker. The Greek word **prophateo** means to speak for another—a spokesman for God. In Hebrew, **naba** means to go forth, like a stream, **nataph** to let drop, like oil, **massa** to lift up, like a banner, and **chazah** to see in vision. - unknown source

1 Corinthians 12:10 lists the gift of prophecy among the ministries of individuals. **Ephesians 4:11,12** lists it in the offices given to the church:

> And He [*Christ*] gave the apostles, the prophets, the evangelists, the shepherds and teachers, to equip the saints for the work of the ministry, for building up the body of Christ ..." - ESV (Shank)

1 Corinthians 12:28-31 Some of the other gifts to individuals are similarly listed as offices or corporate gifts to the church:
> And God has appointed in the church first apostles, second prophets, third teachers, then miracles, then gifts of healing, administrating and various kinds of tongues. Are all apostles? Are all prophets? Are all teachers? Do all work miracles? Do all possess gifts of healing? Do all speak in tongues? Do all interpret? But earnestly desire the higher gifts. – ESV

Because **1 Corinthians 14:31** says that all may potentially prophecy in turn, no one should think that because he can interpret tongues or speak a prophecy in a meeting that he is then like Moses, acting in the *office* of a prophet. God will give ample evidence if we are given such a high calling. Greater wisdom, revelation and power are given to those in the office of a prophet like Elijah or Elisha.

New Testament prophecy has been confused with prediction. But the Greek means telling forth or speaking forth. Apparently Medieval English popularized the notion of prediction as the meaning of the word. Predictions are the venue of a word of wisdom, what God will do. Revealing hidden facts are done with a word of knowledge. Prophecy can carry these other gifts, but the consistent function of the gift of prophecy is to edify, console, exhort, encourage, warn and comfort.

Women may prophecy as freely as men. **Acts 2:17-18** says:
> And in the last days it shall be, God declares, that I will pour out My Spirit on all flesh, and your sons and your daughters shall prophesy, and your young men shall see visions, and your old men will dream dreams; even on My male servants and female servants in those days I will pour out My Spirit, and they shall prophesy. – ESV

In the Old Testament, prophets were God's instruments of revelation for the will of God as it was unfolding in the life of Israel. If Israel disregarded the words of the prophet, there were serious consequences because God was using the prophets to both lead and judge the people, even after the installation of kings. False prophets were put to death for causing the people to believe a lie. Christ was prefigured in three offices then: the prophet, the priest, the king. He was also prefigured as the sacrificial lamb. The nation of Israel was called the people of God.

In the New Testament, prophets are speaking to the Bride of Christ, peopled by all the nations of the world. Now we know Jesus as Prophet, Priest, King and the Sacrificial Lamb of God, the role of prophet has changed for the church age.

1 Corinthians 14:29-32 says:
> Let two or three prophets speak, and let the others weigh what is said. If a revelation is made to another sitting there, let the first be silent. For you can all prophecy one by one, so that all may be encouraged, and the spirits of the prophets are subject to the prophets. For God is not a God of confusion but of peace. - ESV

When a prophecy is given, it is to be *weighed.* This means the word needs to be *tested.* In **Revelation 2:1-2**, the Ephesian church is commended for testing those who call themselves apostles and are not, finding them to be false.

1 John 4:1 says:
> Beloved, do not believe every spirit, but test the spirits to see whether they are from God, for many false prophets have gone into the world. - ESV

When **1 Corinthians 14:29-32** says, "If a revelation is made to another sitting there, let the first be silent," I believe it is not only for order and courtesy that we give pause, but also to allow time for a revelation to touch the one for whom it is intended. There may be a response from that person. Overseers may need to comment. If we all just trample each other to be heard, what good is that? "The spirits of the prophets are subject to the prophets," speaks to both accountability to each other and gracious discretion in not going on and on in the meeting, once two or three have spoken. Is this the Holy Spirit speaking? Can I exercise restraint by faith? The same Lord

Who gives gifts also commands that we are to govern their use. These are good rules for public meetings.

In private prayer meetings with believers only, intercession and spiritual warfare that may go on for some time, I have seen the Holy Spirit speak at length in one case after another as direction is being sought. There are also private prayer meetings where confirmation and encouragement are being sought through the leaders of the church for various members. Discerning spirits, words of knowledge and words of wisdom are often given and are *not in my opinion* limited to the rule of three. But weighing and testing should still be part of those times as well, with all humility.

Prophecy comes in words, pictures, symbols and even theatrical acting out. In the **Book of Ezekiel**, the prophet builds a scale model of Jerusalem and acts out the coming siege. He spends 390 days lying on his side, baking his ration of bread before a dung fire, to illustrate the coming famine. He cuts off all his hair, slashes one third of it with a sword, burns one third of it with fire, and casts a third of it to the wind to scatter it while a sword pursues it. A small amount of his own hair is to be put inside his coat to symbolize the preservation of a remnant, then half of that remnant is thrown away to the wind! That book has many other examples as well.

As was predicted in **Isaiah 11:1-2**, All Israel, including the family of Jesse, would be reduced from being a great tree, to being only a stump, after the Babylonian captivity. The Messiah Who came as a Man in the Incarnation, will return to rule as The King in the future Millennium. He came the first time from a small shoot growing out of that stump which was all that was left of the house of Jesse, David's father:

> There shall come forth a shoot from the stump of Jesse,
> and a branch from his roots shall bear fruit.
> And the Spirit of the Lord shall rest on Him,
> the Spirit of wisdom and understanding,
> the Spirit of counsel and might,
> the Spirit of knowledge and the fear of the Lord.

Acts 21:10 says:

> While we were staying for many days, a prophet named
> Agabus came down from Judea. And coming to us, he
> took Paul's belt and bound his own feet and hands and
> said, "Thus says the Holy Spirit, this is how the Jews at
> Jerusalem will bind the man who owns this belt and
> deliver him into the hands of the Gentiles." – ESV

On hearing those words, the people tried to dissuade Paul from
going on the Jerusalem, but Paul said he was ready to face
whatever the Lord had for him. Agabus was correct and so was
Paul.

A Personal Example

As a young missionary in Amsterdam, I was walking and praying one morning about the need of our fellowship to hear wisdom and encouragement from God's voice. I had also been
praying in tongues. Among other requests, I asked the Lord to
raise up prophets among us. Then He clearly said to me, "Ask
Me this for yourself." "Me?" I exclaimed. "I don't know anything about how to do that." He said to me, "I will teach you."
So, I asked Him for the gift and knowledge of how to use it. I
had received a prophetic gifting, but not the office of a prophet.

In the weeks and months that followed, whenever I asked the
Lord for a word from Him, He gave it to me, sometimes even
when I did not ask. Sometimes I wrote down what He said so I
wouldn't forget, then read it when I thought the time to speak
had come in the worship meetings. I often felt nervous about
when the right moment would be to speak, but I eventually
realized my anxiety was just the enemy trying to make me focus on myself. Sometimes I realized there was more to what I
shared in the meeting and wished I had grasped it more clearly.
But I was comforted by the verses in **1 Corinthians 13:9-10,12**,
which say:

> For we know in part and we prophesy in part, but
> when the perfect comes, the partial will pass away...
> For now, we see in a mirror dimly, but then face to
> Face. Now I know in part; then I shall know fully, even
> as I am fully known. – ESV

<u>Speaking in Tongues</u>
The Holy Spirit's Mind, moving through my submitted will and mouth, in a language that I have not learned or understood, is the gift of tongues. But why on earth would someone want to speak in tongues?

Mark 16:17 says:

> Jesus Himself said, "And these signs will accompany those who believe: in My Name they will cast out demons; they will speak in new tongues ..." – ESV

Acts 2:1-4 says:

> When the day of Pentecost arrived, they were all together in one place. And suddenly there came from heaven a sound like a mighty rushing wind, and it filled the entire house where they were sitting. And divided tongues as of fire appeared to them and rested on each of them. And they were all filled with the Holy Spirit and began to speak in other tongues as the Spirit gave them utterance. – ESV

A similar experience happened in **Acts 10:44-48**, the first "Gentile Pentecost" at the home of Cornelius:

> While Peter was still saying these things, the Holy Spirit fell on all who heard the Word. And the believers from among the circumcised who were with Peter were amazed because the gift of the Holy Spirit was poured out even on the Gentiles. For they were hearing them speaking in tongues and extolling God. Then Peter declared, "Can anyone withhold water from baptizing these people, who have received the Holy Spirit just as we have?" And he commanded them to be baptized in the Name of Jesus Christ. Then they asked him to remain for some days. – ESV

Acts 19:1-7 says:

> And it happened that while Apollos was in Corinth, Paul passed through the inland country and came to Ephesus. There he found some disciples. And he said to them, "Did you receive the Holy Spirit when you believed?" And they said, "No, we have not even heard

that there is a Holy Spirit." And he said, "Into what then were you baptized?" They said, "Into John's baptism." And Paul said, "John baptized with the baptism of repentance, telling the people to believe in the One Who was to come after him, that is, Jesus. On hearing this, they were baptized in the Name of the Lord Jesus. And when Paul had laid his hands on them, the Holy Spirit came on them, and they began speaking in tongues and prophesying. They were about twelve men in all. – ESV

If I have the gift of tongues, God means for me to use it that I may pray by the Spirit beyond the limits of my own understanding. Tongues build me up as I use them to increase boldness and faith for whatever stand I may need to take. I must be prepared for obstacles and not give up because of those hindrances. I have also noticed that when I exercise tongues often, my other gifts seem to come forth with greater frequency and clarity.

1 Corinthians 14:39 says:

So my brothers, earnestly desire to prophesy, and do not forbid speaking in tongues. But all things should be done decently and in order. – ESV

I received this gift shortly after being baptized in the Spirit in 1971 when I was 25 years old. Because I had also gone through deliverance when the Holy Spirit came into me and drove an evil spirit out, I went home exhausted but elated. The Fire Hose had cleaned me out inside. No further manifestations happened that night. It may have been the following week that there was teaching on the gift of tongues, with an invitation offered to have prayer to receive it. Many others joined me, so we were divided into small groups of six or eight around more experienced believers. Each of us prayed aloud to receive the gift, and the leader laid hands on us, and we were encouraged to speak in the tongue the Spirit had given us.

In the time that followed, each of us had problems of unbelief that the leader helped us overcome. Though eager, we all felt foolish making what seemed like nonsense words. This was an alien experience, like the first time I put on Christ as my new identity. I had heard and believed the Scriptural foundation for tongues in the sermon, but this was a whole new way of prayer and I felt I was being asked to walk on water without the solid ground of understanding under my feet.

The Holy Spirit gave wisdom and encouragement to each of us through the leader as we stepped out in faith that the Word of God was now in our mouths. To those who kept saying the same phrase repeatedly, the leader encouraged them that the Lord had given what they had begun to speak, but there was a whole language with an extensive vocabulary the Spirit wanted them to use. What was begun in faith, needed to be continued in faith. To those who tried to control what they were saying, the leader encouraged them to speak faster to break off self-effort. Those who seemed to be exploding in unformed syllables were encouraged to slow down and have faith to exercise more precise articulation. As we became more confident, we were encouraged to sing in the Spirit, extending our vowels in the simple melodies we were making. It was fun!

I must also confess a foolish thing I did during that training time. The girl kneeling next to me was fluent in French, so I started affecting a French accent as I spoke, secretly hoping she would be able to translate my tongue—proving I was speaking a real language. **Ha**! Unbelief unmasked. She took no notice of my words. The crutch I was grasping for was not there. I had to believe in the Holy Spirit moving through me!

Since that day, when I have prayed for others to receive this gift, the wisdom of the leader who prayed with me has helped me help them. Once a person I was praying with, who was studying German in school, began to speak with a German accent. She associated a foreign language to be pronounced as her German class had taught her. I told her to let that assumption go. We had a laugh about it later because I told her what my natural mind did when I first used a French accent. Neither of us was condemned by the Spirit because we were stepping out by faith from what was familiar into something unknown.

In my private prayer times, the enemy often accused me of making it all up and that God was angry at my insulting presumption and rattling nonsense. But as I learned to resist him by continuing to stir the gift, I became stronger.

1 Corinthians 14:4 says, "He that speaks in a tongue edifies himself, builds himself up." But this is *not* to be confused with the 'puffing up" of vanity. The same Spirit Who convicts us of vanity does not work against His Own Nature by encouraging vanity. What I have learned is that in exercising this gift, I invite the intercession of the Spirit through me by praying beyond my limited understanding. Gifts of wisdom and knowledge have been activated in me at different times, so that I could pray more effectively with understanding, as a result of my frequent use of tongues. I have found this to be the way other gifts are "loosened" in me. We are also encouraged to desire and seek the higher gifts, as well. This is not vanity either.

Some churches say that if one does not speak in tongues, one is not filled with the Spirit. Abuse occurs when, as I once heard an evangelist say to someone who had come forward for prayer and spiritual filling, "Manifest your evidence now, manifest your evidence!" Was he looking for proof that the supplicant was supposed to provide? The Scripture says *not all* speak in tongues, *not all* prophesy... We are to encourage each other and build up the church, not shame someone coming forward in repentance. The Holy Spirit is discredited by the spiritual abuse of those in error acting in His Name.

On the other hand, not all those who speak in tongues have a public ministry of exercising that gift. Some do, some don't. But my observation is that the gift seems to be given primarily for personal equipping and strengthening in whatever ministries each of us is called. Stir it, and other gifts are brought to bear on the problem being faced through prayer or by taking courageous action. Yet, some are called to stir the interpreting gift in others, in public meetings.

Interpretation of Tongues
The Holy Spirit shows the meaning of a tongue by interpretation (**hermanea** *to explain thoroughly*). It is not a translation,

314

but an interpretation, wherein the speaker looks to God for the meaning of the tongue. The style can take the form of a picture or a vision. It can also be a plain speaking of the meaning, depending upon the personality of the one interpreting. When we study the Word, we begin to notice the differences in personality of the prophets or the apostles, too. The same Spirit, Who used the different temperaments and personalities of each of them, uses our personalities as well.

Here's a formula that can be deduced from Scripture: tongues + interpretation = prophecy.

1 Corinthians 14:3-5 says:
> On the other hand, the one who prophesies speaks to people for their up-building and encouragement and consolation. The one who speaks in a tongue builds up himself, but the one who prophesies builds up the church. Now I want you all to speak in tongues, but even more to prophesy. The one who prophesies is greater than the one who speaks in tongues, unless someone interprets, so that the church may be built up.
> – ESV

1 Corinthians 14:12-26 gives direction in use of the vocal gifts:
> So with yourselves, since you are eager for the manifestations of the Spirit, strive to excel in building up the church. Therefore, one who speaks in a tongue should pray for the power to interpret. For if I pray in a tongue, my spirit prays but my mind is unfruitful. What am I to do? I will pray with my spirit, but I will pray with my mind also; I will sing praise with my spirit, but I will sing with my mind also. Otherwise, if you give thanks with your spirit, how can anyone in the position of an outsider say "Amen" to your thanksgiving when he does not know what you are saying? For you may be giving thanks well enough, but the other person is not being built up. I thank God that I speak in tongues more than all of you. Nevertheless, in church I would rather speak five words with my mind in order to instruct others, than ten thousand words in a tongue.

> Brothers, do not be children in your thinking. Be infants in evil, but in your thinking, be mature. In the Law it is written, "By people of strange tongues and by the lips of foreigners will I speak to this people, and even then, they will not listen to Me, says the Lord. Thus, tongues are a sign *not for believers* but for unbelievers, while prophecy is a sign *not for unbelievers* but for believers. If, therefore, the whole church comes together and all speak in tongues, and outsiders and unbelievers enter, will they not say you are out of your minds? But if all prophesy, and an unbeliever or outsider enters, he is convicted by all, he is called to account by all, the secrets of his heart are disclosed. And so, falling on his face, he will worship God and declare that God is really among you. – ESV (Shank)

Rarely does one interpret who does not also speak in tongues, hence the exhortation to pray that if we speak in a tongue, we should pray that we may also interpret. People who saw the outpouring of the Spirit at Pentecost accused the disciples of being drunk. Sometimes joyful congregational outpourings happen in church now, too. And I love it! But we must not let it get out of hand with an abuse of order. The same Holy Spirit Who gives gifts also commands order for their use. I have been criticized sometimes for calling for order when things have become wild and disorderly. They said I was quenching the Spirit by insisting we restore order. But quenching the Spirit is when we disobey Him, and order is one of His commands. We are not selves-for-ourselves, we are selves who love and serve the needs of others, like Christ did.

I think the part about tongues being a sign for unbelievers refers to the Old Testament prophets who were warning Israel that judgment was coming from God through the Babylonians, because of their unbelief. **Isaiah 28:11** says:

> For by people of strange lips and with a foreign tongue
> The Lord will speak to this people... – ESV

Israel's disobedience turned a deaf ear to the prophets. So, they were about to receive orders by the lips of Babylonians, in a language they did not understand because they had willfully turned a deaf ear to the Words of the Lord written in their own language and refused to repent. Unbelieving gentiles are also under judgment. The Spirit of God makes no sense—*nonsense*—to them either, because of unbelief.

The remnant in Israel who were still believers listened to the Word of God and were blessed by conviction of sin, being called to account, encouraged, warned, or to be exhorted to keep doing what is right. The language of their captors was accepted as the will of God for them because they knew God and understood what He was doing to prune Israel. So, prophecy is a sign to believers because they will hear it and respond.

But this prophesy which is for believers, also becomes a mercy for unbelievers through the interpreting of tongues, especially the gentiles who never heard the Word. They are given revelation and conviction to repent through the interpretation, as well as through clear prophesy in their own language.

The Church Age has the opportunity for the ingathering of the rest of the world who will *listen* and *repent*. In turning away from Jesus, Israel became blinded and deaf because they rejected their Messiah; the Lord spoke through Isaiah and was quoted by Paul in **Romans 10:20**, regarding the Gentiles:

> I have been found by those who did not seek Me;
> I have shown Myself to those who did not ask for Me.
> – ESV (*Shank*)

After the world that has heard the gospel also turns away, and the true church is raptured, favor will once again return to Israel. When Christ returns to earth to rule in the Millennium, Israel will again listen, repent, and be saved—even though they do not now seek the Lord. **Romans 10:20** will then apply to them:

> I have been found by those who did not seek Me;
> I have shown Myself to those who did not ask for Me.
> – ESV

Romans 11:25-29 says:

> Lest you be wise in your own sight, I want you to understand this mystery, brothers: a partial hardening has come upon Israel, until the fullness of the Gentiles has

317

come in. And in this way all Israel will be saved, as it is written, "The Deliverer will come from Zion, He will banish ungodliness from Jacob: and this will be My covenant with them when I take away their sins."

As regards the gospel, they are enemies of God for your sake. But as regards election, they are beloved for the sake of their forefathers. For the gifts and the callings of God are irrevocable. – ESV

We are to be gracious to each other, taking turns and letting the leaders weigh the message.

As 1 Corinthians 14:26-33 says once again:
> What then brothers? When you come together, each one has a hymn, a lesson, a revelation, a tongue, or an interpretation. Let all things be done for building up. If any speak in a tongue, let there be only two or at most three, and each in turn, and let someone interpret. But if there is no one to interpret, let each of them keep silent in church and speak to himself and to God. Let two or three prophets speak, and let the others weigh what is said. If a revelation is said to another sitting there, let the first be silent. For you can all prophesy one by one, so that all may learn and be encouraged, and the spirits of the prophets are subject to the prophets. For God is not a God of confusion but of peace. – ESV

That phrase referring to the spirits of the prophets being subject to the prophets is important. If I feel myself strongly compelled to prophesy after two or three others in a public meeting, I am still to stop. I am to be responsible for order, which is also a grace given by the Holy Spirit. If the Lord has given me a vital message, I am to have faith to wait until another time or speak to those for whom it is intended, after the meeting. Who is the Lord? Who is really in control? God is faithful to get His message across, even if He uses someone else. Maybe I am not the vessel, but the revelation I have is for confirmation of another, later.

Chapter 18 Study Questions

1. What is the difference between dunamis and exousia power?

2. What are three different faith ways miraculous healing can come?

3. What are some reasons healing may not be forthcoming?

4. What is the gift of discerning spirits and in what situations does it function?

5. What is prophecy and how is it to be governed?

6. What are tongues and interpretation and how are they to be used?

7. How do tongues build up the speaker and prophecy build up the church.

19

Offices & Motivational Gifts of the Spirit

Let's take another look at 1 Corinthians 12:27-31:

> Now you are the body of Christ and individually members of it. And God has appointed in the church first apostles, second prophets, third teachers, then miracles, then gifts of healing, helping, administrating, and various kinds of tongues. Are all apostles? Are all prophets? Are all teachers? Do all work miracles? Do all possess gifts of healing? Do all speak in tongues? Do all interpret? But earnestly desire the higher gifts. - ESV

Ephesians 4:8-16 further expands:

> Therefore it says, "When He ascended on high He led a host of captives, and He gave gifts to men." (In saying, "He ascended," what does it mean but that He had also descended into the lower regions, the earth? He Who descended is the One Who also ascended far above all the heavens, that He might fill all things.) And He gave the apostles, the prophets, the evangelists, the shepherds and teachers, to equip the saints for the work of ministry, for building up the body of Christ, until we all attain to the unity of the faith and of the knowledge of the Son of God, to mature manhood, to the measure of the stature of the fullness of Christ, so that we may no longer be children, tossed to and fro by the waves and carried about by every wind of doctrine, by human cunning, by craftiness in deceitful schemes. Rather, speaking the truth in love, we are to grow up in every way into Him that is the Head, into Christ, from Whom the whole body, joined and held together by every joint with which it is equipped, when each part is working properly, makes the body grow so that it builds itself up in love. - ESV

These gifts make plain their purpose for being given. They are for equipping ourselves and for each other, so that we may become gifts to the church. There is rank in how the offices are described "first apostles, then prophets..." But this is not because of some favoritism on God's part. Charismata means gift of grace. The Holy Spirit gives gifts that are needed according to the calling God has on our lives. It is not our place to envy what God has given to someone else. Neither is it our place to minimize the value of tongues. Some say, "Why didn't I get the gift of healing? Why don't I get to be a prophet?" Tongues seem to be the most widely distributed of the charismatic gifts. Why? I believe it is a faith gate to more blessing. Greater faith is stirred in us by the humble use of tongues, as previously mentioned. On the other hand, if I am called to be only a doorkeeper and someone else is called to be the crusading evangelist, each of us will answer for what we have done with our *calling.* If I am only a doorkeeper, I must be the best doorkeeper I can be. The Kingdom sets me at my post. All I have to do to please God is to be faithful to what He asks me to do, and I will receive a wonderful reward. I must not be like the wicked angels who have left their posts to undermine the Kingdom of God for selfish ambition.

My focus should be on the desire to hear my Lord say as in **Matthew 21:23**:

> Well done good and faithful servant. You have been faithful over a little; I will set you over much. Enter into the joy of your Master. – ESV

But the Lord Who calls us to contentment does not call us to be complacent. As we grow in Him, we want to serve Him more. This will mean more sacrifice and responsibility. God will answer that devotion with higher gifts. That is why the desire to serve as an elder is encouraged. It is a big and sometimes thankless job, demanding greater discipline in our own walk for the sake of those God has entrusted to our care. As our hearts go out to the lost, the suffering, and the deceived, the Spirit for those ministries to which we are called, will appropriately equip us.

The Apostolic Office

Apostolos means one sent forth. The first apostle was Jesus, sent forth by the Father into the world. In the High Priestly prayer in **John 17:3**, Jesus prays:

"... And this is eternal life, that they may know You the only true God, and Jesus Christ Whom You have sent [apostello]." – ESV

Hebrews 3:1-2 says:
Therefore, holy brothers, you who share in the heavenly calling, consider Jesus, the Apostle and High Priest of our confession, Who was faithful to Him Who appointed Him, just as Moses was faithful in all God's house. – ESV

Those who believe the apostolic age is something that ceased to exist at the passing away of the original twelve disciples quote Peter's definition of a replacement-apostle for Judas in **Acts 1:21-22**. They would say there are no more apostles today because no one in our day is a living witness like the original twelve were:
So, one of the men who have accompanied us during all the time that the Lord Jesus went in and out among us, beginning from the baptism of John until the day, when He was taken up from us—one of these men must become with us a witness to His resurrection ...
– ESV

But Paul was called and commissioned by the Lord Himself after He had ascended to heaven. The word **apostolos** is also applied to Barnabas in **Acts 14:4,14**. Andronicus and Junias are also called apostles in **Romans 16:7**, as are Silas and Timothy in **1 Thessalonians 2:6**. Epaphroditus is called "Your apostle" in **Philippians 2:23**. – from Vine's *Expository Dictionary of New Testament Words*

Work and Authority of an Apostle
They are called by God and sent out to plant new churches.
Acts 13:1-3 says:
Now there were in the church at Antioch, prophets and teachers, Barnabas, Simeon who is called Niger, Lucius of Cyrene, Manaen a member of the court of Herod the tetrarch, and Saul. While they were worshiping the Lord and fasting, the Holy Spirit said, "Set apart for Me Barnabas and Saul for the work for which I have called

them." Then after fasting and praying they laid their hands on them and sent them off. – ESV

In **Acts 8:14-17** we see apostles have authority to sanction and impart gifts of the Spirit:

> Now when the apostles at Jerusalem heard that Samaria had received the Word of God, they sent to them Peter and John, who came and prayed for them that they might receive the Holy Spirit, for He had not yet fallen on any of them, but they had only been baptized in the Name of the Lord Jesus. Then they laid their hands on them and they received the Holy Spirit.
> – ESV

Acts 5:12-16 says:

> Now many signs and wonders were regularly done among the people by the hands of the apostles. And they were all together in Solomon's Portico. None of the rest dared join them, but the people held them in high esteem. And more than ever believers were added to the Lord, multitudes of both men and women, so that they even carried out the sick into the streets and laid them on cots and mats, that as Peter came by at least his shadow might fall on some of them. The people also gathered from the towns around Jerusalem, bringing the sick and those afflicted with unclean spirits, and they were all healed. – ESV

Apostles who receive by the Spirit, test what they have received, and transmit revelation to the churches. This often sets policy and precedent going forward. The vigorous debate at the Jerusalem Council in **Acts 15** over the best policy towards Gentile converts, regarding circumcision and the Law of Moses, was resolved in a gathering of apostles. The solution was finally proposed and resolved in **Acts 15:14-21** which says:

> Simeon has related how God first visited the Gentiles, to take from them a people for His Name. And with this the words of the prophets agree, just as it is written, "After this I will return, and I will rebuild the tent of David that has fallen; I will rebuild its ruins, and I will restore it, that the remnant of mankind may seek the

> Lord, and the Gentiles who are called by My Name,
> says the Lord, Who makes these things known from of
> old." Therefore, my judgment is that we should not
> trouble those Gentiles who turn to God but should
> write to them to abstain from the things polluted by
> idols, and from sexual immorality, and from [*eating*]
> what has been strangled, and from [*eating*] blood. For
> from ancient generations Moses has had in every city
> those who proclaim him, for he is read every Sabbath in
> the synagogues. – ESV (*Shank*)

The apostle James reasoned from the prophets before him
what God's policy toward the Gentiles was to be. They were
not to become Jews, but remain whatever their original na-
tionality was, yet they were to separate themselves from unbelieving Gentiles with the four abstinences proposed above.
Both believing Jews and believing Gentiles were to be in the
world, but not of the world. Christians are the called-out-ones,
holy to the Lord! The temple had served its purpose in pointing
to Christ. In thirty years, the temple would be taken away
from the Jews. God was doing a new thing in fulfillment of
words prophesied centuries before.

Apostles also suffer for the sake of the church.
2 Corinthians 1:8-11 says:

> For we do not want you to be ignorant, brothers, of the
> affliction we experienced in Asia. For we were so utter-
> ly burdened beyond our strength that we despaired of
> life itself. Indeed, we felt we had received the sentence
> of death. But that was to make us rely not on ourselves
> but on God Who raises the dead. He delivered us from
> such a deadly peril, and He will deliver us. On Him we
> have set our hope that He may deliver us again. You al-
> so must help us by prayer, so that many will give
> thanks on our behalf for the blessing granted us
> through the prayers of many. – ESV

2 Corinthians 4:7-12 says:

> But we have this treasure in jars of clay, to show that
> the surpassing power belongs to God and not to us. We
> are afflicted in every way, but not crushed; perplexed,

but not driven to despair; persecuted, but not forsaken; struck down, but not destroyed; always carrying in the body the *death* of Jesus, so that the life of Jesus may also be manifested in our bodies. For we who live are always being given over to death for Jesus' sake, so that the life of Jesus may also be manifested in our mortal flesh. So death is at work in us, but life in you. - ESV

Many young Christians will assume that because sin consequences drove them to Christ, they should not have hard things happen anymore, since they have believed and repented. They will say, "I was cursed for my sin, now I am to be blessed. My life should now be smooth." Then, when trials come, they doubt the love of God. They do not yet understand that suffering for the sake of righteousness is what Christ has *called* us all to do. We are to take our cross and follow Him, in order to bear His fruit.

Apostles today are founders of ministries and churches. They are sent out as missionaries into new territories to establish churches. While a pastors shepherd sheep, apostles themselves are sent out as sheep among wolves. They are often put to severe tests, being given over to death in their bodies, that the church may have life. I believe an apostle is an intercessor, identifying with the lost who are under judgment, with their own bodies—by standing in the gap between them and God—extending grace to the deceived to counteract the blindness, deafness and hardness of heart their sins deserve, that they might be saved and placed in a new family of faith, the church.

The Biblical examples seem to show them starting one work, then moving on to start another. Because of this, they do not receive the same support as a pastor who stays with the church he may have planted. Foxes have holes and birds of the air have nests, but like Christ, apostles have no place to rest their heads, at least not for long. Apostles tend to derive their income from the support of the groups of small churches they have planted, remaining long enough with each to appoint elders and train pastors and teachers to take on the day-to-day function of the local congregation.

Miracles seem more prevalent where there is no knowledge of Christ in a culture because those cultures are effectively "pre-Pentecost" and grace abounds to them. Amazing reports of healing and deliverance are coming out of places like India, China and parts of Africa where astonished missionaries, who are not charismatic in their theology or expectation, find the power of God at work in them! Alas, in the West, where Christianity once flourished, hardness of heart has set in and people are complacent or bored in their attitude towards Christ. A detached familiarity breeds contempt: We've heard all this stuff before. Jesus Himself said He could not do many miracles in His hometown because a prophet has no honor in his own land: We know all about his family, he's no big deal. We must pray for revival and be revived ourselves!

The Prophetic Office

A prophet is one who speaks forth openly, proclaiming God's message to the people. Moses also gave Christ the title of Prophet. **Deuteronomy 18:3** says through Moses,

> The Lord your God will raise up for you a Prophet like me from among you, from your brothers, it is Him you shall listen to just as you desired of the Lord your God at Horeb on the day of assembly, when you said, "Let me not hear again the Voice of the Lord my God or see this great fire any more, lest I die." And the Lord said to me, "They are right in what they have spoken. I will raise up for them a Prophet like you from among their brothers. And I will put My Words in His Mouth, and He shall speak to them all that I command Him. And whoever will not listen to My Words that He shall speak in My Name, I Myself will require it of him. – ESV
> *and also cited in* Acts 3:22 & 7:37

As I understand it, one who is in the office of a prophet prophesies, but few who make prophetic utterance hold the office of a prophet. The office is the second highest in rank in **1 Corinthians 12:28**, where only the office of apostle is greater. No doubt a greater blend of gifting is part of the office, whereas the faith of the average believer may speak forth prophetically in a meeting from time to time. **Romans 12:8** says that those who prophesy must do so according to their faith. This takes

seasoned maturity. One who occasionally offers a word of encouragement or exhortation in a meeting is good, but one who
has proven credibility in words being fulfilled is greater and
more likely moving in the office of a prophet. When a congregation looks to or seeks out someone for prophetic insight, the
elders of a biblically minded church should recognize or
acknowledge that person as holding the office if their counsel
proves trustworthy over time.

Once I heard about a meeting where a man asked for prayer for
his diabetic condition. Several said, "Throw away your insulin,
you don't need it anymore, you are healed." But one person
said, "Wait on that." The man seeking prayer listened to the
majority and threw his insulin away. Two or three days later
he had to be hospitalized. The one who had encouraged the
man to wait looked like the man with no faith, but he saw that
what the others were encouraging was not from God. They
may have sincerely meant well, but they had no skin in the
game, so they were prophesying beyond their own faith. The
one who knew there was no real faith behind what the majority was saying spoke truly. God mercifully worked all things
together for the good for all in what was learned, and the man
recovered. This kind of courage and conviction to be willing to
stand up to the majority opinion, needs to be present if one is a
real candidate for the office of a prophet.

The Greek word for a female prophet is **prophetis**. Acts 21:8-9
mentions four unmarried daughters of Phillip the evangelist,
who were prophetically gifted. Luke 2:36-38 describes Anna:

> And there was a prophetess, Anna, the daughter of
> Phanuel, of the tribe of Asher. She was advanced in
> years, having lived with her husband seven years from
> when she was a virgin, and then as a widow until she
> was eighty-four. She did not depart from the temple,
> worshiping with fasting and praying night and day.
> And coming up at that very hour she began to give
> thanks to God and speak of Him to all who were wait-
> ing for the Redemption of Jerusalem. - ESV

Pastors & Teachers

Pastors and teachers are similar in gifting, but Pastors are more
emphasized in shepherding a congregation, while teachers are

more focused on truth in doctrine. Both teach, so both are subject to higher moral standards. **James 3:1-2** says,

> Not many of you should become teachers, my brothers, for you know that we who teach will be judged with greater strictness. For we all stumble in many ways. And if anyone does not stumble in what he says, he is a perfect man, able also to bridle his whole body. - ESV

Those who are called to teach pastorally or doctrinally must be diligent to speak the truth, even to their own hurt. Nothing has made me seek understanding like having to explain what Scripture means. Nothing has made me want to rein in my flesh like interceding for someone I love. The prayers of the righteous avail much and the teaching of a teacher must conform to how the teacher lives out what he is saying.

The corruption of so many seminaries that ordain pastors who are not even born again, or do not stand on the Bible as the Word of Truth, has led to a movement whereby local churches are training their own pastors and teachers. Like the first century church, men with personal integrity are raised up under the tutelage of elder teachers and pastors in an apprentice relationship. Some congregations have formed their own schools, utilizing resources offered by Bible believing organizations online, with courses that ensure the rigors of Biblical scholarship without compromising Biblical truth.

We must take seriously Paul's words in **Galatians 1:6-10**:

> I am astonished that you are so quickly deserting Him who called you to the grace of Christ and are turning to a different gospel—not that there is another one, but there are some who trouble you and want to distort the gospel of Christ. But even if we or an angel from heaven should preach to you a gospel contrary to the one we preached to you, let him be accursed. As we have said before, so now I say again: If anyone is preaching to you a gospel contrary to the one you received, let him be accursed. For am I now seeking the approval of man, or of God? Or am I trying to please man? If I were still trying to please man, I would not be a servant of Christ. - ESV

The Evangelist

It's interesting that the Greek word for evangelist is **euangelistos**, because the word translated as either angel or messenger is **angelos**. Combined with **eu**, which means good, the word becomes good messenger. Evangelists proclaim the gospel to non-believers; they bring the good news, which is what the word gospel means.

A similar dual meaning is in the word **malak** in Hebrew, which also means both angel and messenger. The last book of the Old Testament is named after the prophet Malachi, which either means My messenger, or if it is a shortened form of the name **Malachiah**, it could mean messenger of the Jehovah. - *from the introduction to Malachi*, ESV Study Bible

Like the apostle, the evangelist is a missionary, but not one who plants churches. They both have passion for the lost, but the evangelist is focused on personal salvation, while the apostle wants to establish a church for the new believers in which to grow. An evangelist cannot be an apostle, but apostle can be an evangelist. Both are sent out as sheep among wolves.
In **2 Timothy 4:5** Paul says to Timothy, a fellow apostle:

> As for you, always be sober-minded, endure suffering, do the work of an evangelist, fulfill your ministry. - ESV

True evangelists are deeply interested in people and want to bring them the light of Christ. People seem to open up to them because they inspire trust. They are also fearless of rejection, ready to step up to the challenges of the skeptical and the critical. They want to help the lost to believe. They learn how to defend the faith with apologetics. They want to understand what hinders. They are patient with those who are resistant or afraid. They put great stock in the spiritual power of testimony to sow seeds of faith that will spring to fruitfulness sooner or later. They are truly angels of God's light in places where only darkness was before.

Workers of Miracles

Miracles are rare by definition. They are high above anything a mortal can do. So why are those whom God uses in this way so far down the list in rank? I can only say that it must be because this is a list of offices, ranging from the greatest in diligence and responsibility to the least. Does that mean miracles are no big deal? No. This is the **dunamis** power of God for doing marvelous things. (*See* **Gifts of Power** in **Chapter 18**)

The purpose of miracles is to glorify God, not make life easier for ourselves. When severe obstacles and hindrances must be removed to preserve or advance the revelation of God, miracles can then happen in accordance with His providence. See the many examples in the Old Testament where the enemies of Israel were miraculously destroyed, or where miraculous provision was made, or where even the sun moved back to lengthen the day.

Healers
As we read in the last chapter, healing is a gift that can be given to any believer, and also comes from the authority given in the office of an elder, from **James 5:13-16**. Scripture records apostles and prophets also being equipped in this way. Counselors, too, can be gifted with healing for the soul and the spirit. Deliverance also comes through intercessors guided by the gift of discerning spirits. As we have said, some diseases and afflictions are physical in origin and have only physical symptoms. Some afflictions originate in the soul and express symptoms in the body. Some diseases are demonic, having a spiritual origin.

Healing also comes by the Spirit in the exercise of a word of faith. An interesting lesson comes from **Mark 11:20-26**. We mentioned in the notes from **Chapter 18** on healing that if one prays with confidence and does not doubt in his heart... even a mountain will be taken up and thrown into the sea... if we believe, we shall receive it. But look again at the context for these words from Christ in **Mark 11:12-14**:

> On the following day, when they came from Bethany, He was hungry. And seeing in the distance a fig tree in leaf, He went to see if He could find anything on it. When He came to it, He found nothing but leaves, for it was not the season for figs. And He said to it, "May no one ever eat fruit from you again." And His disciples heard it. – ESV

Something very interesting is to be learned here, so this point bears repeating. Why did Jesus curse the fig tree for not having fruit when it was not even the season for fruit? Wouldn't the Creator of all the earth know this was not the season? What was He teaching His disciples? When they came back the next day, the disciples saw the fig tree had withered because Jesus had cursed it. Peter even pointed it out to the rest. "The tree that was cursed had withered." I speculated over the meaning of this, but could not understand why the fig tree, through no fault of its own, was cursed. How can this be fair? Then I saw it. Jesus was reasoning with the disciples about faith. The logic is this: if the word of faith was answered by God for a trivial thing like withering the fig tree, how much more will God grant the word of faith in a matter that has greater merit!

So, some of us are simply given the gift of healing, but the gift of healing is also part to the office of elder, with its mantel of authority. And the word of faith that is not doubted will not only heal but perform even greater wonders! There is no such thing as a member of the body of Christ not having gifts of the Spirit. There are only those who do not realize this, or those who have not matured to the point where they are stepping out in ministry to discover them. Many are not even taught that they are equipped by the Holy Spirit with gifts or are told the time for gifts of the Spirit has passed.

Those who no longer live off the milk of the Word can chew and swallow the meat of the Word and be mightily strengthened and empowered by it! How can I know what my gifting may be? Start by being one who serves others in the body of Christ. What kind of service are you drawn to? The equipping spiritual gifts will start to show as you are faithful in serving. Where is the place of *unbelief* in Christ? He has none. If I am a new creation in Christ, my old unbelieving nature is now dead. I am now alive to Christ because He is joined to my spirit by His Spirit. I can now move in the power of the Holy Spirit.

Helpers and the Ministry of Service
Helpers are as widely varied in their abilities as there are tasks at hand. Many great works would be severely hindered without the humble service of those with natural or financial re-

sources, or those with skills and talents that are vitally needed and graciously given. They are wonderful people who have been equipped by God for the building up of the Church. Hospitality is the womb in which many new Christians are born and nurtured and is the perfect environment for teaching and Bible study. Those who are passionate about serving often become deacons, who supply the wheels that make the gospel bus go forward. They also powerfully express the grace of God in the testimony and reputation of His people, with good works.

An elder (**presbuteros** – *from* **presbus**, *an older man*) is raised up and qualified by the Holy Spirit to provide leadership, teaching and shepherding roles with the pastors, and are appointed to have spiritual oversight of a local church. 1 **Timothy** 3:1 says that "if anyone aspires to the office of overseer, [**episkopeo**—*the duty*] he desires a noble task." That's because there is a lot of work and responsibility that comes with the office. In order to qualify, the following verses need to be taken seriously.

1 Timothy 3:1-7 says:

> The saying is trustworthy: If anyone desires the office of overseer, he desires a noble task. Therefore, an overseer must be above reproach, the husband of one wife, sober minded, self-controlled, respectable, hospitable, able to teach, not a drunkard, not violent but gentle, not quarrelsome, not a lover of money. He must manage his own household well, with all dignity keeping his children submissive, for if someone does not know how to manage his own household, how will he care for God's church? He must not be a recent convert, or he may become puffed up with conceit and fall into the condemnation of the devil. Moreover, he must be well thought of by outsiders, so that he may not fall into disgrace, into the snare of the devil. – ESV

Titus 1:5-9 says:

> This is why I left you in Crete, so that you might put what remained into order, and appoint elders in every town as I directed you—if anyone is above reproach, the husband of one wife, and his children are believers

and not open to the charge of debauchery or insubordination. For an overseer, as God's steward, must be above reproach. He must not be arrogant or quick-tempered or a drunkard or violent or greedy for gain, but hospitable, a lover of good, self-controlled, upright, holy, and disciplined. He must hold firm to the trustworthy words taught, so that he may be able to give instruction in sound doctrine and also rebuke those who contradict it. – ESV

This is a leadership office the Holy Spirit must confirm in the body of Christ. Since all of us have sinful pasts and would have fallen short in some of these standards, the leadership must discern whether sufficient transformation has occurred. Many times, those of us who have failed in foolishness first and have now become wise, may become all the more able to encourage others in humility. We must not overlook faults, but we must also extend grace where God has shown mercy and real repentance has occurred. Standards are very important, but it is not law that qualifies any of us. In my opinion, the ruling issue is what kind of fruit a man bears now, by the grace of God, and for *how long?*

Romans 12:4-8 says:

For as in one body we have many members, and the members do not all have the same function, so we, though many, are one body in Christ, and individually members one of another. Having gifts that differ according to the grace given to us, let us use them: if prophecy, in proportion to our faith; if service, in our serving; the one who teaches, in his teaching; the one who exhorts, in his exhortation; the one who contributes, in his generosity; the one who leads, with zeal; the one who does acts of mercy, with cheerfulness. – ESV

Spiritual Motivation
There's one more point I'd like to make in this chapter. There is often misunderstanding between those who are *mercy oriented* and those who are *exhortation oriented.* Sometimes they disagree about how to handle a situation because there is a lack of perspective in the point of view of the other. The pro-

verbial saying applies that, "To a hammer, everything is a nail". But we must remember that God has given a whole toolbox with different tools for different uses. What I have learned is that when one is dealing with someone who is defiant and needs to change, the *exhorter* needs to take the lead and confront the sin so they will turn around. But when someone is humble and broken, let the *mercy-person* take the lead to encourage and bring the broken one forward in growth.

If the mercy-person comforts someone who needs to repent, they may unwittingly enable the sinner to continue in his sin by miss-use of sympathy and identification with him. I have seen mercy-people actually side with the defiant one against the exhorter because they have a soulish weakness that cannot bear conflict. On the other hand, I've seen exhorters misread a broken person who has already repented and push the comforter aside to make *yet another point about what needs to change*, when it is now time to show mercy. This is a soulish weakness that cannot rest in what God's goal is at this point in time. Are not all of us in a process of learning to walk in righteousness?

There is a place for shunning and a place for receiving and forgiving the one showing real sorrow for his sin. Wisdom is needed by the Spirit to know which course to take. All of us must be humble and teachable.

2 Corinthians 2:5-8 says:
> Now if anyone has caused pain, he has caused it not to me, but in some measure—not to put it too severely—to all of you. For such a one, this punishment by the majority is enough, so you should rather turn to forgive and comfort him, or he may be overwhelmed by excessive sorrow. So I beg you to reaffirm your love for him. - ESV

As mentioned earlier, excessive sorrow is *morbid shame*. Instead of inspiring faith, it tempts the weak to just give up. If an offender has repented, don't keep him in the doghouse. Real grace and mercy are not enabling. The exhorters may not be satisfied with the depth of remorse if all they can see is more need for improvement. The mercy-oriented may need to take the lead here. But one is not better than the other. Each must play their part, and both should be teachable by the other.

Paul may well be described as an exhorter not afraid to make waves. Barnabas may well be an example of a nurturing mercy-oriented brother. In **Acts 15:36**, Paul did not want to let John Mark come with them on their next journey because Mark bailed out at Pamphlia, leaving them to go on without him, on their previous journey. Paul and Barnabas separated over this. But the Holy Spirit blessed both of them in their work. Paul took Silas and went on to Syria. Barnabas took John Mark with him to Cyprus because he wanted to build him up.

It all turned out right in the end. Barnabas developed the young man into a true minister of Christ. Paul later writes to Timothy in **2 Timothy 4:11**:

> Luke alone is with me. Get Mark and bring him with you, for he is very useful to me for ministry. – ESV

All is forgiven and restored. It is my understanding that this same John Mark wrote the Gospel of Mark at Peter's dictation.

Chapter 19 Study Questions

1. What does Charismata mean?

2. What is the difference between an apostle and an evangelist?

3. How is the office of a prophet different from one who prophesies?

4. Why should not very many of us be teachers of the Word?

5. What are three ways miraculous healing can occur?

6. Why is it not vain to aspire to be an elder?

7. How are exhortation and mercy to be balanced?

20

Judgment and the Household of Faith

The world needs to see Jesus in His people. But a corrupt, hypocritical, idolatrous, and compromised church will give excuses to sinners, not to repent. My personal testimony must also be free of corruption, hypocrisy, idolatry and compromise with the world.

1 Peter 4:17 says:

> For now is the time for judgment to begin at the household of God; and if it begins with us, what will be the outcome for those who do not obey the gospel of God?
> – ESV

The Old Testament has example after example of Israel compromising the testimony of the Most High, to the rest of the world. The Lord punished them with consequences to cause them to repent, both for Israel's sake as well as for the people in the surrounding nations who saw them as the people of Jehovah. They were at various times handed over to their Canaanite neighbors, the Assyrians, all the way to the Babylonian captivity with its massacres and enslavement. By the time Jesus came to earth, the Romans occupied them. There were times when the people who humbly came to the temple to make sacrifices for their sins, were abused. If the very priests who received their sacrifices gave the people an example of contempt, why should they bother to repent if God lets those priests get away with their sin? Unpunished priests made it appear as if there was no righteous God, because wicked people were allowed to serve as His mediators. The story of the cruel and worthless sons of Eli the high priest is an example.

1 Samuel 2:22-25 says:

> Now Eli was very old, and he kept hearing all that his sons were doing to all Israel, and how they lay with the women who were serving at the entrance of the tent of meeting. And he said to them, "Why do you do such things? For I hear of your evil dealings from all the people. No, my sons; it is no good report that I hear the

people of the Lord spreading abroad. If someone sins against a man, God will mediate for him, but if someone sins against the Lord, who can intercede for him?" But they would not listen to the voice of their father, for it was the will of the Lord to put them to death. – ESV

The sons of Eli served as priests. Eli himself was punished by the Lord in **1 Samuel 2:27-36** for only mildly rebuking them when they should have been publicly punished and removed from the priesthood.

And there came a man of God to Eli and said to him, "Thus the Lord has said, 'Did I indeed reveal Myself to the house of your father when they were in Egypt sub-ject to the house of Pharaoh? Did I choose him out of all the tribes of Israel to be My priest, to go up to My altar, to burn incense, to wear an ephod before Me? I gave to the house of your father all My offerings by fire from the people of Israel. Why then do you scorn My sacri-fices and My offerings that I commanded, and honor your sons above Me by fattening yourselves on the choicest parts of every offering of My people Israel?' Therefore, the Lord, the God of Israel, declares:

I promised that your house and the house of your father should go in and out before Me forever, but now the Lord declares: 'Far be it from Me, for those who honor Me I will honor, and those who despise Me shall be lightly esteemed [qalal *cursed, despised*]. Behold, the days are coming when I will cut off your strength and the strength of your father's house, so there will not be an old man in your house. Then in distress you will look with an envious eye on all the prosperity that shall be bestowed on Israel, and there shall not be an old man in your house forever. The only one of you that I shall not cut off from My altar shall be spared to weep his eyes out to grieve his heart, and all the descendants of your house shall die by the sword of men. And this that shall come upon your two sons, Hophni and Phinehas, shall be a sign to you: both of them shall die on the same day.

337

> And I will raise up for Myself a faithful priest, who shall do according to what is in My Heart and in My Mind. And I will build him a sure house, and he shall go in and out before Me anointed forever. And everyone who is left in your house shall come to implore him for a piece of silver or a loaf of bread and shall say, "Please put me in one of the priests' places, that I may eat a morsel of bread." – ESV (*Shank*)

Surely the sins of Hophni and Phinehas provided strong temptation to Israel to be cynical about God. In the verse above, the line should say: ... *those who honor Me I will honor, and those who despise Me shall be cursed.* This more accurately fits the severity of God's response. The same need for integrity and correction has required purification throughout church history. Our sins damage the testimony of Christ if they are not confessed and repented. Unrepented sin leads to apostasy, the falling away and forsaking of Christ. It is the loss of the Wonder of God.

1 Corinthians 10:1-12 says:

> For I want you to know, brothers, that our fathers [*Israel*] were all under the cloud, and all passed through the sea, and all were baptized into Moses in the cloud and in the sea, and all ate the same spiritual food, and all drank the same spiritual drink. For they drank form the spiritual Rock that followed them, and the Rock was Christ. Nevertheless, with most of them God was not pleased, for they were *overthrown* in the wilderness.

> Now these things took place as *examples* for us, that we might not desire evil as they did. Do not be idolaters as some of them were; as it is written, "The people sat down to eat and drink and rose up to play." We must not indulge in sexual immorality as some of them did, and twenty-three thousand fell in a single day. We must not put Christ to the test, as some of them did and were destroyed by serpents, nor grumble, as some of them did and were destroyed by the Destroyer. Now

> these things happened to them as an example, but they were written down for our instruction, on whom the end of ages has come. Therefore, let everyone who thinks that he stands take heed lest he fall. God is faithful, and He will not let you be tempted beyond your ability, but with temptation He will also provide the way of escape, that you may be able to endure it.
> – ESV (*Shank*)

Persevering Faith

Recall from **Chapter 12** in the section concerning **Unconditional Eternal Security**, faith that does not persevere with fruit of a changed life, risks losing salvation. God alone knows the hearts of men, it's not for you or me to say if one has come to the point of apostasy. It is a good thing to work out our salvation with fear and trembling.

As Paul says in **Romans 11:21**:

> For if God did not spare the natural branches [*the Israelites*], neither will He spare you [*Christians*]. Note then the kindness and severity God: severity to those who have fallen, but God's kindness to you, *provided* you continue in His kindness. Otherwise you too will be cut off. – ESV (*Shank*)

Churches that do not repent will have their lampstands *removed* from before the Throne of God! The righteousness of Christ must be manifest in **me** because of who I am in Christ. The righteousness of Christ must be manifest in the Bride of Christ as well. The Great and Terrible Day of the Lord is coming! We must not only persevere in the power of the Spirit for ourselves lest we fall, but also for the sake of others who have no hope unless they see the real Christ in **you** and **me**. The free gift of salvation is received by faith alone, not by works. It is God's doing. We have been given great liberty, but we must not misuse that liberty by giving opportunity for the flesh. My flesh is mine, but it is not me. But faith without works is dead, producing a testimony of death, not life. Even some lukewarm believers Jesus will spit out of His Mouth because they want the free gift but refuse to produce fruit from the obedience of faith.

We are worshipers made for worship of the Most High God, revealed in the Face of His only begotten Son Jesus. We must not worship idols of any kind. What might Mohammed have believed if he had seen the Christian Church without idols in the sixth century, which outwardly appeared no different than all the pagan Arab and Canaanite temples around him, full of images on their altars? At first, he thought the Jews would honor his revelations because they were monotheistic, but when they rightly told him he was in error, he turned against them, too. The Church is commanded to be different than the world. We are called to come out from among them, shining as a bright contrasting light in the midst of darkness. Now Islam is as much an adversary to the church as Canaan was to Israel when she worshiped their idols and became indistinguishable from them. The Real Church of Christ does not put Christ to the test with idols! Moreover, there is little statistical difference between the professing church and the world, in the area of fornication.

Again recall **1 Corinthians 10:7-8**:

> The people sat down to eat and drink and rose up to play. We must not indulge in sexual immorality as some of them did, and twenty-three thousand fell in a single day. – ESV

Do we think that the God Who judged Israel for her sins will not also judge the sins of the church? When the widespread hooking-up culture is inevitably judged, and millions of those of reproductive age fall at the hand of sexual plagues, how many among professing Christians will also die? Aids ravaged the central African countries to such an extent that great numbers of children had to be raised by their grandparents because their natural parents were all dead or dying. Do you think that God will not let this happen to other nations that once believed in Christ and have now largely fallen away?

Do we really think that the God, Who judged Israel for burning their own children as an offering to demons so they would have better economic circumstances, will not judge us for the millions of abortions that have bloodied the hands of nations that once believed in Christ, but have now turned away? Killing children to be better off economically is the same as offering them to Baal or Moloch. It is human sacrifice.

Jeremiah 7:30-34 is very sobering:

> For the sons of Judah have done evil in My sight, declares the Lord. They have set their detestable things in the house that is called by My Name, to defile it. And they have built high places of *Topheth*, which is in the Valley of the Son of Hinnom, to burn their sons and their daughters in the fire, which I did not command, nor did it come to My Mind. Therefore, behold, the days are coming, declares the Lord, when it will no longer be called *Topheth*, or the Valley of the Son of Hinnom, but the Valley of Slaughter; for they will bury in *Topheth*, because there is no room elsewhere. And the dead bodies of this people will be food for the birds of the air, and for the beasts of the earth, and none will frighten them away. And I will silence in the cities of Judah and in the streets of Jerusalem the voice of mirth and the voice of gladness, the voice of the bridegroom and the voice of the bride, for the land will become a waste. – ESV (*Shank*)

Topheth was a place where Israel sacrificed their sons and daughters. That place would later become a killing floor and burial ground for the Babylonians to slaughter the people of Jerusalem. This is an example of symmetry in judgment for the place where abominable practices were once committed in defiance of God. The Bible records a remarkable number of examples of symmetry in the consequences of sin. As you sow, so shall you reap; as you judge, so shall you be judged, et cetera. In the places where sin has abounded, sin has been punished. Infant sacrifice was widespread in the Middle East and along the Northern coast of Africa, Topheths were revered as "sacred cemeteries" for the sacrificial victims. A Topheth excavated in what was once Carthage has yielded thousands of burial jars with the skeletal remains of innocent infants. Does God Who will judge the world for its sins allow His chosen people to go unpunished for these abominations? Shall we go unpunished for the toleration of the slaughter of the innocent pre-born?

I have met Christians who have justified the support of their politics on abortion by saying the Pro-Life movement does not care about the suffering poor. "The church cares more about the lives of children before they are born than they do after." This statement is a smug slander. Cannot one care for both groups? The believing church abounds in mercy to the suffering of all—helping the poor and adopting the unwanted to rescue them from death. Those who advocate abortion say they care more about the living. But the truth is, many poor people also oppose abortion. The irony is that if one applies the same reasoning of their argument back on them, by saying their support for the poor means they don't care about the destruction of the innocent, they get mad. But they still vote for politicians who proclaim a woman's right to abortion to be a "sacred trust."

If what happened to Israel was given as an example to the church, mentioned twice in the verses above, shall we not expect the same if we do not repent? If we have not upheld God's Law, shall we be surprised that He does not uphold our nation's laws, rights and responsibilities? Lawlessness is a curse; with it we curse ourselves. Compromising with the world's values by pushing the Word of God aside, brings a curse on us all. Shall we foolishly believe the wars, famines, plagues and financial collapse foretold will not come also to us, if we do not repent?

Those of us who committed these and other sins in the past can be mercifully forgiven because of the Blood. All of us who have repented and received forgiveness for our sins have been empowered by the Holy Spirit to change. The only sin that is unforgiven is the determined rejection of the conviction of the Holy Spirit. Many of us have sinful pasts that cause us to shutter and cringe when we remember what we did. I know I do. But the love of God has overwhelmed me and made me a new man in Christ. Satan still tries to use my shame to convince me I am hopeless and unusable, but what he intends as evil for me, the Holy Spirit uses for good, to motivate me to press on as a new man in Christ. My old man who sinned outrageously has already been judged in Christ and is now dead. I continue to repent and seek forgiveness when I sin through the weakness of my flesh because sin must no longer reign over me. God has given grace for you and me to grow from faith to greater faith. We who have the Spirit of Christ are one spirit with Him.

A Consequence of Sin is a Strong Delusion

The symmetry of consequences holds true. When we reject God, we get *Notgod*. When we reject the Maker, we get the *Unmaker*. When we reject the truth, we get *untruth*. Then, what is good is considered evil and what is evil is considered good, because the mind follows the heart to obey or disobey. When Christ is pushed away, *Satan* becomes lord by default.

2 Thessalonians 2:9-12 says:

> The coming of the lawless one is by the activity of Satan with all power of false signs and wonders, and with all wicked deception for those who are perishing because they refused to love the truth and so be saved. Therefore, God sends them a strong delusion, so that they may believe what is false, in order that all may be condemned who did not believe the truth but had pleasure in unrighteousness. –ESV (*Shank*)

When the testimony of the household of faith is pure, many of the lost will repent. When the testimony of the church is corrupt, it will become part of the delusion that leads those who remain unrighteous, to hell. The apostate church is likely the whore of Babylon who will be judged for persecuting the true church and for selling out the Truth to get along with the beast. It's interesting to see that the nations on whom the false church rode, will turn on her and destroy her because she led many away from eternal life. This will be God's judgment on the apostate church. See **Revelation 17 and 18.**

Leaving Denomination X

Revelation 18:4-8 says:

> Then I heard another voice from heaven saying,
> "Come out from her, My people, lest you take part in her sins, lest you share in her plagues; for her sins are heaped as high as heaven, and God has remembered her iniquities. Pay her back as she herself has paid back others and repay her double for her deeds; mix a double portion for her in the cup she mixed. As she glorified

herself and lived in luxury, so give her a like measure of torment and mourning, since in her heart she says, 'I sit as a queen, I am no widow, and mourning I will never see.' For this reason, her plagues will come in a single day, death and mourning and famine, and she will be burned up with fire; for mighty is the Lord God Who judges her." – ESV

Come out from her, My people, lest you take part in her sins, lest you share in her plagues... God hates a **mix** of truth and lies because it is such a strong deception. The reason He repays her double for her deeds is first, because of her own sins, and second, for misleading the lost away from true salvation. A serious question that must be addressed is what to do with our participation in an apostate church that has entangled itself with idolatry, heretical doctrine, moral and other worldly compromises. Some of us may be called to stay in them as missionaries, but if that is your calling, be prepared for resistance and eventual rejection if the congregation does not repent.

Without a clear calling from God, most of us should leave and commit to a church family that is following the Word. But before leaving, one should express the concerns over church policies and doctrines. Show in the Word where changes need to be made. This conversation should be about things of greater weight, like idolatry, false doctrine, et cetera, and not petty personal reasons or style preferences.

The procedure in **Matthew 18:15-20** is a good one:

> If your brother sins against you, go and tell him his fault, between you and him alone. If he listens to you, you have gained your brother. But if he does not listen, take one or two brothers along with you, that every charge may be established by the evidence of two or three witnesses. If he refuses to listen to them, tell the church. If he refuses to listen even to the church, let him be to you as a gentile and a tax collector. Truly, I say to you, whatever you bind on earth will be bound in heaven, and whatever you loose on earth shall be loosed in heaven. Again I say to you, if two of you agree on earth about anything they ask, it will be done for them

by My Father in heaven. For where two or three are gathered in My Name, there am I among them. – ESV

Having witnesses who agree in Christ about the issue is important. If I am in Christ and those who are standing with me are in Christ, and also in agreement with me, I know that the Spirit is confirming the need to address the issue. If I am mistaken in what I believe, I can also be corrected by them. If the problem is with a leader, it may be intimidating. An elder should not be accused without two or more witnesses. I think a loving approach expressing personal concern would be good if the issue is a private one. But if it is a doctrinal problem, enlist the help of someone whom you trust knows sound doctrine, and ask if he would stand with you in support of the matter. Sometimes congregational meetings allow for debate. Good. Speak up with respect and a well-reasoned opinion.

Some of us have had to make hard choices regarding official denominational positions that oppose Scripture, even though the local church we attend may be solid. In cases like this, a break with the denomination must happen so the local church can preserve its testimony. In some cases, the denomination owns the church building and the congregation must find somewhere else to meet. If this be the case, one may be encouraged by the example of the priests and faithful believers who left Israel/Samaria because of its idolatry in setting up official high places in Dan and at Bethel in opposition to the temple at Jerusalem. These people moved to Judah, leaving behind all their property and inheritance.

2 Chronicles 11:13-16 says:

And the priests and the Levites who were in all Israel presented themselves to him [*King Rehoboam of Judah*] from all the places where they lived. For the Levites left their common lands and their holdings and came to Judah and Jerusalem, Because Jeroboam [*King of Israel*] and his sons cast them out from serving as priests of the Lord, and he appointed his own priests for the high places and for goat idols and for the calves that he had made. And those who had set their hearts to seek the Lord God of Israel came after them from all the tribes of Israel to Jerusalem to sacrifice to the Lord, the God of their fathers. – ESV (Shank)

When it costs me something to walk in obedience to the Lord, He will remember it and bless me for it, in this life or the next. If I must leave a church that resists repentance, I must shake the dust off my shoes and move on. I must not obsess about them but leave them to God Who is their Judge and mine. So, what constitutes an issue that requires this serious attention? Perhaps this song will be helpful with some of them.

The House of Faith
Blessed are you who keep My Flame,
Who shine My Light, who fear My Name;
Who warn all of those who are falling away
That judgment begins with the house of faith.

You shall not have idols of any kind,
Or change My Word just to suit your times,
To sanction perversion or take innocent lives,
You shall not exchange the Truth for lies.

> Humble yourselves, confess your sins,
> And to each other you must make amends.
> Those who do you wrong you must forgive
> Do these things and you will live.

You shall not pray to those who are dead
Or follow a shepherd who's not born again,
Who does not walk in righteousness,
Who does not call his flock to repent.

> Do what is right, not just what you feel.
> Be humble and not too proud to kneel.
> For those who are honest, for those who are real
> Are the ones I will save and I will heal.

Blessed are you who keep My Flame,
Who shine My Light, who fear My Name;
Who warn all of those who are falling away
That judgment begins with the house of faith.
Shank / Peniel Music & Publishing

346

Changing a church involvement because of personal style preferences or a new ministry call need not involve a confrontation. But remember, no church is perfect, just as no believer is perfect, so don't break fellowship over small matters if the basic Truth of the gospel is being preached and the church is bearing fruit. And if you leave an apostate church, do not become apostate yourself by giving up on all churches. Find another and serve it with your whole heart.

Persecution of the Church

What has happened to Israel will happen to the church. The holocaust of the Jews during World War II was horrible beyond words, but what followed was the return of the promised land to the survivors and their progeny. Before the church receives its promised land, I believe there will be a holocaust persecution for us as well. This would be the wrath of man, *not the wrath of God.* If this is to happen to the saints, some say the Rapture has not yet occurred because the Holy Spirit through the Church is restraining the revealing of the antichrist. (**2 Thessalonians 2:7-8**)

There are good arguments for the remnant to be spared from the wrath of God in the Rapture—the best of Judah were carried off to the king of Babylon before the final massacre in Jerusalem. Lot and his family were led out of Sodom before the fire fell. Noah and his family went into the Ark before the flood rains came.

Revelation 13:5-10 speaks of what will happen to the whole world—*including the saints*—in the wrath of man:

> And the beast was given a mouth uttering haughty and blasphemous words, and it was allowed to exercise authority for forty-two months. It opened its mouth to utter blasphemies against God, blaspheming His Name and His dwelling, that is, those who dwell in heaven. Also, it was allowed to make war on the *saints* and to *conquer them.* And authority was given it over every tribe and people and language and nation, and all who dwell on earth will worship it, everyone whose name has not been written before the foundation of the world in the book of life of the Lamb Who was slain.

> If anyone has an ear, let him hear: if anyone is to be tak-
> en captive, to captivity he goes; if anyone is to be slain
> with the sword, with the sword must he be slain. Here
> is a call for the endurance of faith of the *saints.* – ESV
> (*Shank*)

Revival – Cleaning God's House

The Bride of Christ must be faithful and pure. The Lord is jealous over us. As Paul says in **2 Corinthians 11:2-4**:

> For I feel a divine jealousy for you, since I betrothed you
> to One Husband, to present you as a pure virgin to
> Christ. But I am afraid that as the serpent deceived Eve
> by his cunning, your thoughts will be led astray from
> the sincere and pure devotion to Christ. For if someone
> comes and proclaims another Jesus than the One we
> proclaimed, or if you receive a different spirit from the
> One you received, or if you accept a different gospel
> from the one you accepted, you put up with it readily
> enough. – ESV (*Shank*)

There is only One Christ revealed in the Bible, but there are
many antichrists in the world. Yes, I have my own conceptions
of what the Lord is like, and I know I am incomplete in what I
know. I must grow from being a wavering child in my understanding to mature manhood, to the measure of the stature of
the fullness of Christ. In that process, my opinions must be set
aside when I see they are in conflict with the Word. I have
grace to grow in knowledge of the fullness of God if I have a
heart that is humble enough to receive correction and revelation from the Word. But if I let some selfish or political agenda
define Christ, I will believe in some other Christ or Christ-
consciousness. I will grieve the Spirit of Christ by receiving
some other spirit in a counterfeit experience. That counterfeit
gospel can lead me to put my trust in a lie! If I do not repent, I
will die in my sin. All agendas will be judged by Christ.

False Angels of Light

If I want to merge Christianity with other religions, promote
mystical experiences for their own sake, mix in a feminist or
gay or Marxist or fascist or liberal or conservative agenda, I
misrepresent God's will. To endorse my own aspirations for

riches, or bind you and myself with legalism, or compromise grace with permissiveness, or be dazzled with sensationalism, or justify the use of idols or icons in worship, or pray to human beings dead or alive, or in any way undermine or attack the validity of the Bible as God's Word, I make myself a false teacher, a false prophet and a false apostle of light.

2 Corinthians 11:13-15 says:

> For such men are false apostles, deceitful workmen, disguising themselves as apostles of Christ. And no wonder, for even Satan disguises himself as an angel of light. So it is no surprise if his servants, also, disguise themselves as servants of righteousness. Their end will correspond to their deeds. – ESV

The Ephesian Church in **Revelation 2:2** is commended for their vigilance and perseverance in the truth:

> I know your works, your toil and your patient endurance, and how you cannot bear with those who are evil but have tested those who call themselves apostles and are not, and found them to be false. – ESV

Unity, Duality, & Contention

We are all called to a unity of faith in Christ, even though there is a great range of diversity, gifting and capacity among us as individuals. Paul says in **Ephesians 4:1-6**,

> I therefore, a prisoner for the Lord, urge you to walk in a manner worthy of the calling to which you have been called, with all humility and gentleness, with patience, bearing with one another in love, eager to maintain the unity of the Spirit in the bond of peace. There is one body and one Spirit—just as you were called to the one hope that belongs to your call—one Lord, one faith, one baptism, one God and Father of all, Who is over all and through all and in all. But grace was given to each one of us according to the measure of Christ's gift.
> – ESV

Despite all modern efforts to blend religions, undermine gender roles, compromise moral values, and merge world governments into one, we are called to recognize the distinct opposites of spirituality that are part of God's creation. There is no fellowship of Darkness with Light. The Cross reconciles us with the Light by canceling the Darkness of Sin, not accommodating it.

1 John 1:5-10 says:

> This is the message we have heard from Him and proclaim to you, that God is Light, and in Him is no Darkness at all. *If* we say we have fellowship with Him while we walk in darkness, we **lie** and do not practice the truth. But *if* we walk in the Light as He is in the Light, we have fellowship with one another, and the Blood of Jesus His Son cleanses us from all sin. *If* we say we have no sin, we deceive ourselves, and the truth is not in us. *If* we confess our sins, He is faithful and just to forgive us our sins and to cleanse us from all unrighteousness. *If* we say we have not sinned, we make Him a liar, and His Word is not in us. - ESV (*Shank*)

We are called to recognize that there is also a place for contention in the body of Christ, for iron to sharpen iron. This is not an excuse to justify troublesome quarrels motivated by vanity or to promote political factions, but to contend for the truth, to prove what is good.

Jude 3-4 says:

> Beloved, although I was eager to write to you about our common salvation, I found it necessary to write appealing to you to contend for the faith that was once for all delivered to the saints. For certain people have crept in unnoticed who long ago were designated for this condemnation, ungodly people, who pervert the grace of our God into sensuality and deny our only Master and Lord, Jesus Christ. - ESV

1 Thessalonians 5:19-21 says:

> Do not quench the Spirit. Do not despise prophecies, but *test* everything; hold fast to what is good. - ESV

Romans 12:1-2 says:

> I appeal to you therefore, brothers, by the mercies of God, to present your bodies as a living sacrifice, holy

and acceptable to God, which is your spiritual worship. Do not be conformed to the world, but be transformed by the renewal of your mind, that by *testing* you may discern what is the will of God, what is good and acceptable and perfect. – ESV (Shank)

Image of God & you are gods

A puzzling quotation of Jesus occurs in the Gospel of John. At the Feast of Dedication, at the temple in Jerusalem, He provokes His enemies with this revelation: I and the Father are One. Then He goes on to make a more startling comment.

John 10:31-38 says:

> The Jews picked up stones again to stone Him. Jesus answered them, "I have shown you many good works from the Father; for which of them are you going to stone Me?" The Jews answered Him, "It is not for a good work that we are going to stone You but for blasphemy, because You, being a man, make Yourself God." Jesus answered them, "Is it not written in your Law, 'I said *you* are gods'? *If He called them gods to whom the Word of God came*—and the Scripture *cannot be broken*—do you say of Him Whom the Father consecrated and sent into the world, 'You are blaspheming,' because I said, 'I am the Son of God'? If I am not doing the works of My Father, then do not believe Me; but if I do them, even if you do not believe Me, believe the works, that you may know and understand that the Father is in Me and I am in the Father." – ESV (*Shank*)

When I read this passage as a young man, I was baffled. I was expecting Christ to say only: See the works I do, only God can do them—that proves Who I am! But He puts in this *other thing* about men to whom the Word of God came as being *gods!* It seemed to me He was defusing the issue by spreading divinity around broadly to reduce the sharp contrast with the claim He was making about Himself. He makes this amazing statement about the people of God being gods—then qualifying that remark with the point that Scripture *cannot be broken.*

He was quoting from **Psalm 82** which says:
>God has taken His place at the divine council;
>In the midst of the gods He holds judgment:
>"How long will you judge unjustly
>And show partiality to the wicked?
>Give justice to the weak and the fatherless;
>Maintain the right of the afflicted and the destitute.
>Rescue the weak and the needy;
>Deliver them from the hand of the wicked."
>
>They have neither knowledge nor understanding,
>They walk about in darkness;
>All the foundations of the earth are shaken.
>
>I said, "You are gods,
>Sons of the Most High, all of you;
>Nevertheless, like men you shall die,
>And fall away like any prince."
>
>Arise, O God, judge the earth;
>For You shall inherit all the nations! – ESV

The rulers are to judge rightly, as God does. But they are rebuked in this psalm for not doing so. The wicked Pharisees, scribes and lawyers who wanted to kill the Righteous One sent from the Father are also called gods—what does that mean? These words are not restricted to earthly judges alone, we are all called to judge rightly in our hearts and in our actions! The Lord says to all of us, in **Matthew 5:48**:
>You therefore must be perfect, as your Heavenly Father is perfect. – ESV

The standard of righteousness on Judgment Day is God Himself. The Law cannot be broken in any part if we stand before God apart from Christ. We have not lived in sinless perfection, as God does, and He commands those who seek eternal life to either be perfect themselves, or trust in the Sacrifice of His Perfect Son, Jesus. We are called to be holy, to be godly, but we are not. We who have received the Spirit of God by the Blood of Jesus alone are one spirit with Him. We also are those to whom the Word of God has come because we are made in God's image and are the temple (**naos**) in which He dwells and we are the Bride of Christ. In this sense, we are gods because the Word of God has come to us, and into us. How else could the Bride be a fit consort for Christ forever? How else can we be capable of expressing godliness? Why else are we commanded to be godly? And the Scripture **cannot be broken!** Though made for this high calling, we have fallen because of sin. But the Blood purifies us and the Holy Spirit indwells us to express His godliness!

The Law also says those who commit murder shall be put to death, because we are made in the image of God.

1 Corinthians 3:16-17 says:

> Do you not know that you are God's temple [naos *where God is*] and that God's Spirit dwells in you? If anyone destroys [**phtheiro** *defiles*] God's temple, God will destroy [*defile*] him. For God's temple is holy, you are that temple. – ESV (Shank)

This is why we have an eternal destiny: Heaven forever or Hell forever! Those who believe and receive the Spirit of Christ become partakers of the divine nature! (**2 Peter 1:4**) *But this in no way is an endorsement of New Age or Eastern mystical thinking that we are all gods! They are deceived and they defile and deceive many. They make the sacrifice of Christ meaningless.* But those to whom the word [**logos**] of God has come, the Lord clearly says are gods.

My Wholeness and Healing in Christ

My difficulties with trust come from my habit of trusting in myself and in my old ways—as well as the betrayal of others I have trusted. My old nature and my old **Unmaker**, deceived and destroyed both my family and me. Jesus says the devil was a murderer from the beginning. But my New Father, My **Maker**, shows me the truth and builds me up as a son He loves, in Christ Jesus.

Reckoning

We have all heard of the **Judgment Day**, or the **Day of Reckoning**. This is the Day when our lives will be presented before the Lord. The Judge of all the earth will decide whom He will receive into paradise, and whom He will not.

Romans 4:7-8 says:

> Blessed are those whose lawless deeds are forgiven, and whose sins are *covered;* blessed is the man against whom the Lord will not *count* his sin. – ESV (*Shank*)

A reckoning is a counting of what we have or lack. It is also a navigational term. A sailor sets his course by reckoning by the North Star. He counts the degrees of his compass by it and sets his direction. So are we to do in Christ.

Romans 6:1-14 says:

> What shall we say then? Are we to continue in sin that grace may abound? **By no means!** How can we who died to sin still live in it? Do you not know that all of us who were baptized into Christ Jesus were baptized into His death? We were buried therefore with Him by baptism into death, in order that, just as Christ was raised from the dead by the glory of the Father, we too might walk in newness of life.
>
> For if we were *united* with Him in a death like His, we shall certainly be *united* with Him in a resurrection like His. We know that our old self was crucified with Him in order that the body of sin might be brought to nothing, so that we would no longer be enslaved to sin. For one who has died has been set free from sin. Now if we have died with Christ, we believe we will also live with Him. We know that Christ being raised from the dead will never die again; death no longer has dominion over Him. For the death He died He died to sin, once for all, but the life He lives He lives to God. You must also consider (*count or reckon*) yourself dead to sin and alive to God.

> Let not sin therefore reign in your mortal body, to make you obey its passions. Do not present your members (*body parts*) to sin as instruments of unrighteousness but present yourselves to God as those who have been brought from death to life, and your members to God as instruments of righteousness. For sin will have no dominion over you since you are not under law but grace.
> – ESV (*Shank*)

As I mentioned before, I used to be frustrated with the parts of this passage that say I was baptized into His death that I somehow died with Christ. How could I have died with Him 2000 years ago? Now I see it. When I received Him into me, I was also joined to Him Who died, way back then. If that is true, I will rise from the dead in Him when this mortal body passes away. Even now I can pray from the Right Hand of God in Jesus' Name, with all powers and principalities under my feet.

No longer being under the **law** means my sins are no longer counted, as was said above in **Romans 4:7-8**. This means I have the **grace** to learn how to overcome my old way of **seeing** myself, and my old way of **believing**, and my old way of **doing**.

The Word That Does Not Lie

The following are faith conclusions based on the Word to which I am now to reckon myself in Christ:

- The Scripture says I am to **reckon** myself dead to sin and alive in Christ, by acting *as if* this is true. (**Romans 6:11**)

- I am to **act as if** I am no longer a slave to sin, but a slave to righteousness. His fruit will follow my faith **action**. (**Romans 6:18**)

- I am to **choose** to see myself as a vessel which now contains Christ and no longer Satan. I serve the one I obey. (**Romans 6:16**)

- God is the **Only Autonomous Being** in the Universe. (*God is dependent on no one.*) The Father, the Son and the Holy Spirit are God. They are the only Eternal and Uncreated Beings. The Godhead alone can call into being that which is not. (**Genesis 1 & 2**) All other beings were created by, and are dependent upon, Him for their existence whether they are good or evil.

- I am not the originator of either good or evil, but by my **choices** I express the will of the one I obey. What I take takes me. The one I obey is my master. Repentance restores me to being able to bear Christ's fruit again if I have sinned. (**Romans 6:12-14**)

- I am to no longer regard myself according to my flesh and its desires, but according to my **spirit**, which is joined to the Spirit of Christ. I am now able to bear His fruit because I am joined in union with Him. (**2 Corinthians 5:16,17 & 1 Corinthians 6:17**)

- My old self has been **crucified** with Christ. It is no longer I alone who lives, but Christ Who lives in me. And the life I now live in the flesh I live by the faith **of** the Son of God, Who loves me and gave Himself for me. His faith is upholding my faith. He is my Rock. (**Galatians 2:20** -KJV) *This effectively makes me Christ in my form, as He can now live out through me, as me.*

- I am learning to recognize my soul's *subjective opinion* for what it is and learning to let my **spirit lead** in what I will do.

- I am learning more and more not to live by impulsive thoughts and feelings, but by the obedience of faith, learning to live spontaneously free, in Christ.

- I'm *learning* to believe I am **seated** at the Right Hand of God in Christ. All powers and principalities are under His feet, and I am in His "lap". (**Ephesians 1:20** -**2:7**)

- The Blood of Christ lets me approach God with **bold-ness** and without shame. (**Ephesians 3:11,12**) I can let the Holy Spirit plow my fallow ground to improve my fruitfulness. He will unmask the **conceits** Satan planted and taught me when I was still his, which may still operate as habits to sabotage my fruitfulness and my witness in Christ.

- I have **given** myself to, and have been **received** by God, and I have **received** the Spirit of Christ in my spirit. There are times when the Holy Spirit lavishes His **joy** all over me in worship or in worshipful study of His Word.

- I also **trust** that when I need a manifestation of His Presence, He will give it to me. When there are no outward manifestations, I no longer doubt His Presence is with me because I know Scripture says He is **in** me, to strengthen me to walk by faith and not by sight.

- He knows me because He is living out **through** me and **in** me. He experiences me from the inside and I experience Him inside me, as well as from above. He knows my heart and He is showing me His.

- I am learning to **expect** that He will work through me at any time. I am my Beloved's and He is mine! The areas where I still need to grow are in my **soul**, where Satan will still try to fool me through my soul's subjective, self-interest view. But my **spirit** has been made perfect because the Perfect One has filled my spirit. My **flesh** is hopeless and will be destroyed.

At this point, I want to quote a song from the end of Norman Grubb's book *Yes I Am*. It has the impression of being spontaneously composed by a fellowship group, adding verses as they went along in their joyful celebration of what God has done. I have also found it useful to meditate on three of them a day in my devotions.

If the Lord Says I Am, Yes I Am – from *Yes I Am*, Norman Grubb

If the Lord says I'm a Christian, yes I am,   Acts 11:26
If the Lord says I'm made new, yes I am,   2 Corinthians 5:16,17
If the Lord says I'm one spirit with Himself, 1 Corinthians 6:17
If the Lord says I am, yes, I am.

If the Lord says I'm a son, yes, I am,   1 John 3:2
If the Lord says I'm an heir, yes, I am,   Romans 8:17
If the Lord says I'm a citizen of the kingdom
here and now,   Ephesians 2:9
If the Lord says I am, yes, I am.

If the Lord says I'm a vessel, yes, I am,   2 Corinthians 4:7
If the Lord says I'm a branch, yes, I am,   John 15:5
If the Lord says I'm a temple of His Holy
Spirit in me,   1 Corinthians 6:19
If the Lord says I am, yes, I am.

If the Lord says I'm a saint, yes, I am,   1 Corinthians 1:2
If the Lord says I'm elect, yes, I am,   2 Timothy 2:10
If the Lord says I'm a partaker of His
divine nature,   2 Peter 1:4
If the Lord says I am, yes, I am.

If the Lord says I'm a priest, yes, I am,   Revelation 1:6
If the Lord says I'm a king, yes, I am,   Revelation 1:6
If the Lord says I'm seated in the heavenly
places in Christ,   Ephesians 2:6
If the Lord says I am, yes, I am.

If the Lord says I am holy, yes, I am,   Ephesians 1:4
If the Lord says I am blameless, yes, I am,   Ephesians 1:4
If the Lord says I am un-reprovable
in His sight,   Colossians 1:22
If the Lord says I am, yes, I am.

If the Lord says I'm complete, yes, I am,   Colossians 2:10
If the Lord says I am perfect, yes, I am,   Philippians 3:15
If the Lord says I am as He is in this world,   1 John 4:17
If the Lord says I am, yes, I am.

If the Lord says I am filled, yes, I am,	1 Corinthians 4:8
If the Lord says I am strong, yes, I am	1 John 2:14
If the Lord says I am more than a conqueror	
in this world,	Romans 8:37
If the Lord says I am, yes, I am.	

If the Lord says I'm not I, but He in me,	Galatians 2:20
If the Lord says I am the world's light, yes, I am,	Matthew 5:14
If the Lord says I'm a god to whom the	
Word has come,	John 10:34-35
If the Lord says I am, yes, I am.	

He whom the Son has set free is free indeed!

Bibliography

THE HOLY BIBLE by **The Holy Spirit** *(Primarily ESV Translation)* / Crossway Bibles, Good News Publishers

The Revised Standard Version (RSV) / A. J. Holman Co.

The New International Version (NIV) / AMG Publishers

King James Version (KJV) / AMG Publishers

Expository Dictionary of New Testament Words by **W. E. Vine**/ Revel

The Tense Readings of the Greek New Testament by **Daniel Steele**/ RevivalClassics.com

RSV Interlinear Greek-English New Testament by **Rev. Dr. Alfred Marshall** / Zondervan

Yes I Am by **Norman Grubb** / Overcomer Literature Trust, Zerubbabel Press

Paul's Key to the Liberated Life, Romans Six to Eight by **Norman Grubb** / Zerubbabel Press

Soul & Spirit by **Jessie Penn-Lewis** / Overcomer Literature Trust

IUSTITIA DEI (RIGHTEOUSNESS OF GOD) by **Alister E. McGrath** / Cambridge University Press

How Should We Then Live by **Francis A. Schaeffer** / Revell

Creeds IN Contrast by Dr. Dale Yocum / Schmul Publishing Co, Inc.

Narcissism, Denial of the True Self by **Alexander Lowen, MD** / Collier Books

Escape from Intimacy by **Anne Wilson Schaef** / HarperOne

Out of the Shadows by **Patrick Carnes** / CompCare

Healing the Wounded Heart, The Heartache of Sexual Abuse and Hope of Transformation by **Dan B. Allender** / Baker-Books

The Golden Bough by **Sir James George Frazer** / THE MACMILLAN COMPANY

Inspired sermons and conversations by **many friends and teachers**

Lost booktitles by **authors** I have forgotten

The School of Hard Knocks by **The Holy Spirit**